To my brother
Gary LaVerdiere, S.S.S.,
Religious of the Blessed Sacrament

Contents

Preface

"Do you still not understand?" (Mark 8:21).

The disciples were in the boat with Jesus crossing the Sea of Galilee to the other shore. They had forgotten to bring bread, but they had one loaf with them in the boat. Jesus warned them about the leaven of the Pharisees and the leaven of Herod. They thought Jesus was talking about their lack of bread.

While crossing, Jesus asked the disciples, "Do you not yet understand or comprehend? Are your hearts hardened? Do you have eyes and not see, ears and not hear?" He also asked them how many baskets of fragments they gathered when he nourished five thousand with five loaves and four thousand with seven loaves. Jesus then ends his challenging questions with the resounding final question: "Do you still not understand?"

So ends the first part of the Gospel of Mark. Reflecting on the question, we should recall the title Mark gave to his Gospel: "The beginning of the gospel of Jesus Christ [the Son of God]" (1:1). Throughout the commentary, I kept Mark's title in mind. Over and over again, after each event, I repeated the title. Taking Jesus' final question to heart, I also asked, "Do we still not understand?"

I started this commentary in the summer of 1987. I first presented it in the pages of *Emmanuel* magazine, beginning in November 1987 and ending in July/August 1997. I wanted to introduce Mark's Gospel to people in ministry.

At the time, I was concentrating on the Gospel of Luke. Luke was my home! I lived in the Gospel of Luke and really liked to show my home to everyone. But to understand the Gospel of Luke more deeply,

I had to know one of Luke's principal sources. For a long time, I suspected that Luke knew Mark from memory. Now I am convinced. Writing his Gospel, Luke did not need a scroll of Mark's Gospel before him. After studying Mark and introducing his Gospel to others, I still live mainly in Luke, but I have found a second home. Today, Mark is my condominium!

In my teaching at Catholic Theological Union and Mundelein Seminary in Chicago and at Fordham University in New York, the Gospel of Mark was always with me. Over the years, I also gave many talks and retreats on the Gospel of Mark to various groups. I wanted priests, seminarians, and other people engaged in ministry to appreciate and love the Gospel of Mark, and to ponder and contemplate its presentation of the Christian mystery. I also wanted them to share Mark's awesome sense of Christ's mission, the Christian calling, the universal Church, and its mission. Offering this commentary, my intention is the same.

For this commentary, I revised and sometimes rewrote what I published in *Emmanuel*. Over the years, I learned a lot while commenting on the Gospel, not only in the library, but also while teaching and lecturing. All along, my teachers were my students. I suspect that Mark could also have said that.

Instead of dealing separately with the usual introductory questions—Who was Mark? Where and when did he write, and for whom? What were his sources? What was his guiding intention?—I dealt with the questions while commenting on the Gospel, particularly while introducing Mark's title and preface (1:1). Throughout this commentary, I used the revised edition of the New Testament in The New American Bible.

I am deeply grateful to Anthony Shueller, S.S.S., editor of *Emmanuel* and my provincial superior for his encouragement and fraternal support. I thank my classmate Paul Bernier, S.S.S., for reading the manuscript. His suggestions were invaluable. I also thank my secretary, Maryanne Macaluso, who pored over the manuscript, raised questions of clarity and punctuation. For her, reading the manuscript was an expression of her ministry.

I dedicate this commentary to my brother, Gary LaVerdiere, S.S.S., a fellow religious, who illustrated each installment of the commentary in *Emmanuel*. I think of him and the other members of my family whenever I recall Jesus' question: "Who are my mother and [my] brothers?"

Among Gary's religious responsibilities, he is the manager, art director, and photographer for the magazine. I keep a photograph picturing him at his desk in Cleveland in front of me in New York.

With his art and religious dedication, he inspires and teaches me. I present this commentary to him as an expression of my gratitude.

Eugene LaVerdiere, S.S.S.
August 2, 1998
Feast of St. Peter Julian Eymard,
Founder of the Congregation of the Blessed Sacrament

Table I

A General Outline of Mark's Gospel

Table II

An Outline of the Prologue
The Gospel in Miniature
Mark 1:2-13

I. Biblical inscription: the prologue in miniature	1:2-3
A. God's messenger and his mission (Mal 3:1; Exod 20:23)	1:2
B. The messenger's message (Isa 40:3)	1:3
II. The life and mission of the John the Baptist	1:4-8
A. General mission	1:4-5
1. Proclaiming a baptism of repentance	1:4
2. Popular response	1:5
B. Special mission	1:6-8
1. A new Elijah	1:6
2. Preparing the way for Jesus Christ	1:7-8
III. The life and mission of Jesus	1:9-13
A. The Baptism of Jesus	1:9-11
1. Baptized by John	1:9
2. Divine response	1:10-11
B. Jesus' baptismal life	1:12-13
1. In the desert	1:12
2. A forty-day test	1:13

Table III

An Outline for Part One
Jesus and the Mystery of the Kingdom of God
Mark 1:14–8:21

I. Section One: Jesus and the First Disciples	1:14–3:6
A. Introduction	1:14-20
1. Jesus the proclaimer	1:14-15
2. Jesus calls his first disciples	1:16-20
B. Body	1:21–3:6
1. The beginning of the ministry in Galilee	1:21-45
2. Mounting opposition, climaxing in the hardness of heart in the synagogue	2:1–3:6
II. Section Two: Jesus and the Twelve	3:7–6:6a
A. Introduction	3:7-19
1. Jesus the healer	3:7-12
2. Jesus constitutes the Twelve	3:13-19
B. Body	3:20–6:6a
1. Continuation of the ministry in Galilee	3:21–4:34
2. Going to the other side, climaxing in lack of faith in Jesus' native place	4:35–6:6a
III. Section Three: Jesus and the Mission of the Twelve	6:6b–8:21
A. Introduction	6:6b-30
1. Jesus the teacher	6:6b
2. Jesus sends the Twelve on mission	6:7-30
B. Body	6:31–8:21
1. The mission to the Jews	6:31-44
2. The mission to the Gentiles, climaxing in the disciples' lack of understanding	6:45–8:21

Table IV

An Outline for Part One, Section I
Jesus and the First Disciples
Mark 1:14–3:6

I. Introduction	1:14-20
A. Summary: Jesus the proclaimer	1:14-15
B. Jesus calls his first disciples	1:16-20
II. Body	1:21–3:6
A. The beginning of the ministry in Galilee	1:21–3:6
1. Jesus teaches with authority	1:21-28
2. The raising of Simon's mother-in-law	1:29-31
3. Other cures	1:32-34
4. To the neighboring villages	1:35-39
5. The cleansing of a leper	1:40-45
B. Mounting opposition	2:1–3:6
1. Authority to forgive sins	2:1-12
2. Calling sinners to repentance	2:13-17
3. The new and the old	2:18-22
4. Lord of the Sabbath	2:23-28
5. Saving life on the Sabbath	3:1-6

Table V

An Outline for Part I, Section II
Jesus and the Twelve
Mark 3:7–6:6a

I. Introduction	3:7-19
A. Summary: Jesus the healer	3:7-12
B. Jesus constitutes the Twelve	3:13-19
II. Body	3:20–6:6a
A. Continuation of the ministry in Galilee	3:20–4:34
1. Jesus' teaching at home	3:20-35
2. Jesus' teaching by the sea	4:1-34
B. Going to the other side	4:35–6:6a
1. A storm at sea	4:35-41
2. In the land of the Gerasenes	5:1-20
3. Back on the Jewish shore	5:21-43
4. Jesus in his native place	6:1-6a

Table VI

An Outline for Part I, Section III
Jesus and the Mission of the Twelve
Mark 6:6b–8:21

I

꙳ ꙳

Title and Preface

Mark 1:1

"The beginning of the gospel of Jesus Christ [the Son of God]" (1:1).[1] So begins the Gospel of Mark, the first Gospel ever written. Before Mark, there were stories and clusters of stories about Jesus, and some of them must have been written, but none of those survived. When the Gospel was written, there were no precedents. Each part of the Gospel shows him as an extremely creative writer, beginning with the opening statement.

Deceptively simple, Mark's opening statement fulfills two functions. It is a title for the Gospel and a preface to the readers. As such, we can call it a prefatory title. As a title, it defines and summarizes Mark's Gospel as "the beginning of the gospel of Jesus Christ [the

---

[1] The title, "the Son of God," does not appear in some early manuscripts. For a recent discussion, see Peter M. Head, "A Text-Critical Study of Mark 1:1, 'The Beginning of the Gospel of Jesus Christ,'" *New Testament Studies* 37 (1991) 621–29. After reviewing the external and internal evidence for the longer and shorter reading of Mark 1:1, Head argues for the shorter reading. It is more likely that "Son of God" was added to a shorter text than that "Son of God" was omitted from a longer text. But even if the christological title, "the Son of God," was added later to 1:1, it introduced an extremely important component of Mark's christology (see 1:11; 3:11; 5:7; 9:7; 12:6; 13:32; 14:61; 15:39; see also 8:38).

Son of God]." As a preface, it proclaims "the beginning of the gospel of Jesus Christ [the Son of God]" to Christian readers who thought it was the end of the gospel. As a title for the Gospel and a preface to the readers, the prefatory title stands outside "the beginning of the gospel." The story itself begins with the prologue (1:2-13).

Mark's prefatory title is unique, at least among the Gospels. Matthew's Gospel has a title: "The book *[biblos]* of the genealogy *[geneseos]* of Jesus Christ, the son of David, the son of Abraham" (Matt 1:1), not only for the genealogy (Matt 1:2-17) and the prologue (1:2–2:23), but for the whole Gospel.[2] But Matthew's title is not a preface. Both Luke and the book of Acts have a preface addressed to Theophilus (Luke 1:1-4; Acts 1:1-2), but neither functions as a title.

As a title for the Gospel, the opening verse introduces the entire Gospel of Mark,[3] in doing that, it presents the theme, the general scope, and the purpose of the Gospel. In the second century, Christians added a label, "According to Mark" *(kata Markon),* to distinguish it from the other Gospels.[4] Later, the label developed into a name, "The Gospel According to Mark" *(Euaggelion kata Markon).*[5]

In modern times, very few refer to the Gospel by its title. Instead, most people refer to it by its name, "The Gospel According to Mark," or a variant of it, "The Gospel of (St.) Mark," or more sim-

---

[2] See W. D. Davies and Dale C. Allison, *The Gospel According to Saint Matthew*, ICC, (Edinburgh: T. & T. Clark, 1988) I:149–60; Davies and Allison interpret Matthew's title as the "Book of the New Genesis wrought by Jesus Christ, son of David, son of Abraham," 153.

[3] See M. Eugene Boring, "Mark 1:1-15 and the Beginning of the Gospel," *Semeia* 52 (1991) 43–81; see especially 47–53.

[4] In a short time, the label *kata Markon* was so identified with Mark's Gospel that in early Latin translations the label was simply transliterated instead of translated, giving the Latinized Greek label *cata Marcum* instead of *secundum Marcum*. See Bruce M. Metzger, *The Canon of the New Testament* (New York: Oxford University Press, 1987) Appendix III, "Titles of the Books of the New Testament," 302, n. 5.

[5] In a scroll, the label was placed at the very end of the scroll below the last line. In this way, it was readily seen upon opening the scroll, which was unrolled from the right to the left, that is, from the end of the text to the beginning. In the second century, with the adoption of the codex, the label continued to be written on the last page just below the final column, as would have been done on a scroll. The format invited writing the label at the beginning of the text instead of the end, transforming the label into a name. But even with its new name, the Gospel long retained its concluding label.

ply, "Mark's Gospel." Referring to the Gospel by its name draws attention to the author instead of the gospel itself. As such, it invites inquiry into the author's identity and background and other historical considerations such as when and where he wrote the Gospel and for whom. Today, with our historical consciousness we cannot escape such considerations.

With this development, Mark the author was bound to figure in any discussion of the Gospel's authority. There was no question of the authority of Jesus Christ and his gospel. But what about Mark, the author of the *kata Markon?* Was he reliable? What were his credentials? What were his sources? Such questions could distract us from the Gospel and its meaning.[6]

As a preface, the opening verse allows the author to address the readers or listeners directly, as Paul does at the beginning of his letters when he greets a particular church, and as Luke does in the two prefaces to Theophilus. In the preface, the writer's own person is at the fore. It is the same for the two conclusions of John's Gospel, where a writer addresses the readers directly (John 20:30-31; 21:24-25). In the prologue and the rest of the Gospel, the author continues to address the readers and listeners but indirectly through the narrator.[7] After the preface, the writer disappears, hidden behind the voice of the narrator.

Both as a title and a preface, Mark's opening verse, "The beginning of the gospel of Jesus Christ [the Son of God]" (1:1), is one of the most stirring statements in the New Testament. To read it well, especially aloud, is to appreciate the Gospel it both summarizes and proclaims.

Read as a title, its expressive power as a proclamation can hardly be suppressed. The Gospel was not written for itself but for the readers. Read as a preface, its defining power is very evident. The readers have to hear what the Gospel says. There is no separating the message from its proclamation. For the sake of clarity, however, we will consider Mark's opening verse first as a title for the Gospel and then as a preface to the reader.

---

[6] In the early second century, Papias of Hierapolis defended Mark's authority: "Mark, having become Peter's interpreter, wrote down accurately whatever he remembered of what was or done by the Lord, however not in order." Papias is quoted by Eusebius in his *Ecclesiastical History,* 3.39.15.

[7] In a preface, the author speaks in his name, using the first person ("I" or "we") and addresses the readers or listeners, using the second person ("you"). In the case of Mark, the first and the second person are implied. In a prologue, the author uses the third person ("he," "she," "they").

A Title for the Gospel

Mark's opening verse is clearly a title for the Gospel. First, the statement has no verb, explicit or implied. Second, its first word in Greek, *arche* ("the beginning") has no article, indicating that *arche* is the opening word of a title.[8] Like the title of Matthew's Gospel (Matt 1:1), the opening statement of Mark is not a sentence,[9] nor is the title of the Book of Revelation (Rev 1:1-2).

If Mark's opening verse had a verb, such as, "Here begins the gospel of Jesus Christ [the Son of God]," the verse would point to the next verse, "As it is written in Isaiah the prophet" (1:2a). As such, it would introduce the prologue (1:2-13). Without a verb, it refers and introduces the whole of Mark's Gospel, from 1:2 to 16:8.

To understand what the title means we should return to it after each story or discourse, and especially at the end of a section. For example, after reading this closing, "The Pharisees went out and immediately took counsel with the Herodians against him to put him to death" (3:6) we should recall the title, "The beginning of the gospel of Jesus Christ [the Son of God]." Then, after reading the whole Gospel of Mark, we should start to appreciate what the title means.

The Beginning *(arche)*

Introductory words can be very significant, and it is important not to pass over them too quickly. They invite reflection and meditation. Mark's very first word, *arche* ("beginning" or "the beginning"), evokes the excitement we experience at the beginning of spring, at dawn, at the birth of a child, at a baptism. Indirectly, it also evokes what precedes them, the experience of winter, the darkness of night, the birth pangs of labor, and the abandonment of a former self.

"The beginning" also summons the awesome beginnings announced or described in the Scriptures. Among these, of course, there is ultimate beginning when God first commanded the universe into existence. There is also the birth of Jesus, the long-awaited Savior, and his resurrection from the dead. Such beginnings speak

---

[8] See J. H. Moulton, *Grammar of New Testament Greek*, Vol. I, *Prolegomena*, Third edition (Edinburgh: T. & T. Clark, 1908) 82. Unlike Greek, English style requires the article, and translations into English have to supply it.

[9] The title for the Gospel of Matthew has no verb, and its first word in Greek, *biblos*, has no article. The same is true for the title for the book of Revelation (1:1-2), which has verbs, but only in subordinate clauses, and its first word, *apocalypsis* ("revelation") has no article.

of the mystery of God and the divine presence in creation and history, challenging the imagination and stretching human language to its limits.

From a literary point of view, Mark's "beginning" *(arche)* calls to mind two other books, the book of Genesis and John's Gospel, whose first words in Greek are "in the beginning" *(en arche)*. The similar wording, however, should not obscure the differences in meaning.

In John's Gospel, "the beginning" lies deep in the unfathomable mystery of God, before creation, before ever there was a divine disclosure: "In the beginning was the Word, and the Word was with God, and the Word was God" (John 1:1).

In Genesis, "the beginning" refers to the time of creation. It refers to the time when, at God's command, the light, the earth and sea, the various forms of life, and human life itself emerged from the formless wasteland and the darkness that covered the abyss: "In the beginning, when God created the heavens and the earth" (Gen 1:1).

In Mark, "the beginning" does not refer to the condition of divine existence before creation or to the initial moment of creation when "God said, 'Let there be light,' and there was light" (Gen 1:3). It refers to the beginning of the gospel and the era of salvation in Jesus Christ. "The beginning" includes what Jesus did and taught, his passion and resurrection, and what his followers did and taught, and their participation in Jesus' passion and resurrection.

Mark's story of the beginning opens with a reference to Isaiah (1:2-3), and it is not over until the women run away from the tomb and say nothing to anyone (16:8). "The beginning of the gospel of Jesus Christ [the Son of God]" ends enigmatically with the words, *ephobounto gar* (literally, "they were afraid for"). Mark does not say why the women were afraid. He left the answer to the readers, who live in the continuation of the gospel.

"The beginning of the gospel" continued in the early Church. While telling the story of Jesus' life and ministry with his disciples, Mark told the story of its continuation in the early Church. For Mark, Jesus of Nazareth, his disciples, and their challenges were symbolic of Jesus Christ, the risen Lord, the early Church, and its challenges.[10] As such, Mark's story of the gospel is just as symbolic as John's story of the Word.

---

[10] As Daniel J. Harrington observed, "Mark's presentation of the earliest disciples was based on the parallelism between them and the members of his community" ("The Gospel According to Mark," *The New Jerome Biblical Commentary* (Englewood Cliffs, N.J.: Prentice Hall, 1996) 597.

Reading the Gospel, the Markan community could see themselves mirrored in the life of the disciples with all their hopes, struggles, and even their failures. At the same time, they could see Jesus Christ, the risen Lord, leading them as Jesus of Nazareth led the earliest disciples in his lifetime. In his Gospel, Mark presented the disciples as a model of the Markan community.[11] As such, Mark directs Jesus' teaching beyond the first disciples to the early Church.

Among the Synoptic writers, Mark is the only one who told the story of the early church, including its mission to the Gentiles, in and through the story of Jesus and his disciples. Matthew announced the mission of the apostolic Church among the Gentiles but did not tell its story (Matt 28:16-20). Writing his Gospel, Luke left out passages in Mark that refer to the story of the Church after the ascension.[12] However, he devoted the entire book of Acts to the story of the birth and development of Church and its mission to the nations.[13]

Today, the gospel of Jesus Christ continues in the Church as it faces new situations. Applying the story of Jesus of Nazareth and his first disciples to the early Church, Mark showed us how to apply it today, as we are beginning the Church's third millennium.

The Beginning of the Gospel *(tou euaggeliou)*

The term "the gospel" means "the good news" in Greek *(to euaggelion)*. The term evokes great moments when someone announces the

---

John Donahue connected the process with the very nature of the Gospel: "The Gospels are the good news of the risen one told in the form of stories about the earthly life of Jesus." See his article, "Recent Studies on the Origin of 'Son of Man' in the Gospels," *The Catholic Biblical Quarterly* 48/3 (July 1986) 498.

[11] See Howard Clark Kee, *Community of the New Age, Studies in Mark's Gospel* (Philadelphia: The Westminster Press, 1977) 87–97.

[12] For example, Luke omitted Mark 6:45–8:26 between Luke 9:17 and 18. For a discussion on the relation of Luke to Mark, see Frans Neirynck, "Synoptic Problem," *The New Jerome Biblical Commentary*, edited by Raymond E. Brown, S.S., Joseph A. Fitzmyer, S.J., Roland E. Murphy, O. Carm. (Englewood Cliffs, N.J.: Prentice Hall, 1990) 587–95, especially 589–90; John Drury, *Tradition and Design in Luke's Gospel* (Atlanta: John Knox Press, 1976) 82–119.

[13] Luke wrote the sequel of the Gospel in the book of Acts, beginning with the events after Jesus' passion and resurrection (Acts 1:3-14) until Paul "proclaimed the kingdom of god and taught about the Lord Jesus Christ" (Acts 28:31) where he stayed in Rome for two years.

arrival of good news: a child is born; a good friend is coming to visit; a peace treaty has been signed.

In the Roman world, "good news" heralded the birth of a son, an heir, in the imperial household. In a famous inscription, it refers to the birth of Augustus, announcing that he was the savior of the world.[14] In Luke's prologue, it announces the birth of a savior who is Christ and Lord (Luke 2:10-11).

When Mark spoke of "the beginning of the gospel," the term "gospel" already enjoyed a long Christian history in the preaching and the letters of St. Paul. The creed in 1 Corinthians 15:3-5 summarized the gospel Paul had preached in Corinth and elsewhere (see 1 Cor 15:1). In this context, the word "gospel" announced salvation in Christ. In another early creed, the gospel was about the Son of God, "descended from David according to the flesh, but established as Son of God in power according to the spirit of holiness through resurrection from the dead, Jesus Christ our Lord" (Rom 1:3-4).

In Christian usage, the term resonated especially with the prophetic voice of Isaiah, who proclaimed the coming of the Lord and the return of God's people from a long exile. Isaiah's gospel message addressed the exiles in Babylon, as well as the poor and the oppressed not only in Jerusalem but in all nations (see Isa 40:1-11; 61:1-2). Isaiah spoke most eloquently to those who yearned for good news but did not expect it.

Mark surely was aware of the rich prophetic and Pauline history of the term "gospel." Mark's own use of the term added to its history. Not that Mark referred to "gospel" as a new literary form. At the time Mark wrote, the term "gospel" did not yet designate a special literary genre. As elsewhere in Mark (see 1:14, 15; 8:35; 10:29; 14:9), the gospel referred to the preaching of Jesus and its continuation in the Church.[15]

As proclaimed by the Church, Mark even identified "the gospel" with the person of Jesus. For that, we have two sayings of Jesus. Speaking to the crowd and his disciples, Jesus said, "For whoever

---

[14] See Raymond Brown, *The Birth of the Messiah*, New Updated Edition (New York: Doubleday, 1993) 415–16.

[15] For the term "gospel," applied to a literary genre, see David E. Aune, *The New Testament in Its Literary Environment* (Philadelphia: The Westminster Press, 1989) 17–45; James L. Bailey and Lyle D. Vander Broek, *Literary Forms in the New Testament* (Louisville: Westminster/John Knox Press, 1992) 91–98. In relation to the Gospel of Mark, see Donald Senior, C.P., "The Struggle to be Universal: Mission as Vantage Point for New Testament Investigation" *The Catholic Biblical Quarterly* 46/1 (January 1984) 74–76.

wishes to save his life will lose it, but whoever loses his life for my sake and that of the gospel will save it" (8:35). Later, speaking to the disciples, he said, "Amen, I say to you, there is no one who has given up house or brothers or sisters or mother or father or children or lands for my sake and for the sake of the gospel . . ." (10:29).

In early tradition, the gospel was expressed in the form of creeds (see 1 Cor 15:1-5; Rom 1:3-4). In Paul, the gospel and its implications for Christian life were expressed in the form of apostolic letters. In Mark, the gospel and its implications for Christian life were expressed in a story. Mark's story would soon be recognized as a normative telling of the gospel. Never before had the term "gospel" been so intimately related to a literary work.

The Gospel of Jesus *(Iesou)*

Mark summarizes Jesus' life and mission with one sentence, "Jesus came into Galilee proclaiming the gospel of God" (1:14). In the same summary (1:14-15), Jesus himself summarizes his gospel message: "This is the time of fulfillment. The kingdom of God is at hand. Repent, and believe in the gospel" (1:15). Jesus' proclamation of the gospel was part of "the beginning of the gospel of Jesus Christ." But the term "gospel" also included his whole life, the life and the mission of the disciples, and their gospel concerning Jesus. Jesus and the Church are inseparable in "the beginning of the gospel of Jesus Christ."

For Mark, the gospel was not a mere record of past events, but a new act of proclamation. Just as Jesus proclaimed the gospel in Galilee (1:14-15), his followers were called and sent to proclaim the gospel to all nations (see 13:9-11). The Gospel of Mark, "the beginning of the gospel of Jesus Christ," was a good example of the Church's proclamation. Mark's Gospel was meant for all nations.

In content, Mark's Gospel was a story of the gospel of Jesus and his disciples. After defending the woman that anointed him at the dinner at the home of Simon, Jesus said to his disciples: "Amen, I say to you, wherever the gospel is proclaimed to the whole world, what she has done will be told in memory of her" (14:9). For Mark, the Gospel included the story of the people who came to Jesus as well.

In form, however, Mark's Gospel was an act of proclamation. It made Jesus, the one who was crucified but had been raised from the dead, present to Mark's readers and listeners. Through Mark's Gospel, the gospel proclaimed by Jesus and the Church became the gospel that was Jesus.

"The beginning of the gospel of Jesus Christ" opens with the mission of John the Baptist who appeared in the desert in fulfillment of prophecy. It is in this context, as a follower of John, that the mission of Jesus was conceived, at least from a historical point of view (1:9). Ultimately, however, the mission of Jesus was conceived of the Spirit as Jesus emerged from the waters of John's baptism (1:10-11).

"The beginning of the gospel of Jesus Christ" ends after Jesus' burial with the visit of women to his tomb, with a young man's proclamation of his resurrection, and with the flight of the women from the tomb, saying nothing to anyone because they were afraid (16:1-8). "The beginning of the gospel of Jesus Christ [the Son of God]" ends with the silence of the women. This does appear to be a strange ending for a story that was announced as gospel or good news. But we have to remember that this ending is not the end of the gospel, but only the end of "the beginning of the gospel."

This is how Mark first envisioned the Gospel. From its origins in the desert to a silent flight from the tomb, it included the mission of Jesus in Galilee and its culmination in Jerusalem. It included his passion and resurrection and everything that led to it. Only later, in the second century, would others supplement Mark's original "beginning of the gospel" with brief summaries of the appearances of Jesus as risen Lord told in the Gospels of Luke and John (16:9-20). Today, this alternate ending is part of the canonical Gospel. As such, it is used in the catechesis and the liturgy of the Church.

Jesus Christ [the Son of God] *(Iesou Christou [huiou theou])*

Mark's Gospel is not merely "the beginning of the gospel of Jesus." If it were, we could think of it as a biographical narrative of Jesus. That biography would include his relationship to his followers and his enemies. But Mark's Gospel is "the beginning of the gospel of Jesus Christ [the Son of God]." As such, it is a Christological and ecclesiological narrative, and Christological and ecclesiological concerns determine its structure and development.[16]

After the title (1:1) and the prologue (1:2-13), we can divide the Gospel into two parts. The first raises the question of the identity and mission of Jesus (1:14–8:21). Underlying this question, there is the question of the identity and mission of the Church. The first part begins with Jesus coming into Galilee proclaiming the gospel

---

[16] Papias of Hierapolis may have had a biographical narrative in mind when he wrote that Mark wrote down accurately what he remembered but not in order (see Eusebius, *Ecclesiastical History,* 3.39.15).

of God (1:14-15) and the call of the first disciples (1:16-20). It ends with Jesus' dramatic challenge to the Twelve, "Do you still not understand?" (8:21).

The second part answers the question of Jesus' identity and mission and the underlying question of the identity and mission of the Church (8:22–16:8).[17] The second part begins with Jesus opening the eyes of a blind man (8:22-26) and it ends with the silence of the women, "They said nothing to anyone, for they were afraid" (16:8).

We can entitle the first part, "Jesus and the Mystery of the Kingdom of God" (1:14–8:21). In this part, "the beginning of the gospel of Jesus Christ [the Son of God]" emphasizes the mystery of the gospel, of the person of Jesus and the kingdom of God. From the point of view of the Church, it emphasizes the breadth of the Church and its universal mission. In this first part, the major symbols are the sea *(he thalassa)* and the bread *(ho artos)* and everything associated with them.

We can entitle the second part, "Jesus and the Coming of the Kingdom of God" (8:22–16:8). In this part, "the beginning of the gospel of Jesus Christ [the Son of God]" emphasizes the implications of the gospel, the passion and resurrection of Jesus, and coming of the Kingdom of God. From the point of view of the Church, it emphasizes the depth of commitment required to make the Church truly universal. In this second part, the major symbols are the way *(he hodos)*, and the cup *(ho poterion)*, and everything associated with them.

Every Gospel—and Mark is no exception—views Jesus from certain points of view. For Mark, Jesus is above all the Christ and the Son of God (1:1). The Gospel includes many other titles of Jesus, such as Teacher, Rabbi, the Nazarene, and King of the Jews. Of these various titles, two, Son of Man and Son of David, explain what it means for Jesus to be the Christ and the Son of God.

Today the title "Christ" is so closely associated with the name Jesus that it has become part of his name, and we tend to forget that it began as a title. It was not so in the first century, when Christians added Christ to the name of Jesus. Instead of calling him Jesus of Nazareth, they called him Jesus Christ *(Iesous Christos)*. But at the same time, they continued to use *Christos* as a

---

[17] In recent years, the tendency has been to emphasize the Christological concerns of Mark's Gospel, but the ecclesiological concerns are just as important. See Donald Senior, C.P., "The Struggle to be Universal: Mission as Vantage Point for New Testament Investigation," *The Catholic Biblical Quarterly* 46/1 (January 1984) 63–81.

title.[18] Doing that, they referred to Jesus as "the Christ" *(ho Christos)* with the definite article.

It is only here in the title (1:1) that Mark refers to Jesus with the full name, Jesus Christ. In 9:41, he refers to Jesus simply as Christ: "Anyone who gives you a cup of water to drink because you belong to Christ (literally "you are of Christ," *Christou este*), amen, I say to you, will surely not lose his reward." Elsewhere, when Mark refers to Jesus as "the Christ" with the article, he uses "Christ" as a title (8:29; 12:35; 13:21; 14:6; 15:32).

In Mark, therefore, the use of the name, "Jesus Christ" or "Christ," is very close to the title, "the Christ." As such, the name, "Christ," retains the Christological meaning of the title and its association with Jesus' passion and resurrection and Christian baptism (see 1 Cor 15:3-5). In Mark, the name evokes the title and vice versa.

When a New Testament writer wants to refer to Jesus Christ with his proper name, the article is not used. St. Paul, for example, frequently refers to Jesus as "Christ Jesus," or more simply, "Christ." In these cases, the Christological meaning of "Christ" is not emphasized but assumed. In the New Testament, the titular use of Christ clings to the name, Jesus Christ.

When the same author wants to identify Jesus as the Christ, the definite article is used: Jesus is the Christ. This is the case in Peter's confession of faith, "You are the Messiah *[ho Christos]*" (8:29), and elsewhere in the Gospel. In these cases, the christological meaning of "Christ" is emphasized.

Like the title, "the Christ," the title, "the Son of God," is also closely associated with Jesus (see 1:11; 3:11; 5:7; 9:7; 12:6; 13:32; 14:61; 15:39; see also 8:38). In Jesus' interrogation before the Sanhedrin, the high priest associates the two titles: "Are you the Messiah *[ho Christos]*, the son of the Blessed One *[ho huios tou eulogetou]*" (14:61). Usually, the title, "the Son of God" or its equivalent, includes the definite article (1:11; 3:11; 9:7; 12:6; 13:32; 14:61) very much like the title, "the Christ." Used as a vocative and in apposition, "Jesus, son of the Most High God," the title does not need the article (5:7).

Here in the opening verse, the Greek expression for "[the Son of God]" *(huiou theou)* does not have the article. Mark or a later editor associated the title with the name of Jesus Christ. At the end of the

[18] Today, we refer to Jesus as "the Messiah" but rarely as "the Christ." The meaning of the two titles is the same, "the Anointed One," with "the Messiah" coming from the Hebrew and "the Christ" coming from the Greek.

Gospel, the centurion also does not include the article when he proclaims: "Truly this man was the Son of God!" *(alethos houtos ho anthropos huios theou en)* (15:39). But in this case, the absence of the article may not be significant. When the noun, "Son" *(huios),* is followed by the genitive, "of God" *(theou),* it does not need the article. We could translate the centurion's proclamation as a title, "the Son of God," or as a description, "a son of God."[19]

As a subtle writer, Mark may have intended both, from different points of view. From the point of view of the centurion, who was not a Christian, it was a description: "Truly this man was a son of God!" But from point of view of the author and the narrator, it was a title: "Truly this man was the Son of God!"

In the title of the Gospel of Mark (1:1), "Son of God," could be a Christological title. We would then translate it as "the Son of God." But its close association with the name, Jesus Christ, invites the translation, "Son of God." "Son of God" remains a title, but extremely close to the name Jesus Christ.

A Preface to the Readers

We have seen how Mark's opening verse, "the beginning of the gospel of Jesus Christ [the Son of God]," is a title for the Gospel. As a title, it summarizes and defines the Gospel. We have also seen how the opening verse is also a preface to the readers. As a preface, it proclaims "the beginning of the gospel of Jesus Christ [the Son of God]" to the readers.

In the opening verse, Mark surely had his readers in mind. With his prefatory title, he addressed the readers directly. In the prologue and in the Gospel, while summarizing a series of events, telling stories, and presenting the teaching of Jesus, he continued to keep the readers in mind.

At various points, he even interrupts a story or a discourse to address the readers directly, parenthetically explaining Jewish customs (see 7:3-4), pointing out the implications of Jesus' teaching (see 7:19), or translating a Semitic phrase into Greek for the sake of Greek-speaking readers (see 5:41; 7:34; 15:22; 15:34). In Jesus' eschatological discourse, describing the great tribulation, he even

---

[19] See Maximilian Zerwick S.J., *Biblical Greek*, English edition adapted from the fourth Latin edition (Rome: Pontifical Biblical Institute, 1963) 59, #183.

calls on the reader: "Let the reader understand *(ho anaginoskon noeito)*" (13:14).

Viewed as a title, all the emphasis is on the beginning of the good news and the Gospel it introduces. Viewed as a preface, it also draws attention to the author and his readers, their background, and their present situation, as well as to the message. In a title, the author is invisible. In a preface, the author is very visible as he addresses the readers directly.

Considering Mark's opening verse as a preface, we now focus on the author and the readers, that is the setting of Mark's Gospel, as well as the message.[20] In relation to that, we have many questions. Who was the author? Do we know anything about him? When and where did he write the Gospel and for whom? What was his purpose? To answer these questions, we could look at external sources, beginning with other books in the New Testament and the quotations of Bishop Papias of Hierapolis included in Eusebius' *Ecclesiastical History*. But our primary answers have to come from the Gospel itself.[21]

What then does the Gospel assume concerning the author and the readers? In the title, why did the author entitle his story as "the beginning of the gospel?" Why did he announce it as good news? And why did he refer to Jesus as Jesus Christ instead of Jesus of Nazareth? If he included the title, "the Son of God," why did he not choose another title, such as "the Son of Man"?

The answers to these questions are far from evident. The authors of the Gospels had a choice. Matthew entitled his Gospel, "The book of the genealogy of Jesus Christ, the son of David, the son of Abraham" (Matt 1:1). Luke described his Gospel as "a narrative of the events that have been fulfilled among us" (Luke 1:1). John referred to his Gospel as the signs Jesus did in the presence of his disciples (see John 20:30). Mark opted to present his Gospel as "the beginning of the gospel of Jesus Christ [the Son of God]." He must have thought that his readers urgently needed to hear this.

Anticipating the story of the prologue, why did the author emphasize the themes of proclamation, repentance, baptism, and the

---

[20] For an excellent discussion of the setting of the Gospel, see John R. Donahue, S.J., "Windows and Mirrors: The Setting of Mark's Gospel," *The Catholic Biblical Quarterly* 57/1 (January 1995) 1–26.

[21] In the same way, Paul's letters are the primary source for the life of Paul, his relationship to coworkers and the churches to whom he wrote, and his purpose for writing. After examining Paul's letters, we turn to the Acts of the Apostles as a secondary source.

way of the Lord? Why did he give so much prominence to the desert, to Jesus' divinity, and to his forty-day period of testing? Again, he must have thought that these themes responded to the situation of the readers.

The themes also say a lot about the author. Mark was a proclaimer, like John the Baptist, calling people to repentance. Through his Gospel, Mark was preparing the way for the Lord's definitive coming. Doing that, he reminded his readers of their baptism.

Anticipating the story of the Gospel, why did Mark summarize Jesus' mission as proclaiming the gospel of God? Why did he present Jesus as an exorcist, a healer, who had authority to forgive sins, and one who taught with authority? Why did he emphasize that Jesus called disciples to follow him, constituted them as the Twelve, and sent them on mission? Why did he give so much importance to the universality of the Church and its mission to the nations? Why did he focus on the kingdom of God and the passion of Christ as primary themes? Why did he stress the disciples' lack of understanding?

Being a Christian was not a birthright. The disciples were called to be Christians, to be the followers of Christ. Jesus also established his followers as the new Twelve. As the Twelve, they would be the foundations of the Church that was open to Gentiles as well as Jews. In the midst of a turbulent world, internal conflicts, and persecution, it was a great temptation to return to their origins in the Jewish community. Baptized with the baptism with which Jesus was baptized, they died with Christ. Mark reminded them that their mission was to all nations. The kingdom of God was intended for everyone. That is why the Church has to be universal.

This says a lot of the Markan Church. In terms of the history of the early Church, the Markan Church was born within a culture permeated by Jewish beliefs and practices, but had moved beyond that. It entered the imperial world of Rome, whose culture was permeated by Hellenistic culture and civilization.[22] It had moved from a predominantly Jewish culture, but its memories were still fresh, at least among some of the members. The temptation was to look back to an idealized past instead looking forward. Mark's Gospel directed them to the future.

This also says a lot of Mark and his Gospel. Following Jesus, Mark proclaimed the gospel of God. Unlike the women who fled from the

---

[22] With respect to the early history of the Church seen from the perspective of Vatican II, see Karl Rahner, "Towards a Fundamental Theological Interpretation of Vatican II," *Theological Studies* 40 (1979) 716–27.

tomb and said nothing to anyone, Mark proclaimed "the beginning of the gospel of Jesus Christ [the Son of God]" to everyone who listened.

Like Paul, Mark dedicated himself to the mission to the nations. Becoming a Christian, he became a member of a particular community. As he matured, he brought the gospel to others, preparing them to be baptized. Over the years, he must have visited many communities, preaching and teaching. Eventually, he wrote his Gospel for those whom he evangelized, catechized, and prepared for baptism.

This would explain why it is so difficult to identify the Markan community and pinpoint where and when the Gospel was written. Instead of one Markan community, we should think of many communities. My hypothesis is that Mark addressed the Gospel to the growing Church of his time. As an itinerant preacher, a missionary, Mark may have developed the Gospel over many years and in many places.

This would also coincide with the data from the New Testament and Papias. Luke associated Mark with the primitive community in Jerusalem, where he knew Peter, and with the church in Antioch, where he knew Paul and Barnabas.

In the Book of Acts, Luke tells how Peter "went to the house of Mary, the mother of John who is called Mark, where there were many people gathered in prayer" (Acts 12:12). Later, when Barnabas and Paul completed their relief mission, they took "with them John, who is called Mark" (Acts 12:25). Mark would be their assistant on the first mission from Antioch (Acts 13:5-13), but not on the second (15:37-39).

In the second century, when the label *kata Marcon* ("According to Mark"), was added to the scroll of Mark, Christians in general identified Mark, the author of the Gospel, as the one Luke referred to in the Acts of the Apostles. They also identified him as the Mark mentioned in Colossians 4:10 as the cousin of Barnabas, in Philemon 24 as Paul's co-worker together with Aristarchus, Demas, and Luke (see also 2 Timothy 4:11), and the one referred to in 1 Peter as "Mark, my son" (1 Pet 5:13).

In a historical matter like this, we do not expect an absolute conclusion. But everything points that the author of the Gospel was the one referred to in the Book of Acts, the Pauline letters and 1 Peter.[23]

[23] Mark was not a disciple of Jesus, let alone one of the apostles. According to Papias of Hierapolis, Mark heard nothing of the Lord until Peter instructed him (see Eusebius, *Ecclesiastical History* 3.39.15). This argues in favor of Markan authorship. By the final decades of the first century and

It explains why Mark was steeped in the early tradition. In Jerusalem and in Antioch, he got to know Peter, James, Barnabas, Paul, and many others. With them, he participated in the most creative period that the Church has ever known.

Finally, why did Mark end the first part of the Gospel with a question, "Do you still not understand?" (8:21). Then, why did he end the whole Gospel with the flight of the women: "Then they went out and fled from the tomb, seized with trembling and bewilderment. They said nothing to anyone, for they were afraid" (16:8).

Did the Markan communities understand? Did they understand that Jesus was the Christ and the Son of God? Did they understand that, being the Christ, Jesus had to undergo the passion? Did they understand the implications of Jesus' passion for those who became his followers? Mark tried to make them understand with "the beginning of the gospel of Jesus Christ [the Son of God]." Were they afraid to proclaim the gospel of God, including the passion and the resurrection? Why were they afraid?

Surely, Mark thought that these themes and emphases corresponded to what the Church needed to hear. To answer these questions requires a close reading of the whole Gospel. For now, we will consider a few factors in relation to the meaning of the preface and its proclamation of "the beginning of the gospel" to the readers.

The Beginning of the Gospel

Why did Mark entitle his work "The beginning of the gospel of Jesus Christ [the Son of God]" rather than "The gospel of Jesus Christ [the Son of God]?" We could think of him as modest and apologetic, or realistic. As the latest author or editor of John's Gospel wrote: "There are also many other things that Jesus did, but if these were to be described individually, I do not think the whole world would contain the books that would be written" (John 21:25). No one could tell the whole story. Whether or not Mark was modest, his modesty would account only for what he did not attempt, not for what he presented in "the beginning of the gospel."

Mark referred to "the beginning" because he was convinced that "the beginning of the gospel" began with the mission of John the

---

throughout the second century, the tendency was to lend authority to a Christian writing by attributing it to someone like Peter or Paul. Unlike them, Mark would not have enhanced the authority of the Gospel. That is why Papias of Hierapolis had to defend its authority, at the very time when the label *kata Markon* ("according to Mark") was being added to its scroll.

Baptist and ended with the mission of the early Church. He was convinced that the Church he addressed now lived in the continuation of "the gospel of Jesus Christ [the Son of God]." Living in the continuation, they had to learn from the beginning. *good*

Many in the Church thought they were seeing the end. Mark responded with the story of another time when people thought it was the end of the gospel, the time when Jesus was put to death and buried, when everyone abandoned him, either at his arrest (14:50-51) and condemnation (14:66-72) or when a young man proclaimed his resurrection (16:1-8). The disciples thought it was the end, but it turned out to be the beginning.

In effect, Mark was telling his readers, "Now, you think it is the end!" To understand the continuation of the gospel in the Church they had to understand the beginning of the gospel. As a preacher and teacher, Mark fulfilled his mission by proclaiming "the beginning of the gospel."

The entire Gospel is relevant for the situation when Mark wrote "the beginning of the gospel." But the eschatological discourse (13:5-37) has special relevance. In the discourse, Jesus spoke to his closest disciples, Peter, James, John, and Andrew, the first four Jesus called to be fishers of human beings (1:16-20). The setting for the discourse is the Mount of Olives overlooking Jerusalem (13:1-4). The discourse speaks of what would happen in the future, of the various conflicts and persecutions that the community would have to experience. Many in the Church thought that the future had come and that the ultimate tribulation was upon them, heralding the end of the gospel.

For Mark, conflicts among nations and kingdoms, even a war that would level the walls of Jerusalem, were not signs of the end. Nor were natural calamities such as earthquakes and famines. All these things were but the beginning of labor pains (13:9), for a birth which would take place at some unknown time in the future (13:32) once the gospel was preached to all nations (13:10). Mark needed to bolster the faith of the community that it might be faithful in its witness to the end (13:9-13). For that, he counted on the authority of Jesus. *good*

Such is the context for Mark's telling the story of the beginning of the gospel. At a time when nearly everyone felt it was the end, Mark boldly told the story of the beginning. When so many were overwhelmed by what seemed to be bad news, he proclaimed the story of the beginning of the good news. *post J-R war, post 70*

Jesus Christ [the Son of God]

Knowing the historical context of Mark's community helps us understand why the Gospel dwells so much on the disciples' lack of understanding and hardness of heart, on the inability to see, hear, speak, and walk, also on the overwhelming presence of unclean spirits and demonic forces. It helps also to understand why the Gospel emphasized the passion (14:1–16:8) and the conflicts and controversies (see 2:1–3:6; 11:27–12:40) that led to it.

The name "Jesus Christ" and the title "Christ" were already long associated with the passion and resurrection of Jesus, as well as with Christian baptism. Mark emphasized especially its relation to the passion. Not that the passion in itself was more important than the resurrection. But from a pastoral point of view, he had to emphasize the passion and the baptismal participation in it. The communities had to know that there would not have been a resurrection without the passion. In relation to their baptism, there is no rising with Christ without dying with Christ.

Mark's story of Jesus Christ emphasized the passion, what seemed to be the end, because all knew that it had proven to be the beginning. He told the story of Jesus' journey to Jerusalem as a journey to the passion. What people thought as the end was a prelude to new life for Jesus and his followers.

How could they have forgotten? As followers of Jesus Christ, they should expect to suffer some of the resistance and violence Jesus had suffered. Did they not live in the continuation of the gospel? Recognizing that, they should know that they lived in the continuation of the passion. What seemed to be bad news, the triumph of evil, and the end of everything, would prove to be good news, the triumph of the gospel, and a new beginning.

The title "the Son of God" was associated with the Davidic kingship. But the Markan communities had to be reminded that Jesus was not a political, earthly king. And so, Mark associated the title "the Son of God" with Jesus' exaltation and his coming in glory. With the name "Jesus Christ," he made his readers face their passion in faith. If he included the title "the Son of God," he offered them ultimate hope in the kingdom of God.

As a preface, Mark 1:1 is thus a bold proclamation, a fresh statement of the gospel of Jesus, and an eloquent challenge to the readers. Such a proclamation was eminently suited to tell how Jesus had proclaimed the gospel and how the first disciples had proclaimed the death and resurrection of Jesus the proclaimer. Mark's Gospel, which speaks of proclaiming the gospel is itself a literary act of proclamation. His Gospel is indeed the beginning of the gospel of Jesus Christ, the Son of God.

II

༒ Prologue ༒

The Gospel in Miniature

Mark 1:2-13

Mark's Gospel has a name, the "Gospel According to Mark." The name was added long after it was written when the Gospels were collected in a book. Of course, Mark himself never referred to his Gospel as the "Gospel According to Mark." Beginning in the second and third centuries, Christians used the name to distinguish the Gospel of Mark from other Gospels, particularly for the purpose of public reading in the Christian assembly.

Mark's Gospel also has a title, "the beginning of the gospel of Jesus Christ, [the Son of God]" (1:1). In relation to Mark's Gospel, the title introduces the Gospel and tells what it is about. As such, it is summary of the Gospel. In relation to the readers, the title addresses the readers and tells what the Gospel is for. As such, it is a preface to the readers.

As an introductory summary, the "beginning of the gospel of Jesus Christ, [the Son of God]" (1:1) is very concise. Like a signpost or marquee, it introduces Mark's story as the beginning of the gospel or good news. Mark did not attempt to write the entire story of the gospel, but only the beginning. The story proper then begins with a second introduction, now in the form of a prologue (1:2-13).[1]

---

[1] Many have concluded that Mark's prologue extends to 1:15. As the conclusion of the prologue, the summary in 1:14-15 would be its climax. See

Like the prefatory title, the prologue has two functions. It is an introduction for the Gospel. At the same time, it is a prologue to the reader. As an introduction, it presents the main themes of the Gospel in story form. As such, it can be described as the Gospel in miniature. As a prologue, it addresses the readers and attunes them to the purpose of the Gospel. As such, it can be described as a preliminary proclamation of the gospel.[2]

Since the opening statement that constitutes the title and preface (1:1) is very short, its two functions were considered separately. For the prologue (1:2-13), however, which is much longer, the two functions will be considered together.

As with Mark's opening statement, we need a close reading of the whole Gospel to appreciate the prologue's Gospel in miniature and its message to Mark's readers. But for now, respecting the prologue's nature as a symbolic overture, we will introduce it as a narrative synthesis of the Gospel and show how its various units are related to the Gospel.

A Narrative Synthesis

Like every other segment of the Gospel, the prologue tells a particular story that can be read and appreciated on its own. It begins with a biblical inscription or epigraph (1:1-2) that relates the prologue and the entire Gospel to the Scriptures. After the inscription, the prologue continues with the story of John the Baptist, highlighting his identity as a new Elijah, whose mission is to prepare the way of the Lord (1:4-8). It concludes with the story of the baptism of Jesus, announcing his identity as God's beloved Son whose mission is presented symbolically as a forty-day test in the desert (1:9-13).

Every gospel story must be read and interpreted in light of the entire Gospel. This applies in a special way to the prologue because of its unique function. Besides being a story in itself, it announces the

---

M. Eugene Boring, "Mark 1:1-15 and the Beginning of the Gospel," *Semeia* 52 (1991) 43–81, especially 53–59. In view of the summary's literary relationship to the call of the first disciples (1:16-20) and to other summaries of Jesus' mission and ministry, (3:7-12; 6:6b), 1:14-15 can also be considered as an introduction for the first section of the Gospel (1:14–3:6) and through it the entire Gospel.

[2] For the prologue's relationship to the Gospel, see John R. Donahue, S.J., "Windows and Mirrors: The Setting of Mark's Gospel," *The Catholic Biblical Quarterly* 57/1 (January 1995) 9–12.

major themes that are developed in the Gospel. Its story seems very simple, but actually it is a narrative synthesis of the entire Gospel.

Mark's prologue, like that of John, Luke[3] and Matthew, is a literary key to the Gospel, providing a brief guide for the reader. We saw that to understand the title and preface (1:1) we have to be familiar with the whole Gospel. It is the same with the prologue. Like the title and preface, the prologue has to be read in the light of the Gospel, and the Gospel has to be read in the light of the prologue. It is very helpful to reread the prologue after reading each section, asking how the prologue introduced the section.

The prologue can be compared to the overture of an opera, which gathers the major themes of the opera in an orchestral introduction. Those who are unfamiliar with the opera can enjoy the music. Many overtures are performed apart from their operatic context. But only those that are familiar with the opera can recognize how its basic themes have been gathered into a new musical synthesis. So it is that we can read Mark 1:2-13 apart from Mark's Gospel, especially in the liturgy. But only those that are familiar with the whole Gospel can appreciate Mark's achievement in the prologue.

Like John the Baptist, who prepared the way of the Lord, the prologue prepares the way of the Gospel. It does this with a short symbolic narrative. Relating "the beginning of the gospel of Jesus Christ [the Son of God]" to Scripture and the mission of John the Baptist, the prologue announces their fulfillment in the person and mission of Jesus. To appreciate such a prologue and how John the Baptist prepared the way for the Lord, we must read the entire Gospel.

An Overview

The prologue can be divided in three parts. The first part is a biblical inscription attributed to Isaiah the prophet (1:2-3). The second part presents John the Baptist and his prophetic mission (1:4-8) and the third Jesus and his divine mission (1:9-13).

The biblical inscription (1:2-3) introduces the missions of John and Jesus, but without naming them. Attributed to Isaiah the prophet, the inscription is actually a synthesis of three passages, including Malachi 3:1, Exodus 23:20, and Isaiah 40:3.[4] The components of

---

[3] Luke's second volume, the Acts of the Apostles, has also a prologue in Acts 1:3-14.

[4] In his book, *The Way of the Lord, Christological Exegesis of the Old Testament in the Gospel of Mark*, Joel Marcus presented Mark 1:2-3 as "the Gospel According to Isaiah" (Louisville: Westminster/John Knox Press, 1992) 12–47.

the inscription can be found in various parts of Matthew and Luke, but only Mark brought them together in a literary and theological synthesis.

The inscription announces John's mission as a divine messenger to prepare the way for the Lord. The life and mission of John the Baptist and of Jesus of Nazareth are thus anchored in biblical prophecy. It is only later, and in looking back, that we learn how the messenger actually prepared the way of the Lord. By presenting the biblical synthesis at the very beginning, Mark expands our imagination. After reading the inscription, we expect to encounter biblical personages that are larger than life. We are also ready for biblical wonders and signs.

As such, the inscription itself can be considered as a biblical prologue for the prologue of Mark's Gospel. If the prologue (1:2-13) is the Gospel in miniature, the inscription is the prologue in miniature.

The inscription first provides a biblical frame of reference for the prologue's story of John of Baptist (1:4-8). The prologue then tells John's story in two parts. The first describes his general mission, how he proclaimed a baptism of repentance and how many people accepted his message (1:4-5). The second describes his special mission as a new Elijah, preparing the way for the Lord (1:6-8).

John the Baptist was God's messenger, one who was sent to prepare the way for the Lord. He did this as a voice of one crying in the desert, calling everyone to join him in preparing the way of the Lord (1:2-3) through a baptism of repentance for the forgiveness of sins (1:4).

The people's response to John's preaching was enormous. People came to him from the whole of Judea as well as from Jerusalem to be baptized in the Jordan River as they confessed their sins (1:5). Later, Jesus too would attract large crowds, as Mark frequently notes (e.g., 1:28, 33, 37, 45; 2:2; 3:7-12). In both cases, the crowds that they attracted do not impede their violent deaths (see 6:14; 14:2). Nor would it impede the martyrdom of some of Jesus' followers.

John's general mission and its popular success (1:4-5) provide the setting for John's special mission as a new Elijah (1:6-8). John is identified as Elijah through a description of his clothing (1:6; see 2 Kgs 1:8). John exercised his mission as a desert ascetic subsisting on the desert's hospitality.

As a new Elijah, John's mission was to proclaim the advent of one of his followers, one that would be mightier than John. His follower would also baptize, but unlike John, who baptized with water alone, he would baptize with the holy Spirit. Much later in the Gospel, Mark will show how the way of the Lord was the way to Jerusalem, where the Son of Man would be put to death and rise after three days (10:32-34). The baptism that Jesus offers associates his followers with his death (10:38-39) as his supreme act of service (10:45). If some of Mark's readers were persecuted, they were participating in the baptism in which Jesus was baptized.

The inscription (1:2-3) also provided a biblical setting for the life and mission of Jesus (1:9-13). The biblical voice in the inscription first addresses Jesus, "Behold, I am sending my messenger ahead of you *[pro prosopou sou]*; he will prepare your way *[ten hodon sou]*" (1:2). Having addressed Jesus, it then addressed everyone who reads Mark's Gospel (1:3).

John's life and mission (1:4-8) also introduces Jesus, who came from Nazareth of Galilee and was baptized by John in the Jordan (1:9). Jesus was one of many who responded to John's baptismal proclamation (1:5). But, as John had announced, Jesus was mightier than John (1:7-8).

Like John's story, Jesus' story is told in two parts. The prologue first describes Jesus' baptism by John, the descent of the holy Spirit, and the heavenly voice that addressed Jesus as God's beloved Son (1:9-11). Second, it describes the baptismal life of God's beloved Son in the desert (1:12-13).

After introducing Jesus (1:9), the prologue tells why he was mightier than John. As Jesus emerged from the waters of John's baptism, he saw the Spirit descending on him (1:10). Anointed by the Spirit, Jesus would baptize with the Spirit (see 1:8). Then Jesus heard a heavenly voice announcing that he was God's beloved Son. As a follower of John, Jesus was also God's beloved Son. John the Baptist was preparing the way for God's beloved Son with whom God was well pleased (1:11). Divine love is very demanding. In the case of Jesus, the anointed one and God's beloved Son, it demanded the gift of his life.

The prologue's final scene presents the baptismal life of Jesus. Driven by the Spirit into the desert, he was tempted by Satan for forty days. He was among the wild beasts while angels ministered to him (1:12-13). In the Gospel, what would be the wild beasts? Better, who would be the wild beasts? Who would be the angels? As Mark ends the prologue, he leaves us wondering and pondering.

Basic Themes

The overview of the prologue introduced us to its structure, its sub-units, and how they contribute to the prologue's over-all development. It also gave us a glimpse of the Gospel's basic themes, including Isaiah's prophetic message. Isaiah has a special place in

Mark's biblical theology, as we see in 4:12 (Isa 6:9), 7:6-7 (Isa 29:13), 11:17 (Isa 56:7) and 12:10 (Isa 28:16). No other prophet, indeed no other biblical book receives so much attention in Mark's Gospel. Interpreted by Mark, Isaiah calls his readers to "prepare the way of the Lord" (1:3).

With Isaiah, Mark also introduced the theme of the desert (1:1-3), which frames the mission of John and Jesus in the prologue (1:4, 12-13). In Mark's Gospel, the desert is much more than a geographical region. Evoking the exodus of the people of God, it is a symbolic place associated with repentance (1:4), temptation or testing (1:12-13), prayer (1:35), solitude (1:45), and rest (6:31-32). It is also the place where Jesus broke the bread, providing nourishment for the five thousand (6:34-44; see 6:35) with a new manna, and later for the four thousand (8:1-9; see 8:4).

The prologue also introduces the theme of the way (*he hodos*, 1:2-3), a major image in the second part of the Gospel (8:22–16:8). In relation to the way, the prologue also emphasizes the one who goes before (*pro prosopou*, 1:2) and those who come after (*opiso*, 1:7) him on the way (see 1:16-20; 8:33, 34; 10:32-34; 14:28; 16:7).[5]

Then, of course, there are the themes of proclamation, repentance, forgiveness of sins, the role of the prophet Elijah, the region of Galilee, the holy Spirit, Jesus' divine Sonship, and baptism. All of these play a very prominent role in the Gospel. But as the most prominent theme in the prologue, baptism is in a category apart.

Baptism is clearly the central theme of the prologue. John came to baptize in the desert and to proclaim a baptism of repentance (1:4). Many from Judea and Jerusalem came to him and were baptized (1:5). John baptized with water, but one of his followers would baptize with the holy Spirit (1:8). Jesus came from Nazareth of Galilee to be baptized by John (1:9). Anointed by the Spirit, Jesus pursued his baptismal life in the desert (1:12-13).

After the prologue, there is no explicit reference to baptism until Jesus asks James and John if they were willing and able to be baptized with the same baptism with which Jesus was baptized (10:38-39). If the prologue is indeed the Gospel in miniature, and if the prologue sets the basic themes of the Gospel, how is it that there is so little mention of baptism in the Gospel?

[5] In 10:32; 14:28; 16:7, the verb *proago* describes Jesus as he leads, precedes, or goes before his followers. In the inscription, the expression *pro prosopou* describes the one who goes ahead and prepares the way.

We should not underestimate Jesus' challenge to James and John and its critical role in the Gospel. It associates Christian baptism with Jesus' passion and resurrection, particularly the passion. Would Jesus' followers stay with him as they enter the passion? Would they abandon him? Would they deny him? Denying him, they would deny their relationship to him. Were they able to die with him, be buried with him, and live with him, all in view of rising with him?[6]

Jesus' dialogue with the James and John refers to his passion and resurrection as a baptismal event. Even if baptism is seldom referred to in the Gospel, at least explicitly, it underlies the whole of the passion and resurrection account (14:1–16:8). And since the entire Gospel, beginning with the very first section (see 1:20-28; 2:1–3:6), leads to the passion, the Gospel as a whole must be read in the light of Christian baptism. In the baptism of Christ's passion-resurrection, Jesus' followers share in the life and mission of the beloved Son who was anointed by the Spirit (1:8, 10, 12).

Mark's Gospel thus tells the story of Jesus and his followers as the story of baptismal proclamation, initiation, and commitment. Every other theme is related to this central theme. If so, the source for Mark's Gospel may well be the baptismal catechesis of the communities in which Mark ministered and fulfilled his mission.[7]

Biblical Inscription (1:2-3)

"As it is written *[kathos gegraptai]* in Isaiah the prophet" (1:2a). So begins the prologue of Mark. With this seemingly perfunctory statement, Mark announces that "the beginning of the gospel of Jesus Christ [the Son of God]" (1:1) unfolded "as it is written in Isaiah the prophet." As such, the statement introduces not only the mission and ministry of John the Baptist, but also the good news of Jesus Christ.

After the opening statement, Mark presents a biblical inscription for the prologue and through it for the entire Gospel. Deceptively simple, this programmatic inscription is a brilliant synthesis, composed with elements from the prophet Malachi and the book of Exodus as well as Isaiah the prophet, but focused on Isaiah. Hence the introduction: "As it is written *[kathos gegraptai]* in Isaiah the prophet"

---

[6] Mark's theology of baptism is very close if not identical to that of Paul in Romans 6:1-11.

[7] Many stories in the Gospel, including the passion narrative, can be read as baptismal stories. This commentary will test this hypothesis.

(1:2a). The expression *kathos gegraptai* ("as it is written") is a common formula in the Septuagint for citing a biblical passage.[8]

The inscription opens with a reference to Malachi: "Behold, I am sending my messenger to prepare the way before me" (Mal 3:1). This oracular message is part of "the word of the LORD to Israel through Malachi" (Mal 1:1). The Lord's messenger is sent to prepare the way for the Lord, that is, for God, who is coming to visit the people of Israel.

In the prologue, Mark modifies Malachi 3:1 with a reference to Exodus: "See, I am sending an angel before you" (Exod 23:20).[9] The same verse then specifies the role of the angel: "to guard you on the way and bring you to the place I have prepared." Combining the two references, Mark transforms Malachi 3:1 into: "Behold, I am sending my messenger ahead of you; he will prepare your way" *(ten hodou sou)* (1:2b). In the inscription, the messenger no longer prepares the way for God ("before me") but for God's beloved Son ("ahead of you," *pro prosopou sou,* literally, "before you").

In a slightly different form, this theological synthesis of Malachi 3:1 and Exodus 23:20 was solidly embedded in early Christian tradition. Drawing from Q, both Matthew and Luke used it to describe John's mission and its relation to that of Jesus (Matt 11:10; Luke 7:27).[10] In Mark, the combined text is a proclamation, a prophetic announcement that touches the spirit and challenges the imagination. It raises questions. Who? Where? When? How? In Matthew and Luke, the text is a biblical catechesis, explaining the meaning of John's mission. Instead of raising questions, it provides answers.

In the Synoptic tradition, the presentation of John as "my messenger"[11] is extremely significant. Later, the book of Malachi identifies "my messenger" with Elijah: "Lo, I will send you Elijah, the prophet" (Mal 3:23a). At the very beginning of the inscription, Mark thus raises expectation regarding the return of Elijah, who was ex-

---

[8] See Vincent Taylor, *The Gospel According to the St. Mark* (London: Macmillan & Co. LTD, 1963) 153.

[9] Exodus refers to the angel of God in several places, including Exod 14:19; 23:20, 23; 32:34; 33:2. In Exodus, the angel of God is the presence of God leading and protecting the people of Israel.

[10] In many Byzantine icons, John the Baptist is presented with the robes and wings of an angel, an iconographic interpretation of Mark 1:2, Matt 11:20 and Luke 7:27.

[11] In Hebrew, the name "Malachi" means "my messenger." The anonymous author of the Book of Malachi referred to himself as "My Messenger," that is, Malachi (see Mal 1:1; 3:1).

pected to come "before the day of the LORD comes" (Mal 3:23b). As such, the biblical inscription not only introduces the mission of John but also the coming of Jesus, from his coming to Galilee (1:14-15) to his coming with the clouds of heaven with great power and glory (see 13:26; 14:62).

According to Mark, many identified Jesus with Elijah (6:15; 8:28), but as Jesus told the disciples, Elijah had already come "and they did to him whatever they pleased, as it is written of him" (9:13; see 6:17-29). John the Baptist, not Jesus, came as Elijah. But as Elijah, John prepared the way for Jesus.

Everything is prepared for the prologue's description of John the Baptist as the prophet Elijah paving the way for the coming of the Lord Jesus (1:6-8). John's Gospel, which explicitly denies that John the Baptist was Elijah (1:21), does not refer to the theological synthesis of Malachi 3:1 and Exodus 23:20.

In the first verse of the biblical inscription, the Lord addresses Jesus in the second person. Later in the prologue, a voice from heaven addresses him again in the second person: "You are my beloved Son." In both cases, the proclamation is for the readers' benefit. This is made clear as the inscription moves into its second verse, now using the third person.

The passage from Isaiah reads like this:

> "A voice of one crying out in the desert *[en te eremo]*:
>   'Prepare the way of the Lord *[ten hodou kyriou]*,
>   make straight his paths'" (1:3; see Isa 40:3).

Matthew, Luke, and John used the same text to introduce and interpret the mission of John the Baptist (Matt 3:3; Luke 3:4; John 1:23).

In the context of Deutero-Isaiah (Isa 40–55), the passage refers to the Israelites' return from Babylon after a long exile comparable to their years of servitude in Egypt. When a king or an important public servant was to travel to a foreign capital, a road crew was sent in advance to prepare the way for his coming. So would it be with the coming of Jesus. John the Baptist was to prepare the way for his coming.

The genius of Mark was to transform Malachi 3:1 with Exodus 23:10 and to use the conflated text as an introduction to Isaiah 40:3. In this way, Mark identified the way of Jesus (1:2b) with "the way of the Lord" (1:3). As such, he also identified God's new saving action with the way of Jesus.[12]

---

[12] See Joel Marcus, op. cit., 37–41.

Composing the biblical synthesis, Mark viewed the Scriptures through the lens of the mission of John the Baptist and the mission of Jesus. In this way, he provided a biblical theology for "the beginning of the gospel of Jesus Christ [the Son of God]," that is, for the entire Gospel.

The Life and Mission of John the Baptist (1:4-8)

The biblical inscription at the head of Mark's prologue announces God's messenger as the voice of one crying in the desert (1:2-3). The messenger is then introduced as John the Baptist,[13] who appeared in the desert baptizing and proclaiming a baptism of repentance for the forgiveness of sins (1:4).[14] John was both a baptizer and a preacher.

In this second part of the prologue (1:4-8), the attention focuses on John and his mission. But as with the biblical inscription (1:1-2), Mark does not present John's prophetic mission for its own sake but in view of preparing the way of Jesus and his transcendent mission (1:6-8; see 9-13).

Like the biblical inscription, the life and mission of John the Baptist can be divided into two parts. The first part describes John's general mission as a baptizer and proclaimer (1:4-5). The second describes John's specific mission as Elijah (1:6) and his relation to Jesus (1:7-8).

John, Baptizer and Proclaimer (1:4)

John's preaching or proclaiming ministry was known to Mark's readers from Israel's prophetic tradition as well as from their own Christian tradition. Jesus was a preacher, proclaiming the kingdom of God. So did his followers, including many of Mark's readers.

For John's baptizing ministry, however, as far as we know, there was no precedent when he came on the scene. There was a precedent for his reforming movement, but not for his baptismal movement. John's baptism was somewhat comparable to the Jewish ritual

---

[13] The title, "the Baptist" *(ho baptizon)* is used in 6:14 and 6:24. In 1:4, many ancient manuscripts did not include the article. Without the article, the reading would be "John appeared baptizing in the desert."

[14] For a discussion of the textual options of 1:4 and the syntax of 1:1-4, see M. Eugene Boring, "Mark 1:1-15 and the Beginning of the Gospel," *Semeia* 52 (1991) 47–50.

of purification with water that can be traced to that era among the Essenes and in relation to early synagogue worship.

Evidence for this comes from the rich Essene library and the installations discovered at Qumran,[15] from the archeological remains of purification pools at some of the early synagogues,[16] and private homes in Jerusalem dating before the Roman destruction in A.D. 70.[17] The practice of ritual purification in ancient Judaism may have provided a general context for John's baptism. But unlike the ritual purification practiced by the Essenes and the synagogue, the baptism of John was not to be repeated. John called for a definitive conversion to welcome the eschatological coming of the Lord.[18] For Mark and his readers, the primary point of reference for John's baptism was the Christian practice of baptism, which also expressed a definitive commitment.

John's baptism called for a profound change of heart or conversion, for a *metanoia,* as it was called in Greek. *Metanoia,* the essential condition for the forgiveness of sins, was the direct purpose of John's baptism. The Greek term for sin, *hamartia,* refers to a personal offense as well as to the resulting break in a personal relationship.

Forgiveness *(aphesis)* is a personal gesture that dismisses the offense and restores the relationship that had once existed. For someone to be forgiven, *metanoia* was a condition, but forgiveness remained a free and gracious gesture. That is why John's baptism did not effect the forgiveness of sins. Rather, it expressed a *metanoia* in view of the forgiveness of sins.

So it is that John prepared the way for the coming of the Lord, the one who had "authority to forgive sins on earth" (2:10) and save everyone from sin and death. Jesus gave "his life as a ransom for many" (10:45) and offered the cup of his blood that would "be shed for many" (14:24).[19]

[15] See A.R.C. Leaney, *The Rule of Qumran and Its Meaning,* The New Testament Library (Philadelphia: The Westminster Press, 1966) 141–42; Jerome Murphy-O'Connor, *The Holy Land, An Archeological Guide from Earliest Times to 1700,* New Edition (New York: Oxford University Press, 1986) 321–25.

[16] See Yigael Yadin, *Masada, Herod's Fortress and the Zealous Last Stand* (Jerusalem: Steimatzky, 1966) 164–67.

[17] See Nahman Avigad, *Discovering Jerusalem* (Nashville: Thomas Nelson Publishers, 1980) 139–43.

[18] For Mark, the end-time or *eschaton* began with the mission of Jesus Christ and will end with his final coming in glory.

[19] In 10:45 and 14:24, "many" is not opposed to "all" but to "one."

Popular Response (1:5)

John's mission met with great success, if we judge by the crowds that came to hear him and be baptized by him (1:5). According to Mark's account, people came from the entire Judean countryside, and all who lived in Jerusalem came to be baptized by John in the river Jordan. In their baptism, they indicated their *metanoia* by confessing their sins.

There is no mention of people coming to John from Galilee. Later, when the prologue announces that Jesus came from Nazareth of Galilee (1:9), it highlights the singular nature of the baptism of Jesus. The crowds came from Jerusalem and Judea. Jesus came all the way from Nazareth of Galilee. In his limited mission, John prepared the way for Jesus' universal mission, when people would come to him from Galilee, from Judea, from Jerusalem, as well as from Idumea, from Transjordan, and from the region of Tyre and Sidon (3:7-8).[20]

Mark gives no indication of where John baptized other than that it was somewhere along the Jordan. The provenance of the crowd, which came from Judea and Jerusalem, points to a site not far from the Dead Sea. Here Mark differs from John's Gospel, in which John baptized in a place called Bethany across the Jordan (John 1:28). The context of John 1:19-51 presupposes a place not far from the Sea of Galilee.

A New Elijah (1:6)

From the beginning, the prologue's biblical inscription announced that God's messenger was Elijah (1:2; see Mal 3:1, 23). Introducing John right after the inscription, the prologue invites us to think of John the Baptist as this new Elijah (1:4-5). Now, with a brief but very graphic description of John's clothing (1:6), it tells us in unmistakable terms that John was indeed Elijah.

Like Elijah of old, John came clothed in camel's hair and with a leather belt around his waist. This clothing was so characteristic of Elijah that it proclaimed his identity. When messengers came to king Ahaziah with the announcement that his infidelity would result in

---

[20] As Luke tells it, the crowds did not come to John. Rather, he went about the whole region of the Jordan seeking people to address (Luke 3:3). This fits Luke's general emphasis on John's prophetic mission rather than on his baptizing ministry. Mark's presentation sets the stage for the great crowds that would come to Jesus later in the Gospel (3:7-8).

death, he inquired who told them these things. They answered, "He wore a garment of haircloth, with a belt of leather around his loins." To that Ahaziah responded, "It is Elijah the Tishbite" (2 Kgs 1:5-8). Now, when Mark describes John's garments in similar terms, we are expected to exclaim, "John is Elijah the Tishbite!"

Like Elijah, John the Baptist was a true prophet. The prophet Zechariah had spoken of the day when prophecy would cease: "On that day,[21] every prophet shall be ashamed to prophesy his vision, neither shall he assume the hairy mantle to mislead" (Zech 13:4). Zechariah was referring to the day of the Lord. John the Baptist would be an exception. As a new Elijah, preparing the way of the Lord, John the Baptist was not ashamed to prophesy. Like the prophets of old, he wore his garment of camel's hair as a sign of his calling.

Garments in the ancient world and many parts of the world today are very significant. They protect a person from the elements, but they also speak the person's identity. When Paul describes Christian baptism as "putting on" Christ, he means that a baptized person has a new identity (see Gal 3:27; Rom 13:14). When Mark describes the garments of John, he is speaking of his personal identity.[22]

Elijah was a man of God, a reformer, a protector of widows, and a worker of signs and wonders. He nourished the hungry and even raised the dead to life. Mark's description of John leads us to expect something similar of him. Later, we are not surprised that John denounces Herod for taking his brother's wife and that John was recognized as a righteous and holy man (6:17-19). Like Elijah, dressed in rough garments, John spoke tough words to the powerful of his day, calling them to repentance in order that their sins might be forgiven.[23]

We are also told that John survived on locusts and wild honey, the harsh staples of desert hospitality. His diet calls to mind Jesus'

[21] In the book of Zechariah, the phrase, "on that day," refers to eschatological times. Punctuating the chapters 12–14, it is used seventeen times (12:3, 4, 6, 8a, 8b, 9, 11; 13:1, 2, 4; 14:4, 6, 8, 9, 13, 20, 21). See Carol L. Meyers and Eric M. Meyers, *Zechariah 9–14,* The Anchor Bible, vol. 25c (New York: Doubleday, 1993) 316–17.

[22] See Erik Peterson, *Pour une theologie du vetement,* translated by M.-J. Congar, O.P., La Clarte-Dieu VIII (Lyon: Editions de L'Abeille, 1943); Edgar Haulotte, S. J., *Symbolique du vetement selon la Bible,* Theologie 65 (Paris: Aubier, 1966); E. LaVerdiere, "A Garment of Camel's Hair" *Emmanuel* 92 (1986) 545–51, and "Robed in Radiant White" *Emmanuel* 90 (1984) 138–42.

[23] For the story of Elijah, see 1 Kings 17–19, 21; 2 Kings 1–2.

instructions for the Christian missionary journey. The disciples were
to take no provisions. As they went about preaching repentance,
they were to accept whatever local hospitality provided (6:8-10).
John did the same, but in the desert wilderness by the Jordan River,
where the local hospitality consisted in locusts and wild honey.

John and Jesus (1:7-8)

We now come to the climax of the prologue's story of John (1:7-8).
As a new Elijah, John came for a special mission. John himself describes his special mission while summarizing his preaching. Jesus
also would describe his mission in a short summary (1:15). Everything John said and did proclaimed the coming of one far mightier
than he. John was not even worthy to stoop and loosen the thongs
of his sandals (1:7).

The one who was mightier than John would also come to baptize,
but with a difference. John baptized with water. He would baptize
with the holy Spirit, the purifying Spirit of God, that would make
those who repent holy, as God is holy (1:8). Later, the Gospel will
also speak of Jesus' baptism as a baptism in his passion (10:38-39).

In all of this, Jesus is never explicitly identified. All we know is that
one of John's followers was mightier than John. Such is the meaning
of the expression "after me" *(opiso mou)* in the summary of John's
preaching: "One mightier than I is coming after me" (1:7a). The preposition *opiso* with the genitive *mou* or *autou* does not refer to a temporal but to a personal relationship. The same expression, "after me"
(opiso mou), is used when Jesus calls his first disciples: "Come after
me" *(Deute opiso mou,* 1:17). Responding, they "followed him," or more
literally, "they came after him" *(apelthon opiso autou,* 1:20).[24]

The same expression, *opiso mou,* is used later when Jesus re-
proaches Peter, "Get behind me" *(Hypage opiso mou,* 8:33), more literally, "Get back after me," meaning, "Get back into my following"
see 1:17). In this case, the expression, "behind me" *(opiso mou)* does
not refer to a local but to a personal relationship. The same expression, *opiso mou,* is used immediately afterwards when Jesus says,
"Whoever wishes to come after me *[opiso mou]* must deny himself,
take up his cross, and follow me *[akoloutheito moi]*" (8:34).

The biblical inscription (1:2-3) had raised expectations. Who was
this messenger? Who was this new Elijah? Who was this prophet

---

[24] In 1:16-20, "after me" *(opiso mou)* or "after him" *(opiso autou)* is equivalent to "follow me" or "following him." When Jesus calls Simon and Andrew
to come after *(opiso)* him, they followed *(ekolouthesan)* him (1:17-18).

who would raise his voice in the desert? The prologue's story of John the Baptist (1:4-8) has raised further expectations. Who was this follower who was mightier than John? Who was John's follower who would baptize not with water but with the holy Spirit?

The Life and Mission of Jesus (1:9-13)

In the first part of the prologue, that is, in the biblical inscription (1:2-3), God addressed Jesus, but without naming him: "Behold, I am sending my messenger ahead of you; he will prepare your way" (1:2). Most of the inscription focused on John the Baptist, God's messenger, the one who would prepare the way for Jesus.

In the second part, in the story of the life and mission of John the Baptist (1:4-8), John announces that one of his followers was mightier than he was (1:7), again without naming him. John then describes his follower's mission in relation to his: "I have baptized you with water; he will baptize you with the holy Spirit" (1:8).

The third part of the prologue focuses on the life and mission of Jesus (1:9-13). Like the first and second part, it can be divided into two related units, one telling about the baptism of Jesus (1:9-11),[25] the other about Jesus' baptismal life (1:12-13).

The Baptism of Jesus (1:9-11)

In the third and climactic part of the prologue, the one who was mightier than John is finally named. His name was Jesus, and he came from Nazareth of Galilee. The central question of Mark's Gospel is Jesus' identity. As the Gospel in miniature, the prologue now focuses on Jesus' identity (1:9-13). Luke and Matthew presented Jesus' identity in the stories of his conception, birth, and manifestation. John presented Jesus' identity in a poetic meditation on the Word of God made flesh. Mark presented Jesus' identity in the story of his baptism by John.

As with John the Baptist, Mark assumes we are familiar with Jesus: "It happened in those days that Jesus came from Nazareth of Galilee and was baptized in the Jordan by John" (1:9). In the Gospel, Jesus is associated with both Galilee (1:14; 14:67, 70) and Nazareth (16:6).

At first sight, it may appear problematic that Jesus accepted John's baptism. After all, John's baptism called for a change of heart

---

[25] For a theological analysis of 1:9-11, especially for its references to Scripture and how Mark integrated them in his Christology, see Joel Marcus, op. cit. 48–79.

(*metanoia*) in view of the forgiveness of sins. How could Jesus, who was not a sinner, have accepted such a baptism? In John's Gospel, John the Baptist gives testimony to Jesus as the Lamb of God, but he does not baptize Jesus (see John 1:29-34).

For readers who approach life's challenges in individualistic terms, the baptism of a sinless person makes no sense because the baptism has no meaning beyond the individual who is baptized. For readers, however, who view life's challenges in interpersonal terms, the baptism of a sinless person makes a lot of sense.

Jesus did not have to be a sinner to accept John's baptism. All he needed was to be in personal solidarity with men and women who are sinners and in need of salvation. Jesus' baptism by John presented him as a person in solidarity with all human beings, and it demonstrated his willingness to bear the weight of our sins on his own sinless shoulders.

The prologue has emphasized the enormous popular response to John's mission (1:5). It now presents the divine response to Jesus' baptism by John (1:10-11). Jesus' baptism by John revealed Jesus' humanity and his solidarity with and commitment to sinners. What followed the baptism revealed his divinity and his solidarity with and commitment to God his Father.

As Jesus came up (*anabainon*) from the waters of baptism, "he saw the heavens being torn open" (*schizomenous tous ouranous*) (1:10a). As the heavens were torn open, he saw the Spirit of God coming down (*katabainon*) upon him in the form of a dove (1:10b). The heavens were torn open rending in response to Isaiah's prayer: "Oh, that you would rend the heavens [*anoixes ton ouranon*] and come down, / with the mountains quaking before you" (Isa 63:19).

At Jesus' baptism, the rending of the heavens announced the beginning of the eschatological age. At the end of his ministry as Jesus breathed his last, the veil of the sanctuary would be rent from top to bottom (15:38). In the eschatological age, the holy of holies and the ancient sacrifices would be no more.

Isaiah had prayed that the heavens be rent and that the Lord come down (Isa 63:19) to bring his flock up from the sea, to put his holy Spirit in the midst of his people (Isa 63:11) and to guide them in a new exodus (Isa 63:14). The image of the dove, a symbol for Israel (see Hos 11:11), reveals Jesus as the personal embodiment of a new Israel. As the Christ, the Anointed One, Jesus fulfilled Isaiah's prayer.

Jesus is not only the Christ. He is also the Son of God. Once the Spirit has descended upon Jesus, he hears a heavenly voice declaring him God's beloved Son, one in whom God is well-pleased (1:11). To tell the story, Mark invoked the biblical language of biblical hope.

According to Mark, only Jesus saw the vision and heard the voice. Those present at Jesus' baptism did not see and hear anything. But, thanks to Mark, his readers can see and hear as well as understand the fulfillment of Scripture in Jesus life and mission.

As God's Son (Ps 2:7), Jesus is associated with God's universal dominion. As such, Jesus has authority *(exousia)* over all peoples, including both Jews and Gentiles. This is also the basis of the authority he exercised over unclean spirits in his mission.

Jesus is also God's beloved Son *(ho agapetos),* a Son beloved by God as Isaac was beloved by Abraham. Just as Abraham was willing to offer his beloved son to God in sacrifice (Gen 22:2), God was willing to hand over his beloved Son. But like Isaac, whom God saved from death on the third day (Gen 22:4-14), Jesus would be raised from death on the third day. Jesus, God's beloved Son, is also the Servant of the Lord, the suffering Servant, upon whom God sent his Spirit and in whom God is well pleased (Isa 42:1).

In three short verses (1:9-11), Mark has introduced the major lines of his Christology. Baptized by John the Baptist, Jesus is human. Anointed by the Spirit, Jesus is divine. Jesus is both the Son of Man and the Son of God. In the royal line of David, Jesus is royal Messiah. But as the Son of God, Jesus far transcends David's line and will reign with God in the kingdom of God. Jesus is the Christ, the anointed embodiment of a new Israel. Like Isaac, Jesus is a beloved Son that would be handed over but saved on the third day. Jesus is also God's suffering Servant.

All of these themes are richly developed in the course of Mark's Gospel. For the present, we are asked to reflect on them in relation to Jesus' baptism. While reading the Gospel, we shall appreciate how Jesus' baptism summarized his life and mission. At the same time, we shall appreciate how baptism summarizes a Christian's life and mission, indeed the life and mission of the Church.

Testing in the Desert (1:12-13)

After Jesus' baptism, the Spirit that descended upon him drove him into the desert (1:12) where he was tested as Israel was tested in the desert of their exodus. The prologue thus presents Jesus' baptismal life as a test, a symbolic forty-day test which evokes the forty days and forty nights which Moses spent with God on the mountain as he received the words of God's covenant (Exod 34:27-38). It also evokes the forty-day and forty-night walk of Elijah as he too made his way to the mountain of God (1 Kgs 19:8). Later in the Gospel, both Moses and Elijah will join Jesus on the mountain of his transfiguration (9:4).

Here in the prologue, Jesus' forty days in the desert represent his entire baptismal life, culminating in his passion.[26] Sent by the Spirit to lead the people in a new exodus, Jesus was tested by Satan. Satan is the adversary of Jesus Christ, the Son of God. Representing the power of evil, Satan was the obstacle that Jesus had to overcome.

The setting for Jesus' baptismal test is extremely simple. All but the bare essentials have been stripped away. Gone is John the Baptist and the crowds that came to be baptized by him. Jesus' life is presented as a conflict between the one anointed by the holy Spirit and his adversary, Satan, the spirit of evil.

In the course of the Gospel, the conflict will be spelled out in relation to various situations and contexts. There were even those who accused Jesus of being possessed by Satan and of driving out demons by the prince of demons (3:22-30). At one critical point, Simon Peter himself will be called Satan for playing Satan's role, trying to dissuade Jesus from the test of the passion (8:31-33).

In the desert Jesus found himself among wild beasts, but at the same time, the angels ministered to him *(diekonoun auto)*. The scene evokes a number of passages in the Old Testament, most especially the story of Daniel in the lion's den, where God's angels ministered to him: "My God has sent his angels and closed the lions' mouths so that they have not hurt me. For I have been found innocent before him" (Dan 6:23).

The description evokes several other passages. Mark might also have had in mind the primal contest of creation where human beings had dominion over wild beasts (Gen 1:24-28). The same imagery played an important role in the prayer of Israel (Ps 8) and in Isaiah's articulation of messianic hope (Isa 13:21-22). Be that as it may, with the angels ministering to Jesus, the wild beasts would not overwhelm him, even in his passion.

As we end the prologue, it leaves us with a number of questions. The wild beasts and the angels may evoke biblical passages, but they also represent those who challenged or ministered to Jesus. To know who they were we have to read the entire Gospel. Who then are the wild beasts in the life of Jesus? And who then are the angels that ministered to him as he ministered to others? Some of them are evident. Others are not.

---

[26] For the relationship of the testing of Jesus in the desert (1:12-13) to Mark's passion narrative, see Ernest Best, *The Temptation and the Passion: the Markan Soteriology,* 2nd ed. (New York: Cambridge University Press, 1990); Donahue, op. cit. 10–11.

III

᭠ Part One ᭟

Jesus and the Mystery
of the Kingdom of God

Mark 1:14–8:22

Introduction

We have seen how Mark provided his Gospel with a title and preface, "The beginning of the gospel of Jesus Christ [the Son of God]" (1:1). As a title, it summarizes the Gospel. As a preface, it is a bold proclamation to Christians who thought it was the end not the beginning of the gospel.

We have also seen how Mark provided "the beginning of the gospel" with a prologue (1:2-13). He opened the prologue with a biblical inscription attributed to Isaiah (1:2-3). He then told of the mission of John the Baptist, who proclaimed a baptism of repentance and announced that one of his followers would baptize with the holy Spirit (1:4-8). He concluded the prologue with the story of the baptism of Jesus and his forty-day test in the desert (1:9-13).

Introducing the principal themes of the Gospel, the prologue is the Gospel in miniature. It relates John the Baptist and Jesus to biblical prophecy and to one another. John was God's messenger, sent to prepare the way of the Lord. Jesus is the Christ, one anointed by the Spirit, and the beloved Son of God. Describing Jesus' baptismal life as among wild beasts but ministered to by the angels, it also relates Jesus' life and mission to his passion and resurrection.

Addressing the readers, the prologue reflects the challenges they had to face. Describing the mission of John as preaching repentance and baptizing all those who came to him, the prologue put the readers in touch with their own baptism and reminded them of their Christian identity. Baptized with Jesus' baptism, they shared in his passion and resurrection (see 10:38-39). Like Jesus, they had to undergo the passion in order to share in the divine life of God's beloved Son (see 1:11; 9:7). As Christians, they had to act and speak, not as ordinary human beings, but as God does (see 8:33; 13:11).

Having heard the title and preface (1:1) and listened to the prologue (1:2-13), we are now ready for the Gospel story they introduce. The main body of the Gospel can be divided in two parts. The first tells about Jesus and the mystery of the kingdom of God (1:14–8:21). The second tells about Jesus and coming of the kingdom of God (8:22–16:8). In the first, the kingdom of God is near but it is hidden in mystery. In the second, the kingdom of God is revealed in the passion and resurrection of Jesus, the Christ and the Son of God, and in the baptism of those who are baptized in his passion and resurrection.

This introduction provides an overview of the Gospel's first part. In it, we examine its literary characteristics, its most significant symbols and images, and the general lines of its structure and movement.

Literary Characteristics

It is helpful to stand back from the Gospel and look at some of its principal characteristics. They can tell us a lot about the nature and the purpose of the Gospel. The following observations pertain to the whole Gospel, but they are especially characteristic of the first part.

In reading Mark 1:14–8:21, we notice that it is very much an action story. Unlike the Gospel's second part (8:22–16:8), the first has relatively little dialogue and only two extended discourses (4:1-34; 7:1-23). We are far away from the Gospels of Matthew, Luke, and John, where the discourses of Jesus figure prominently. In Mark, Jesus is a preacher and teacher, but he preaches and teaches mainly by what he does rather than what he says. The second part of the Gospel devotes a lot more space to Jesus' message and discourses, long and short.

That does not mean that the dialogue and the discourses in the first part are insignificant. On the contrary, they stand out. The dialogue engages the various personages in the story with one another. This gives the Gospel a great sense of immediacy, quite unlike what we experience in reading John, where the author directs the discourses and dialogues beyond the personages to the readers.

Mark does have his readers in mind, but he reaches them principally by having the readers identify with the personages in the story. As readers, we are drawn inside the story. In this way, Mark respects the literary integrity of personages like Simon Peter, Simon's mother-in-law, and all those who figure in the Gospel. When Jesus grasps the hand of Simon's mother-in-law and raises her up (1:31), he grasps the readers' hand and raises them up. Instead of looking past the personages to the readers, Mark leads us to think and feel like them. Identifying with them in the story, we are then open to Jesus' challenge. When Jesus teaches the disciples and others, he teaches us.

What little dialogue there is consists of brief sayings, questions, and prophetic challenges, intimately wedded to the action. But its simplicity and brevity do not weaken the dialogue. Combined with vivid and concrete imagery, they strengthen it. Once Jesus has said, "Come after me, and I will make you fishers of men" (1:17), what more is there to say?

Mark's narrative style is just as simple and energetic as his dialogue style.[1] The sentences are short, the language imaginative and very concrete, save for the little summaries that repeatedly sum up Jesus' preaching and ministry and the reaction of the crowd.

Some summaries are introductory. For example, the first section of the Gospel (1:14–3:6) opens with introductory summary of Jesus' mission and ministry (1:14-15). The introduction also summarizes all of 1:14–3:6). Some summaries are transitional (see 1:32-34), and some are concluding (see 1:28, 39, 45b,c). Linking a new section or unit with the previous, introductory summaries also have a transitional function.

Whether introductory, transitional, or concluding, the summaries bring a sense of amplitude to an event or a series of events. For example, note the effect of this concluding summary, "His fame spread everywhere throughout the whole region of Galilee" (1:28). The summary relates the story of a cure in the synagogue at Capernaum (1:21-28) to the summary that introduces Jesus' mission: "After John had been arrested, Jesus came to Galilee proclaiming the gospel of

---

[1] For Mark's vocabulary, style and syntax, see Vincent Taylor, *The Gospel According to Mark* (London: MacMillan & Co LTD, 1963) 44–54; Howard Clark Kee, *Community of the New Age, Studies in Mark's Gospel* (Philadelphia: The Westminster Press, 1977) 50–54.

God." So far, Mark has told only a few things about Jesus' preaching activity, yet we have the feeling that we know a lot. And so, we can understand how Jesus' fame spread everywhere throughout Galilee.

The Gospel consists of little episodes, each of which is tightly written and very spare. Apart from the brief summaries, there are no restful pauses. Each event is alive with movement. The energetic verbs, very often in the historical present, along with the repetition of "and" *(kai)*, "immediately," "suddenly," or "just then" *(euthys)*, give the stories a sense of urgency. There is no time to lose. "The kingdom of God is at hand" (1:15). The gospel has to be proclaimed.

As the story progresses, the Gospel very often associates a new event with a previous event, even with a series of events, contributing to the unity of the story. For this, Mark uses the adverb "again" *(palin)*.[2] The link always enhances the story. For example, *palin* links the breaking of the bread for the four thousand (8:1-9; see 8:1) with the breaking of the bread for the five thousand (6:34-44). With this simple device, Mark invites us to interpret the new story in the light of the previous story.

Using the adverb *palin* ("again"), Mark recalls a particular theme developed earlier, at times a few stories ago. With "again," he resumes the theme and continues to develop it. In the stories of the breaking of the bread, the theme was the great crowd of hungry people: "In those days when there again *(palin)* was a great crowd without anything to eat" (8:1; see 6:35-36).

Mark also uses a literary device referred to as an intercalation or interpolation. Popularly, it is also called a Markan sandwich. It is also typical of Mark to drop a story in midstream and to start a new and seemingly unrelated story. After completing the second story, he continues the first and brings it to a conclusion (see, for example, 3:20-21 [22-29] 31-35; 5:21-24a [25b-34] 35-43; 6:7-13 [14-29] 30; 11:12-14 [15-19] 20-25). With this device, Mark provides a new literary and theological context for both stories. Each story has to be understood in light of the other.[3]

A good example is the story of the Herod's opinion of Jesus and the death of the John the Baptist (6:14-29) that is inserted into the

[2] For the literary function of the adverb *palin* ("again") in Mark's Gospel, see David Barrett Peabody, *Mark as Composer,* New Gospel Studies 1 (Macon, Ga.: Mercer University Press, 1987) 115–58.

[3] See James R. Edwards, "Markan Sandwiches: The Significance of Interpolations in Markan Narratives," *Novum Testamentum* XXXI/3 (1989) 193–216; see also Howard Kee, *Community of the New Age,* 54–56.

story of the mission of the Twelve (6:7-13, 30). With the sandwiching technique, Mark invites the readers to reflect on the relationship between the mission of the Twelve and Jesus' identity as well as the death of John the Baptist.

The episodic nature of the Gospel makes it especially suitable for dividing it in distinct liturgical and catechetical readings. Such readings could very well have been their immediate source in the early tradition. If so, the Gospel witnesses to the high quality of Christian story telling in the liturgical assembly and of the baptismal catechesis in the first few decades of Christianity.

Symbols and Images

Symbols are realities, persons and things, which speak to us very profoundly and evoke various aspects of our personal and communal inner world. In the Scriptures symbols are surrounded with mystery and evoke particular biblical stories and experiences, and sometimes a general theme. Symbols touch us at every level, the conscious, the subconscious and the unconscious. The Gospel, of course, is literature, and as such it is made up of words not symbols, although in a limited sense words could be thought of as symbols.

The Gospel contains a great deal of symbolic language, words and expressions, which call symbols to mind. Symbolic language speaks primarily through images rather than ideas. The world of Mark is filled with images, to the point where a good deal of the Gospel's message escapes us when we read it without engaging our imagination.

The first part of the Gospel is dominated by two great images, the sea *(he thalassa)* and bread *(artos),* each of which is surrounded by an entire set of subordinate images. Mark's images come in clusters with many interrelated elements. The first part also has other important images, such as the desert *(ho eremos* or *eremos topos)* and the mountain *(to oros),*[4] but these are limited to one or two sections.

The Sea *(he thalassa)*

The first set of images revolves around the Sea of Galilee or simply the sea.[5] It includes everything that concerns the sea *(thalassa).*

---

[4] For the significance of the desert and the mountain, see Elizabeth Struthers Malbon, *Narrative Space and Mythic Meaning in Mark* (Sheffield: JSOT Press, 1991) 72–75 and 84–89.

[5] For the literary and theological significance of the Sea of Galilee in Mark's Gospel, see Elizabeth Struthers-Malbon, "The Jesus of Mark and

There is the boat, getting into the boat, stepping out of the boat, fishing, nets, casting the nets and repairing them. There is also rowing, crossing the sea, strong headwinds, storms, and huge waves. Finally, there are the shores. In Mark's Gospel, these are extremely important, since the Gospel at times distinguishes the Galilean Jewish shore from the other shore, especially the Gentile shore of the Decapolis.

Actually, the Sea of Galilee is not really a sea at all. It is a lake, and not a very large one at that. In most of the ancient literature, the Sea of Galilee is called a lake, in Greek, *limne*. By calling it a sea, Mark and other early Christians associated the lake with the primal abyss, the watery chaos that prevailed when God first created the heavens and the earth. The sea was the abode of the great monsters, such as Leviathan, and jaws of death that swallowed Jonah. The sea was the dwelling place of the dark and ever-threatening unknown. As we learn from the story of Jonah, who was thrown out of a boat into the sea, the netherworld lay in its depths.

Obviously, the sea was an object of fear and prudent respect. The depths of the sea were a good place for unclean animals, especially those that were filled with a legion of unclean spirits. In this context, it should be easy to understand why Jesus' walking on the sea and his calming of a storm at sea were extremely powerful christological images. Jesus was the Lord of creation. Like God, his Father, he could command order into the unformed and chaotic universe. In his company, no one needed to fear the abyss.

We can understand also why Mark could present the great transitions and transformations in the Christian community as a stormy crossing of the sea.[6] The Christians began as a small, Jewish, Galilean community of men, but in a few years they opened their mission and their communities to Gentiles and women as well as Jewish men. This must have been a very stormy crossing. They must have encountered very strong contrary winds.

---

the Sea of Galilee," *Journal of Biblical Literature* 103 (September 1984) 363–77; see also her book *Narrative Space and Mythic Meaning in Mark*, op. cit., 76–79.

[6] See Donald Senior, "The Struggle to be Universal: Mission as Vantage Point for New Testament Interpretation," *The Catholic Biblical Quarterly* 46/1 (January 1984) 76–78. As Senior pointed out, "Mark uses geography as theological symbolism" in relation to the universality and the mission of the Church.

Bread *(artos)*

The second set of images revolves around the symbol of bread *(artos)*. Since bread was the basic element in every meal, this second set includes everything that has to do with nourishment. In general, bread corresponds to food and meals.

Some of Mark's references to bread are hidden beneath our English versions. Instead of translating the Greek expression, "to eat bread," they simply refer to eating. A good example is the translation of 3:20: "Again [the] crowd gathered, making it impossible for them even to eat" *(mede arton phagein)*. The Greek expression is *arton phagein* ("to eat bread"), not just *phagein* ("to eat").

Something similar happens in Jesus' instructions for the missionary journey of the Twelve: "He instructed them to take nothing for the journey but a walking stick—no food [*arton*, literally, "bread"], no sack, no money in their belts" (6:8). Instead of "food" *(trophe)*, the Greek text reads "bread" *(arton)*. This departure from the literal text is unfortunate. It conceals the relationship between Jesus' instructions and what happened later when the disciples wanted to send everyone away because they had no bread (6:34-44).

The verbs are especially important in this second cluster of images. They include taking, breaking, giving, all of which evoke the early Christian context of the Lord's Supper. Other verbs include having or not having, assembling, and bringing or not bringing. Besides the verbs, there are references to a formal banquet *(symposion)* and fragments *(klasmata)*, that is, bread that has been broken.

Both sets of images, that of the sea and that of the bread, are almost completely absent from the second part of the Gospel (8:22–16:8). The sea is mentioned only twice in the second part of the Gospel. But unlike the first part, neither situates an event beside the sea or in relation to the sea. And neither refers particularly to the Sea of Galilee. Both are general references to the sea in a saying of Jesus. The first is about scandal: "Whoever causes one of these little ones who believe [in me] to sin, it would be better for him if a great millstone were put around his neck and he were thrown into the sea" (9:42). The second is about faith: "Amen, I say to you, whoever says to this mountain, 'Be lifted up and thrown into the sea,' and does not doubt in his heart but believes that what he says will happen . . ." (11:23).

The bread is mentioned only once in the second part of the Gospel, as an element in a liturgical text that Mark quotes in the story of the Last Supper (14:22), connecting the Last Supper with the breaking of the bread (6:34-44; 8:1-9). At the Last Supper, however, the emphasis is on the cup (14:23-25) rather than the bread.

The second part of the Gospel also has two major clusters of images, but they are quite different. In place of the sea *(he thalassa),* we find the way *(he hodos).* In place of the bread *(ho artos),* we find the cup *(to poterion).* We shall review these images while introducing the second part of the Gospel.

Structure and Movement

The first part of the Gospel unfolds in three sections, which lead to the introduction (8:22-30) of the second part. That introduction includes the opening of the eyes of a blind man (8:22-26) and Peter's response to the question of Jesus' identity (8:27-30). At the end of the first part, Jesus asks the disciples: "Do you have eyes and not see, ears and not hear?" (8:18). In the introduction of the second part, Jesus begins to open their eyes (see also 10:46-52). In the first part, the question of Jesus' identity is raised over and over again, but the response comes in the second part, beginning with Peter's response.

The first part of the Gospel is divided into three sections:

Section One: Jesus and the First Disciples (1:14–3:6),

Section Two: Jesus and the Twelve (3:7–6:6a),

Section Three: Jesus and the Mission of the Twelve (6:6b–8:21).

All three sections are built up in the same way. From the point of view of the structure, each has a double introduction, and each concludes with a statement of rejection, unbelief or not understanding. Parallel in structure, the three sections move the story forward. Each section presupposes the previous and builds on it.

The introduction opens with a summary concerning Jesus and his ministry (1:14-15; 3:7-12; 6:6b). The summary is followed immediately with a basic statement concerning the disciples (1:16-20; 3:13-19; 6:7-30). There follows the body of the section (1:21–3:6; 3:20–6:6a; 6:31–8:21). All three conclude with an episode in which an entire category in the world of Jesus rejects him or fails to believe or understand who he is, first the Pharisees (3:1-6), then the people of his native town (6:1-6a), and finally the disciples themselves (8:14-21). In one way or another, everyone was blind.

We can now look at this very general outline more closely. In the following synopsis, the emphasis is on the parallel structure of the three sections. In the commentary, I will treat the parallel concluding units (3:1-6; 6:1-6b; 8:14-21) as part of the body.

Section One: Jesus and the First Disciples (1:14–3:6)

Throughout the first section, the focus is on Jesus and the call of his first disciples. Jesus calls the disciples to follow him, fulfilling and extending his mission. In this section, Mark shows how Jesus' proclamation of the gospel led to conflicts with religious and political leaders and how it had implications for those who followed him and took on his mission.

1. **Jesus the Proclaimer (1:14-15).** A short summary describes Jesus' entire mission and ministry as a proclamation that the kingdom of God was at hand. The kingdom called for repentance and faith.

2. **Jesus Calls His First Disciples (1:16-20).** After the summary of Jesus' mission, a short unit describes how he called his first disciples. It too can be considered a summary of the mission and ministry of the disciples. It presupposes that their mission has already unfolded. Looking back, the four fishermen became followers of Jesus to fish for human beings.

3. **The Beginning of the Ministry in Galilee (1:21-45) and Mounting Opposition (2:1–3:6).** The body of the section shows Jesus teaching and forming the disciples as he went about his ministry to others. The body unfolds in two units. In the first, Jesus evokes amazement from the growing crowds (1:21-45). In the second, he provokes conflict with the scribes and the Pharisees (2:1–3:6). The last of the five conflicts or controversies (3:1-6) forms the conclusion of this section.

4. **Hardness of Heart (3:1-6).** The first section concludes with a note of anger and grief on the part of Jesus because of the hardness of heart he observed in the synagogue. As the section ends, the Pharisees leave and take counsel with the Herodians in search of way to destroy Jesus. Already we are at the threshold of the passion.

Section Two: Jesus and the Twelve (3:7–6:6a)

In this second section, the Gospel focuses on how Jesus made or created the Twelve as the foundation of the Church, a new Israel. We are shown what constitutes the new Israel, and how those who were closest to Jesus and the scribes from Jerusalem failed to understand it. They had no faith.

1. **Jesus the Healer (3:7-12).** Like the first section, the second begins with a summary of Jesus' mission and ministry. This time, however, it describes Jesus' preaching ministry as healing and exorcising. The summary also describes how the crowds came to Jesus from beyond Galilee, Judea, and Jerusalem. The description calls to mind the crowds in Jerusalem for Pentecost (see Acts 2).

2. **Jesus Constitutes the Twelve (3:13-19).** After the summary of Jesus' ministry, like the first section, the second has a story concerning the disciples. This time, Jesus creates the Twelve to be the foundation for a new Israel. Again the story can be considered a summary of the mission of the disciples. One of the Twelve, Simon, is given a new name, Peter. For the foundation of the new Israel, he would be the bedrock. The list of the Twelve also includes the name of Judas, the betrayer.

3. **The Continuation of Jesus' Ministry in Galilee (3:20–4:34) and Going to the Other Side (4:35–6:6a).** The body of the second section shows how Jesus formed the new Israel. Again the body unfolds in two units. In the first, Jesus addresses his relatives and the scribes, who do not understand how the new Israel is based on a faith relationship to Jesus and the Twelve. It is here also that Jesus speaks of his teaching in parables (3:20–4:34). In the second unit, Jesus and the Twelve cross the sea to the Gentile shore, bringing the gospel, healing, and exorcising among the Gentiles. They then return to their ministry on the Jewish shore (4:35–6:6a).

4. **Lack of Faith (6:1-6a).** The second section ends with Jesus' amazement at the lack of faith among those in the synagogue of his native place. The small unit should be read in relation to 3:20-35, in which Jesus' relatives and the scribes from Jerusalem symbolically remain outside Jesus' home.

Section Three: Jesus and the Mission of the Twelve (6:6b–8:21)

In the third section, the Gospel turns to the mission of the disciples, those Jesus called to follow him and created as the Twelve. It tells the story of the mission of the Church, the new Israel, while telling the story of Jesus and his disciples.

1. **Jesus the Teacher (6:6b).** Like the first and second sections, the third begins with a summary of Jesus mission and minis-

try, describing how he went about the villages teaching. This time, however, the summary is remarkably short. The emphasis in the third section is on the mission of the Twelve.

2. **Jesus Sends the Twelve on Mission (6:7-30).** After the summary, the section again includes a basic story concerning the disciples. In story form, it summarizes the mission of the Twelve. Jesus sends them with staff in hand, sandals on their feet and one tunic. The description calls to mind the ancient Israelites as they prepared to embark on the Exodus. The mission journey of the Twelve is a new exodus. The story includes the martyrdom of John the Baptist.

3. **Jesus Forms the Missionary Church (6:31-8:21).** The body of third section shows how Jesus formed the Twelve and the Church for their mission. Again, the body is divided in two units. The first focuses on the mission in the Jewish people from whom the Church emerged (6:31-44). The second unit shows how Jesus and the Twelve crossed to the other side of the sea, laying the foundations for the mission of the Church to all peoples (6:45–8:21). In both units, the key passage is a story of the breaking of the bread (6:34-44; 8:1-9).

4. **Lack of Understanding (8:14-21).** The conclusion of the first section showed how the Pharisees and the scribes hardened their hearts (3:1-6). The conclusion of the second section showed how the people of Jesus' native place had little or no faith (6:1-6a). Now, the conclusion of the third section shows how the Twelve could not understand who Jesus was. Being blind to Jesus' identity and his mission to all peoples, they were also blind to their own identity and their mission to all peoples (8:14-21).

In this introduction for the Gospel's first part (1:14–8:21), we have reviewed some of its major literary characteristics. We have also reviewed the symbols and images that dominate this first part, namely the sea *(thalassa)* and the bread *(artos)*. Finally, we proposed a literary structure for the first part, showing how it moves to climax to climax.

Now, we are ready to enter the first section, "Jesus and the First Disciples" (1:14–3:6), beginning with a summary of Jesus' mission (1:14-15) and the call of the first disciples (1:16-20).

IV

ᖰ Section I ᖳ

Jesus and the First Disciples

Mark 1:14–3:6

Jesus began his mission in Galilee, where he called his first disciples, those who would form the nucleus of the Church. In the New Testament, particularly in Mark's Gospel, the beginning of the mission of Jesus and the call of the disciples are inseparable. Each Gospel connects the origins of the Church to the mission of Jesus. At the same time, each Gospel has its own way of telling the story of the origins of the Church in the mission of Jesus.

Part One of the Gospel according to Mark (1:14–8:21) opens with a section on Jesus' mission and ministry and the call of the first disciples (1:14–3:6). It tells how the mission of Jesus began and how he called and formed the first disciples. The section is a synopsis of the whole Gospel, from Jesus' preaching in Galilee (see 1:14) to his passion and resurrection (see 3:1-6). In the process, the section introduces many of the basic themes of the Gospel.[1]

Like the title (1:1) and the prologue (1:2-13), the first section (1:14–3:6) can be seen as the Gospel of Mark in miniature. In capsule form, the section tells the entire story of "the beginning of the

---

[1] Later, Luke would do the same, presenting the whole life and mission of Jesus and the basic themes of Luke-Acts in the story of the beginning of Jesus' ministry in Galilee (Lk 4:14-44); see Eugene LaVerdiere, *Luke,* New Testament Message #5 (Collegeville: The Liturgical Press, 1990) 62–73.

gospel of Jesus Christ [the Son of God]" (1:1). As such, the Gospel's opening section is told from the point of view of its climax in the passion and resurrection. From the very beginning, the cross casts its shadow on the beginning of the Jesus' mission in Galilee and the call of the first disciples.[2]

When Jesus was dying on the cross, he continued to proclaim the gospel of God, even as he did in Galilee. To the very end of the Gospel, in the story of the women's visit to the tomb (16:1-8), the disciples are still called to follow Jesus. As such, the first section must be considered as extremely basic. The rest of the Gospel is built on its foundations.

An Overview

The section opens with a double introduction,[3] including a summary of Jesus' life, mission and ministry (1:14-15) and a succinct story of how Jesus called his first disciples (1:16-20). The summary presents Jesus as a proclaimer of the gospel of God. The story presents the disciples as his followers.

The two introductory units, one concerning Jesus, the other concerning the disciples, set the stage for the whole section (1:14–3:6), indeed for the rest the gospel. Mark's Gospel is not just a story of Jesus. It is a story of Jesus and his disciples. Everything Jesus said and did, every event in Jesus' life, including his passion and resurrection, had implications for his disciples.

The summary of Jesus' mission begins with a general introductory statement: "After John had been arrested, Jesus came to Galilee proclaiming the gospel of God" (1:14). Such was Jesus' basic mission. The summary then becomes more specific with a synopsis of Jesus' proclamation: "This is the time of fulfillment. The kingdom of God is at hand. Repent, and believe in the gospel" (1:15). Such was Jesus' basic proclamation.

The story of the call of the first disciples shows how Jesus called four fishermen, Simon and his brother Andrew, James and his brother

---

[2] For a discussion of the importance and significance of the beginning of the Gospel of Mark, see M. Eugene Boring, "Mark 1:1-15 and the Beginning of the Gospel," *Semeia* 52 (1990) 43–81. The entire issue of *Semeia* is devoted to how the gospels begin.

[3] Like the first section, the second and third also begin with a double introduction, including a summary of Jesus' mission and ministry (3:7-12; 6:6b) and a major passage on the disciples (3:13-19; 6:7-30).

John, to be his followers. As his followers *(hoi akolouthountes)*, they would also be his disciples *(hoi mathetai)*. Like the summary of Jesus' mission, the story of the call of the disciples is very stylized, suggesting that the story is also a summary, giving only the highlights or the very essence of the event.

After the double introduction (1:14-15, 16-20), the body of the section (1:21–3:6) begins and ends on the Sabbath in the synagogue at Capernaum (1:21-28; 3:1-6). In the opening unit (1:21-28), a man with an unclean spirit confronted Jesus and identified him as the Holy One of God (1:24). Rebuked by Jesus, the unclean spirit convulsed the man and came out of him (1:26). In the closing unit (3:1-6), the Pharisees confronted Jesus when he healed a man with a withered hand. Reduced to silence (3:4), the Pharisees came out of the synagogue and took counsel with the Herodians to find a way to put Jesus to death (3:6).

The body (1:21–3:6) unfolds in two closely related parts, showing first how Jesus' mission and ministry began and developed, putting him in conflict with unclean, demonic spirits (1:21-45). The first part prepares the second, where Jesus' disciples come in conflict with the scribes and the Pharisees, and through them with the Herodians (2:1–3:6). It also shows how Jesus' mission, responding to various situations, was expressed in a range of ministries, anticipating the ministries of his followers and of the early church.

Unlike the scribes, Jesus taught with authority (see 1:22, 27; 2:10), expelling demons, healing the sick, as he proclaimed the kingdom of God in deed and word. From the beginning, filled with the holy Spirit, Jesus, the holy one of God, was bound to come into conflict with unclean spirits (1:21-28, 32-34, 39). As his fame spread (1:28, 45) and the crowds continued to grow (1:33, 37, 45; 2:2, 4), conflict with the scribes and the Pharisees was inevitable.

The first part of the section shows Jesus going further and further from the synagogue in Capernaum. After teaching in the synagogue (1:21-28), Jesus went to the home of Simon and Andrew (1:29-31), to the door of the home (1:32-34), then to a desert place *(eis eremon topon,* 1:35-38), from which he went to synagogues throughout Galilee (1:39-45). By the end of the section, Jesus was staying outside *(exo)* the towns and villages in desert places *(ep' eremois topois,* 1:45).

In a series of five conflict stories, the second part shows how Jesus' mission and ministry met resistance from the scribes, the interpreters of the Law (2:1-12), and from the Pharisees, the rulers of the synagogue (2:13-17), and from people in general, because, unlike the disciples of John and of the Pharisees, his disciples did not fast (2:18-22). Jesus again met resistance from the Pharisees because his disciples picked heads of grain on the Sabbath (2:23-28). The series of five conflicts and the first section climax with the Pharisees consulting the Herodians on how to put Jesus to death (3:1-6). With that, we find ourselves on the threshold of Jesus' passion. The second part also shows how the disciples, as followers of Jesus, would face conflicts from every side.

Setting and *Dramatis Personae*

We begin our reflections on the mission of Jesus and the call of the first disciples (1:14–3:6) by examining the setting, where and when the events are situated, and the personages who play a role in the story. While the story of Mark is not a drama, it is very dramatic, allowing us to refer to its personages as *dramatis personae*.

The Gospel of Mark has an extraordinary sense of place. For Mark, the geography of the gospel and the location of various events were very significant. For Mark, many places were symbolic, including, Galilee, the Sea of Galilee, and desert places. On the other hand, except for the Sabbath, the Gospel of Mark pays comparatively little attention to specific times, at least until the passion and resurrection. For Mark, the chronology of the gospel and the time of various events were much less significant than where they occurred. The Gospel of Mark also includes a large cast of personages. Some of them are named, but most of them remain anonymous, such as the man with the withered hand (3:1-6).

Geographical Setting: Jesus in Galilee

Galilee is a very important place in the Gospel of Mark. Galilee is the place where Jesus began his mission (1:14), called and formed disciples to be his followers, and preceded them during his historical mission (see 10:32-34), preparing them for the baptism of his passion (see 10:38-40). It was also there where he preceded them as the risen Lord after his passion and resurrection (see 16:6).

Galilee is a real place, a geographical area in northern Palestine stretching west-east (*circa* 35 mi.) from the Mediterranean Sea to the Jordan valley and the Sea of Galilee and south-north (*circa* 50 mi.) from the plain of Esdraelon (Jezreel) to Syro-Phoenicia and the regions of Tyre and Sidon. The region, much of which is mountainous, includes Upper Galilee, where the mountains reach an altitude of four thousand feet, and Lower Galilee, where rolling hills reach fifteen hundred feet. Nazareth is situated in Lower Galilee.[4]

Because of Galilee's many associations with the life of Jesus and his disciples, it had a special meaning for the early Christians. The very name "Galilee" evoked a whole series of places, towns, and events included in Mark's Gospel. Because Galilee provided the setting for most of the early Christian stories of Jesus, it became more than a geographical place. For the early Christians, it was a symbolic place, inseparable from the story of the gospel.

When Mark wrote "the beginning of the gospel of Jesus Christ [the Son of God]" (1:1), Galilee also became a literary place. In Mark, Galilee is the world of discipleship, the setting for the following of Christ, the place where men and women learned to live with and like Jesus Christ and where their eyes were gradually opened in faith.

As told by Mark, the opening of the eyes began in Jesus' lifetime when he healed a blind man at Bethsaida (8:22-26) and another in Jericho (10:46-52). After the passion and resurrection, Galilee was the place where Jesus' followers would see him. Such was the message confided to the women by a young man in the tomb: "But go and tell his disciples and Peter, 'He is going before you to Galilee; there you will see him'" (16:7; see 14:28).

In this first section (1:14–3:6), the literary setting never moves away from Galilee. Within Galilee, the story unfolds close to the Sea of Galilee,[5] where Jesus called his first disciples (1:16-20; 2:13-14). Jesus' Galilean ministry took him to many towns and villages, but only one of these, Capernaum *(Kapharnaoum),*[6] is mentioned by name (1:21; 2:1). Jesus had come from Nazareth in Galilee (see 1:9), but his ministry unfolded in and around Capernaum on the shore of the Sea of Galilee.

---

[4] For the geography of Galilee, see Rafael Frankel and Sean Freyne, "Galilee," *The Anchor Bible Dictionary,* Editor-in-Chief, David Noel Freedman (New York: Doubleday, 1992) 2:879–99. The section of the article concerning "Prehellenistic Galilee" (279–895) was written by Frankel. The section concerning "Hellenistic/Roman Galilee" (895–99) was written by Freyne.

[5] The significance of the Sea of Galilee in Mark, see Elizabeth Struthers Malbon, "The Jesus of Mark and the Sea of Galilee," *Journal of Biblical Literature* 103 (September 1984) 363–77.

[6] For a report on the excavations at Capernaum, see Virgilio C. Corbo O.F.M., *Cafarnao I, Gli Edifici della Citta* (Jerusalem: Francisan Printing Press, 1975). For a good summary, see the same author's article, "Capernaum," in *The Anchor Bible Dictionary* 1:866–69.

Capernaum was a small fishing (see 1:16-20) and farming (see 2:23-28) village situated just north of Tiberias, the Roman capital of Galilee. Capernaum was surrounded by desert places (see 1:35), but most of the events took place along the Sea (1:16-20; 2:13-14), in the synagogue (1:21-28; 3:1-6), and in two homes, that of Simon and Andrew (1:29-34; 2:1-12) and that of Levi the tax collector (2:15-17).

In addition, Jesus sometimes went to desert places to pray (1:35-38; see also 1:45), and on one occasion he walked with his disciples through a field of ripe grain (2:23-28). Away from Capernaum, in the other towns and villages of Galilee, Jesus also preached in the synagogues (1:39), but there is no reference that he stayed at a particular home. For Jesus, home was being with his disciples, and at this early point in Jesus' ministry, home was at Capernaum.

Such is the literary geography and the setting for the first section of the Gospel of Mark. Jesus began his mission, called the disciples and formed them as followers in Galilee, mainly in and around Capernaum. At Capernaum the events unfolded by the sea, at the synagogue or in a home, in contrast with the desert places, where Jesus retired to pray or to avoid the press of the crowd.

Temporal Setting: After John Was Handed Over

In the first section, as in most of the Gospel of Mark, chronology is much less significant than geography.[7] Every event and development is joined to every other by the conjunction "and" *(kai)*. This literary device, which is of Semitic inspiration, provides the gospel story with a strong sense of movement, succession, and urgency. The sequence unfolds so rapidly—"just then" *(euthus)*—that each event, while being really new, seems to collapse into the previous one. The kingdom of God was at hand! There was little time to lose. There are many events in Mark's story, but they form a single tightly knit story, "the beginning of the gospel of Jesus Christ [the Son of God]" (1:1).

Mark shows little interest in distinguishing different periods of history. Like Matthew and Luke, he does distinguish the period that preceded Jesus' passion and resurrection from the period that followed them. But, while maintaining the distinction theologically, he did not separate the two periods in his story. Instead, he told the story of the historical Jesus and that of the risen Lord in the same

---

[7] By contrast chronology is very important in the story of the passion-resurrection, which notes not only the day but also the time of the day when an event took place.

story. While telling the story of the first disciples, he also told the story of the early Church and the various challenges it encountered after the passion and resurrection of Jesus.

In the Gospel of Mark, the historical Jesus is the image or icon of the risen Lord and first disciples and the enemies of Jesus are the image or icon of the early church and its enemies. In Mark's Gospel, Jesus' mission and ministry reflects the mission and ministry of the Church.[8]

There was one major chronological event, however, that made a difference for "the beginning of the gospel," the arrest or handing over of John the Baptist. The ministry of Jesus began after John's ministry was completed. John, the forerunner, prepared the way of the Lord to the very end of his life. The next important chronological event would be the handing over of Jesus himself. This second event would be announced later in the Gospel (9:31; 10:33) and would be fulfilled in Jesus' passion (14:21). The period of Jesus' ministry unfolded between the handing over of John and the handing over of Jesus.

In Mark's Gospel, as in the tradition from which he drew, the verb "to be handed over" *(paradidomai)* evoked the biblical songs of the suffering servant (Isa 42:1-4; 49:1-6; 50:4-11; 52:13–53:12), particularly the fourth. Like the servant, Jesus was handed over or delivered up for our sins when he gave *(dounai)* his life "as a ransom for many" (10:45; see Isa 53:12, LXX).

Mark carefully distinguished the active use of the verb "to hand over" from its passive use. When used in the active voice, the verb refers to the way Jesus was betrayed and arrested by human beings. Its subject, for example, is Judas, who betrayed Jesus, and the chief priests, who handed him over to the Gentiles. When used in the passive voice, without a complement,[9] the verb implies an underlying activity of God. The servant in Isaiah's songs was handed over

---

[8] In the United States several decades of research on the Gospel of Mark has focused on its Christology, neglecting the Gospel's ecclesiology and its missionary perspective. In his article, "The Struggle to be Universal: Mission as Vantage Point for New Testament Investigation" *(The Catholic Biblical Quarterly,* 46/1 (January 1984) 63–81, Donald Senior underlined "the *impact* of the early church's mission consciousness and missionary experience on the NT writings" (65). He treated the mission perspective in Mark's Gospel from the point of its genre, its geography and its salvation history (74–81).

[9] The passive is used with a complement at the Last Supper: "For the Son of Man indeed goes, as it is written of him, but woe to that man by whom the Son of Man is betrayed *(paradidotai)*" (14:21).

by God. So were John the Baptist and Jesus. So would be Jesus' followers (see 13:9-13).[10]

When used in the New Testament, an expression like "to be handed over" evokes more than a particular verse from a song of the suffering servant where the verb is actually used. It brings the entire song to mind and invites reflection on how John and Jesus were handed over in light of the extremely rich context of Isaiah's poem.

The handing over of John is the only chronological event indicated in the first section of the Mark's Gospel. Jesus' ministry began after this unique and religiously significant event, whose story would be told later in 6:7-29 as a flashback. Every other reference to time situates an event or episode on a day of the week or at a particular time of day.

For Mark, the Sabbath is very important. Like the synagogue, the Sabbath was a primary institution in Judaism. Together, the synagogue and the Sabbath frame the body (1:21–3:6) of the first section (1:21-28; 3:1-6). Mark wrote for communities that had their historical roots in Judaism but had also developed a specific Christian identity. Those communities included many Gentiles as well as Jews. In that light, the stories of Jesus with a Sabbath setting were extremely significant.

It is on the Sabbath that Jesus revealed himself as a powerful and authoritative teacher (1:21-28) and healer (1:29-31). It is also on the Sabbath that Jesus challenged some of the human traditions that distorted the meaning and purpose of the Sabbath: "Then he said to them, 'The sabbath was made for man, not man for the sabbath. That is why the Son of Man is lord even of the sabbath'" (2:27-28). Opening on the Sabbath (1:21-28, 29-31) the section also ends on the Sabbath with two conflict stories (2:23-28; 3:1-6). Among the Christians, Sabbath observance had become a controversial issue. Through Jesus, Mark was responding to the controversy.

The first section of the Gospel also refers to "evening, after sunset" (1:32-34), that is, when the Sabbath was over (1:21-31), and to "very early before dawn" of the next morning (1:35-38). Apart from these two temporal indications, which speak wonderfully to the imagination, the only other reference to time is the very vague "after some days" (2:1).

---

[10] For the background of the term *paradidonai* and its theology, see Norman Perrin, "The Use of *(Para)didonai* in Connection with the Passion of Jesus in the New Testament," *A Modern Pilgrimage in New Testament Christology* (Philadelphia: Fortress Press, 1974) 94–103.

This leaves many of the episodes in 1:14–3:6 outside any temporal framework. It also contributes to the Gospel's sense of universality. It is not so much that the call of the first disciples and the other events took place at a specific time in the past. Rather, they were an integral part of the life of the church. Recalled over and over again in preaching and catechesis, they were taking place over and over again.

Dramatis Personae

The first section of the Gospel introduces an interesting array of personages. There is Jesus, of course, and there are the first disciples, but there are also a number of other people, only some of whom are named. Most of the personages remain nameless. The way Mark identifies and presents them tells us much about the Gospel and helps us appreciate Mark's message and pastoral intentions.

Jesus is the principal personage is this section of the Gospel, as he is throughout the Gospel. The narrator always refers to him by the simple name Jesus (1:14, 17, 25; 2:5, 8, 15, 17, 19) or by a pronoun, never by a title. Not that Mark avoided the titles of Jesus (see 1:1), but he usually attributes the titles to a personage within the story, including Jesus himself.

In the first section (1:14–3:6), a man with an unclean spirit cries out, "Jesus of Nazareth" (*Iesou Nazarene,* 1:24) and identifies Jesus as "the Holy One of God" (*ho hagios tou theou,* 1:24). Jesus twice refers to himself as "the Son of Man" (*ho huios tou anthropou,* 2:10, 28), one of the most significant titles of Jesus in the Gospel of Mark.[11] In both instances, the title is used in relation to Jesus' authority *(exousia),* that is, the authority that flowed from his mission and ultimately from his identity.

---

[11] Jesus is the only one who uses the title, "the Son of Man," in the Gospel of Mark. See Norman Perrin, *A Modern Pilgrimage in New Testament Christology* (Philadelphia: Fortress Press, 1974) 23–40, 57–93. For the state of the question, see John R. Donahue, "Recent Studies in the Origins of 'Son of Man' in the Gospels," *Catholic Biblical Quarterly* 48/3 (July 1986) 484–98, and William O. Walker, Jr., "The Son of Man: Some Recent Developments," *Catholic Biblical Quarterly* 45/4 (October 1983) 584–607.

For the background, the history, and the use of the title, see George W. E. Nickelsburg, "Son of Man," *The Anchor Bible Dictionary* 6:137–50; Carsten Colpe, *"huios tou anthropou," Theological Dictionary of the New Testament* (Grand Rapids, Mich.: Wm. B. Eerdmans, 1972) 400–77.

In 2:10, we read that "the Son of Man has authority to forgive sins on earth." In 2:28, Jesus affirms that "the Son of Man is lord even of the sabbath." Jesus was responding to the scribes and the Pharisees who were objecting to his ministry. In and through Mark's Gospel, Jesus was also addressing important issues in the Church for Mark's readers.

The title "the Son of Man" *(ho huios tou anthropou)* is not found outside the Gospels, but it has a rich background in the Old Testament and in early Jewish literature. It has many literary associations, of which the best known is the apocalyptic figure announced in Daniel 7.[12] Not that the expression itself was used in the Old Testament as a Messianic or eschatological title. The title "the Son of Man" has to be credited to the early Christians reflecting on the Scriptures.

Daniel had a vision in a dream in which he saw "one like a son of man" approach "the Ancient One" to be presented with everlasting dominion, glory, and indestructible kingship (Dan 7:13-14). Notice that Daniel referred to "one like a son a man," that is a human being, not to "the Son of Man." Nonetheless, Mark was well aware of this richly imaged context for the title "the Son of Man," as shown in Jesus' eschatological discourse: "And then they will see 'the Son of Man coming in the clouds' with great power and glory" (13:26; see also 14:61).

In the Old Testament, the expression "son of man," is a way of emphasizing someone's humanness, as we can see from Psalm 8 and from the book of Ezekiel, whom God repeatedly called "son of man." Mark's use of the title in 2:10 and 28 is based on this generic usage. With the title, Mark emphasizes Jesus' humanness, as we can see from Jesus' statement in 2:27-28: "The sabbath was made for man, not man for the sabbath. That is why the Son of Man is lord even of the sabbath."

Jesus, it should be noted, is not just "a son of man," that is, an ordinary human being. Jesus is "the Son of Man," the ultimate human being, in whom humanity finds complete fulfillment according to the plan of the creator. It is as the Son of Man that Jesus declares himself able to forgive sins on earth and lord of the Sabbath.[13]

---

[12] W. E. Nickelsburg defines "son of man" as "a Semitic expression that typically individualizes a noun for humanity in general by prefacing it with "son of," thus designation a specific human being, a single member of the species" ("Son of Man," op. cit., 137).

[13] John Donahue makes this telling observation, "A Christology where Jesus constantly describes himself as 'the Son of Man' with its overtones of solidarity with the human condition underscores the true humanity of the

Earlier in the first section, Jesus was called "the Holy One of God" (1:24) by a man with an unclean spirit. The possessed man addressed Jesus directly as "Jesus of Nazareth" and proceeded to challenge him: "I know who you are—the Holy One of God!" Jesus answers by silencing and expulsing the unclean spirit (1:25). He would do the same later by not permitting demons to announce who he was (1:34).

At first glance, Jesus' response seems strange. Here is one who acts, speaks and does everything to present himself as the Holy One of God. At the same time, he forbids others to declare him as such. Since the beginning of the twentieth century, this phenomenon has been referred to as the Messianic Secret.[14]

There is a simple explanation for Jesus' seemingly contradictory behavior. Being able to identify Jesus and knowing one or more of his titles may fall far short of a confession of faith. Faith is primarily a matter of knowing a person, not just knowing about a person, in this case, the person of Jesus. Such personal knowledge is a trusting knowledge, an aspect well expressed when we say that we have faith in someone.

The unclean spirits or demons may have known who Jesus was, but they did not have faith in him. Coming from a demon, a proclamation of Jesus' identity could only distort the meaning of Jesus' life and mission. Jesus, therefore, silenced the demon, as he would do for others who did not have faith.

Besides Jesus, the first section of the Gospel speaks of a number of people by name. There is Simon and his brother Andrew, James, the son of Zebedee, and his brother John, and Levi, the tax collector. The first four, Simon in particular, continue to play an important role in the rest of the Gospel. After Jesus called them, their presence is assumed throughout the first section (1:21–3:6). It is quite striking that, apart from John the Baptist (1:14), no one else is mentioned by name. Except John the Baptist, all those named have this in common: Jesus personally called them to be his followers. As such, Mark presents them as historical personages.

---

one who was proclaimed as risen Lord." See "Recent Studies on the Origin of 'Son of Man' in the Gospels," *The Catholic Biblical Quarterly* 48/3 (July 1986) 498.

[14] See William Wrede, *The Messianic Secret,* translated by J. C. G. Greig, (London: James Clarke & Co. Ltd., 1971). Wrede's work, first published in 1901 under the title *Das Messiasgemeimnis in den Evangelien,* has been extremely influential, showing that the Gospel of Mark should be taken seriously as a work of theology.

Besides Jesus' followers, there are also a number whom Jesus heals and reconciles or from whom he expels demons. There is a man with an unclean spirit (1:21-28), a leper (1:40-45), a paralytic (2:1-12), tax collectors and sinners (2:13-17), and a man with a withered hand (3:1-6). All these remain anonymous. As such, Mark presents them as symbolic personages, representing all those in need of Jesus' ministry and the ministry of the Church. Others are related to Simon, namely, his mother-in-law (1:30) and "those who were with him" (1:36). The expression, "those who were with him" indicates their solidarity with Simon.

Some of those who remain anonymous did become followers of Jesus, including Simon's mother-in-law, "those who were with him," and probably the leper that Jesus cleansed (1:40-45; see 1:45a). All of them benefited from Jesus' extraordinary healing, reconciling, and exorcising power. But with a few exceptions there is no indication that they took on Jesus' ministry on behalf of others.

A third group consists of those who opposed Jesus and challenged him publicly. These include some of the scribes (2:1-12), scribes who were Pharisees (2:13-17), the Pharisees (2:23-28), and the Pharisees and the Herodians (3:1-6). Apart from the Herodians, all of them are associated with the same basic group of people. They too play an important role in the rest of the Gospel.

Finally, there is the crowd, an anonymous mass of people, sometimes referred to as "all," "everyone," or "many." In this section of the Gospel, the crowd shows how Jesus' fame was growing and his reputation was spreading far afield (1:28, 44-45). At the same time, the crowd could be an obstacle. Because of its size, the crowd made it harder for Jesus to fulfill his ministry, forcing him to stay in desert places for prayer and solitude (1:35; 45). Later, Jesus would invite his disciples to come away from the crowds to a desert place to rest a while (6:31).

Jesus the Proclaimer (1:14-15)

Mark's story of Jesus and his first disciples (1:14–3:6) begins with a general summary of Jesus' mission, message, and ministry (1:14-15). In just a few words Mark captures the essence of Jesus' life and mission.

The opening summary describes Jesus' entire mission and ministry as "proclaiming *(kerysson)* the gospel of God" (1:14). In the prologue, Mark summarized the mission and ministry of John the Baptist as "proclaiming *(kerysson)* a baptism of repentance for *(eis)* the forgiveness of sins" (1:4). John's proclamation of a baptism of repentance prepared the way for Jesus' proclamation of the gospel. It also found its fulfillment in Jesus' proclamation.

In Mark, John's preparatory mission is over with the advent of Jesus' mission. In Matthew and Luke, the mission of John and Jesus overlap chronologically (see Matt 11:2-19; Luke 7:18-35), as they very likely did. In that, Matthew and Luke are more sensitive to the historical reality. By introducing Jesus' mission "after John had been arrested" *(meta de to paradothenai ton Ioannen)* or handed over (1:14), Mark was making a theological statement. Being handed over, John was preparing the way for Jesus. As John was handed over, Jesus would be handed over. At the same time, it was a message both for Jesus' followers and the early Church.

John had proclaimed a baptism of repentance "in the desert" *(en te eremo),* a traditional place of purification and formation, to which people came to him from the whole of Judea, even from Jerusalem (1:4-5). Jesus proclaimed the gospel of God in Galilee (1:14), in the towns and villages where people lived, worked and attended synagogue. He went to a "desert place" *(eis eremon topon)* in search of solitude (1:45) especially for prayer (1:35).

The proclaiming or preaching aspect of Jesus' mission and ministry was the most basic. All of Jesus' activities showed how in fact Jesus went about proclaiming the gospel of God. This can be seen from how Mark presented Jesus' proclamation ministry.

The verb "proclaim" *(kerysso)* appears only in general summaries of Jesus' ministry (1:14, 38, 39). Very likely, Mark was the author of these summaries. If some of their elements were traditional, Mark at least reshaped them as the redactor. When the Gospel tells stories of Jesus' ministry, it refers to it as teaching *(didasko,* 1:21, 27), healing *(therapeuo,* 1:34), casting out demons *(daimonia ekballo,* 1:34, 39), and cleansing or purifying *(katharizo,* 1:40-45). Such stories very likely came from tradition but were reshaped by Mark.

We conclude that Mark viewed Jesus' proclaiming mission and ministry as extremely important. It responded to a primary need in the Church of his time. The Church needed to hear Jesus' proclamation. It also needed to proclaim it. For Mark, among all the ministries, proclaiming the gospel, that is, evangelization, was primary. Every other ministry was an expression of Jesus' proclaiming ministry.

Jesus' message is described as "the gospel of God" *(to euaggelion tou theou,* 1:14), that is, the gospel that comes from God.[15]

---

[15] The genitive *tou theou* ("of God") is subjective, not objective. As an objective genitive, the expression would mean, "the gospel about God." As a subjective genitive, it means "the gospel from God."

The expression, "the gospel of God," was traditional (1 Thess 2:2, 8, 9; 2 Cor 11:7; Rom 1:1; 15:16). In 1 Thessalonians, the expression "the gospel of God" is parallel to "the word of God," that is, the word that comes from God (1 Thess 2:13).

Paul used the expression to introduce himself to the Romans: "Paul, a slave of Christ Jesus, called to be an apostle and set apart for the gospel of God, which he promised previously through his prophets in the holy scriptures, the gospel about his Son" (Rom 1:1). Paul then summarizes "the gospel of God" with a traditional creed: "the gospel about his Son, descended from David according to the flesh, but established as Son of God in power according to the spirit of holiness through resurrection from the dead, Jesus Christ our Lord" (Rom 1:3-4).

Mark then adds a resume of Jesus' message, quoting Jesus directly (1:15). The first part of Jesus' proclamation focuses on the time of fulfillment and the kingdom of God: "This is the time of fulfillment *[Peplerotai ho kairos]*. The kingdom of God is at hand" *(kai eggeken he basileia tou theou)* (1:15a).

After this solemn announcement, the second part is an urgent exhortation to seize the opportunity *(kairos)* and not let the moment pass unattended: "Repent *[metanoeite]*, and believe *[pisteuete]* in the gospel *[en to euaggelio]*" (1:15b). In Greek, Jesus' message emphasizes the verbs: "Fulfilled is the time; at hand is the kingdom of God; repent and believe in the gospel." Later, once the disciples had been constituted as the Twelve, they too would be sent to proclaim repentance *(metanoia*, 6:12).

The designated time *(kairos)*, the opportune moment, the moment of decision is now. God's plan for the history of salvation is now fulfilled.[16] This is the time to repent and believe in the gospel of God. The time is fulfilled because the kingdom of God is imminent, the reign of God, for which we pray in the Lord's prayer (see Matt 6:9-13; Luke 11:2-4), is at hand. To enter the kingdom of God, one has to repent, change their way of living, and believe, that is, put their trust in the gospel.

The kingdom of God is for the entire human race, including Jews and Gentiles from every nation. As such, welcoming the kingdom of

---

[16] As Donald Senior observed, today the term, "the history of salvation," is usually associated with Luke-Acts and Matthew, not with Mark. But Mark also emphasizes the history of salvation. See Donald Senior, "The Struggle to be Universal: Mission as Vantage Point for New Testament Investigation," *The Catholic Biblical Quarterly* 46/1 (January 1984) 78–81.

God requires a radical *metanoia*. Relating that *metanoia* to the passion of the Christ, the second part of the Gospel (8:22–16:8) will show how radical it has to be.

The summary of Jesus' message was at the same time a summary of the message of his followers and of the early Church. It thus represents the voice of Jesus of Nazareth, who fulfilled his historic role in Galilee, as well as the voice of Jesus the risen Lord, who preceded his followers in Galilee after the passion-resurrection.

Mark's summary of Jesus' proclamation is rich in the traditional language of Christian evangelization. It also drew on the early Christian reflection on the Scriptures, particularly in the book of Isaiah. Proclaiming the gospel of the coming of the kingdom of God had been Deutero-Isaiah's central message, giving hope to the Israelites exiled in Babylon (see Isa 40:9-10; 52:7). Drawing on Isaiah's classic imagery, Mark had Jesus proclaim the gospel of the coming of the kingdom of God, rekindling the prophetic hope for Israel's return from exile in a new exodus. In Mark, Jesus' gospel was a message of eschatological hope. Like Isaiah, Jesus was announcing a new exodus, but for Jesus, the new exodus would be a definitive exodus.

Jesus Calls His First Disciples (1:16-20)

After summarizing Jesus' mission and message (1:14-15), Mark tells how Jesus called four disciples to follow him. As his followers, they would also proclaim the gospel of God. Their message would be the same as Jesus: "This is the time of fulfillment. The kingdom of God is at hand. Repent, and believe in the gospel" (1:15).

Note that the word "disciple" *(mathetes)* is not used in the story of their call (1:16-20).[17] Nor would it be used later in the story of Levi's call (1:13-14).[18] Jesus did not call disciples just to be disciples. He called them to follow him. There is a difference.

Following Jesus is more fundamental than being a disciple. Following is a matter of being and living. Being a disciple is a matter of learning. The correlative for disciple is teacher *(didaskalos)* or

---

[17] The word "disciple" *(mathetes)* is not used in any of the synoptic accounts in which Jesus calls his first disciples (Mark 1:16-20; Matt 4:18-22; Luke 5:1-11). In John it is used only for the disciples of John (1:35, 37).

[18] The same is true of the call of Levi or Matthew (Mark 1:13-14; Matt 9:9; Luke 5:27-28), only at the dinner that follows the call (Mark 1:15-17; Matt 9:10-13; Luke 5:29-39).

scribe *(grammateus)*. The correlative for following *(akoloutheon)* is leading *(proagon;* see 10:32; 16:7). For Jesus' followers, following meant three things: being with Jesus, patterning their lives on his life, and taking up his mission. For that, they had a lot to learn. To be good followers of Jesus, they had to be his disciples.

Later in the Gospel, Mark shows how following Jesus is following him as the Christ (8:29), the Son of Man, one "must suffer greatly and be rejected by the elders, the chief priests, and the scribes, and be killed, and rise after three days" (8:31, 33; see 9:31; 10:32-34). Mark also connects the following of Christ with the Eucharist and baptism (10:38-39, 52).

The first time Mark refers to the disciples is in the context of a dinner at Levi's home: "While he was at table in his house, many tax collectors and sinners sat with Jesus and his disciples; for there were many who followed him" (2:15-16). The same is true in Luke's Gospel (see 5:30). In the Gospel of Matthew, the term "disciples" first appears in the introduction for the Sermon on the Mount: "When he saw the crowds, he went up the mountain, and after he had sat down, his disciples came to him" (5:1).

To describe the following of Jesus, Mark uses two different expressions interchangeably, the verb "to follow" *(akoloutheo)* and the preposition "after" or "behind" *(opiso)* and the pronoun, "me" *(mou)* or "him" *(autou)*. Both expressions are used in 1:16-20. When Jesus called Simon and Andrew, he said, "Come after me" *(deute opiso mou,* 1:17), and they "followed him" *(ekolouthesan autou* 1:18). When he called James and John, they came after him *(apelthon opiso autou,* 1:20).

Mark had already used the expression *opiso mou* ("after me") to describe Jesus' relationship to John the Baptizer: "One mightier than I is coming after me" *(opiso mou)* (1:7). Later, Mark uses the same expression when Jesus rebukes Peter: "Get behind me *[hypage opiso mou],* Satan" (8:33) and instructs the crowd: "Whoever wishes to come after *[opiso mou elthein]* must deny himself, take up his cross, and follow me" (8:34).

In every case, the expression *opiso mou (autou)* describes the personal relationship of a follower to the one who leads, either John the Baptist or Jesus Christ. *Opiso* ("after" or "behind") does not refer to time or place. John the Baptist refers to Jesus as his follower, not as one who would come later. Jesus does not say to Peter, "Get out of my sight," but "Get back into my following." In his instruction (8:34), Jesus addresses the future as well as the present, the Markan community and all of Mark's readers as well as a his first followers.

The story of the call of the first disciples is very succinct. In a sense, it also represents a summary, but this time in story form. In

1:14-15, Mark summarized the mission and message of Jesus. In 1:16-20, he summarizes the following of Jesus.

Short as it is, the summary contains two distinct episodes. First, Jesus calls Simon and his brother Andrew. They had been fishermen. As Jesus' followers, they would leave their nets and become another kind of fisherman. Instead of fishing for fish, they would fish for people (1:16-18). Second, Jesus calls James and his brother John. At the time they were mending their nets. To follow Jesus they would leave their father Zebedee and the hired men and mend the nets used in fishing for human beings (1:19-20).

The two episodes are very traditional, representing how the call of the disciples was presented in the catechesis of the early Church. In the background there was the biblical story of Elijah and Elisha (2 Kgs 2:1-18). But since Jesus was not Elijah, but much greater (1:1-13), the parallel breaks down.

The call of the disciples may recall how Elijah called Elisha (2 Kgs 2:1-18), but the stories are very different. Elijah was Elisha's master *(kyrios)*, and Elisha followed Elijah on his final journey. Elijah did not call Elisha to follow him but to succeed him. The disciples would follow Jesus to his passion and resurrection, but they would never succeed him.

The event takes place as Jesus passes by the Sea of Galilee, where he sees one or more busy at their occupation. He calls them to follow him, and they leave their occupation to follow him. In the case of Simon and Andrew, and James and John, the occupation was fishing (1:16-18, 19-20). In the case of Levi, it was tax collecting (2:13-14).

In these stories, Jesus does not introduce himself to those whom he calls, nor does he prepare the future disciples for their call. The disciples themselves do not ask who Jesus is, nor do they ask what will be expected of them as his followers. Everything focuses on the call of Jesus and the response of the disciples. So stylized a presentation presupposes the passage of many years and the emergence of a traditional catechetical form. All but the barest essentials have been dropped. What remains is the heart of the matter inviting everyone to ponder.

Jesus' call of the first disciples shows what is involved in becoming his follower. Fishers of men must leave their nets, their father, and the hired men with whom they have worked. Their occupation, their human relationships, even the most intimate, must be transformed. Later in the Gospel, these themes will be developed at much greater length (see, for example, 3:31-35; 10:28-31). For Jesus' followers and disciples, the call story shows what the time of opportunity *(kairos)* and the kingdom of God mean for them. It also shows what it means to repent and believe in the gospel.

The story opens with a reference to Jesus passing by the Sea of Galilee. As the first reference to the sea, Mark uses the full expression, "the Sea of Galilee." He does the same when he refers to it for the last time (7:31). In between he refers simply to "the sea."

Actually, the Sea of Galilee, was just a lake *(limne,* see Luke 5:1, 2; 8:22, 23, 33), but Mark never calls it a lake. Everyone knew it was a lake, and outside the gospels there are extremely few references to it as a sea. Calling it a sea, Mark associated the lake with the sea and its symbolic evocation of primitive chaos, where the jaws of death lurk, and where the netherworld lies.

Galilee is a particular geographical and historical region. Accordingly, the Sea of Galilee is a particular body of water. Symbolically, Galilee is also the region for the following of Christ. In the same way, the Sea of Galilee is also symbolic, evoking various aspects including the chaos encountered in the following of Christ.

One of the central images in the story is that of fishermen *(halieis)* casting nets *(amphiballein)* in the sea. Mark's term for net *(diktuon,* 1:18, 19) is a general designation for many kinds of nets, including the dragnet *(sagene,* see Matt 13:47) and the casting net *(amphiblestron,* Matt 4:18).[19] The image is that of a circular net with small weights attached on the edge. Cast by a single person, the net flares over the water and the weights slowly drag it down. Pulled by the fisherman, the net encloses the fish.

The followers of Jesus were called to take up his mission, to proclaim the gospel of the kingdom of God, calling people to repentance and belief in the gospel. In their mission, the kingdom of God would already be present, but like a mustard seed, almost invisible (see 4:30-32). Jesus' followers would continue to be fishermen, but from now on, they would fish for human beings for the kingdom of God. Since the kingdom of God is universal, their net would flare until it included the entire human race. Like the kingdom of God, the mission would be universal.

In the story, Mark introduces another image that would be extremely important for the whole first part of the Gospel, the boat *(ploion,* 1:19, 20), that is, a fishing boat. The boat would be the vehicle for the mission of Jesus and the Twelve to the Gentiles (see 4:35-41; 6:45-52).

---

[19] See Wilhelm H. Wuellner, *The Meaning of "Fishers of Men"* (Philadelphia: The Westminster Press, 1967).

The Beginning of the Ministry in Galilee (1:21-45)

We have seen how Jesus proclaimed the gospel of God (1:14-15) and called disciples to follow him in that mission (1:16-20). Now Mark begins to show what this would mean for Jesus and his followers. The primary focus is on Jesus' mission and ministry and on how the crowds responded, but the disciples are ever present.

As followers, the disciples had to learn to be with Jesus, to live like Jesus, and to take on his mission. They accepted these three aspects of the following of Christ when they first accepted the call to follow him. But what actually their call would involve they had to learn by participating in Jesus' mission.

In a series of five units or scenes, the story demonstrates the centrifugal nature of the gospel and its proclamation. The first scene shows Jesus proclaiming the gospel in the synagogue at Capernaum (1:21-28). In the second scene, Jesus moves out of the synagogue and into the home of Simon and Andrew (1:29-31).

Among the Jews away from Jerusalem, religious life unfolded in two principal settings, the synagogue and the home. In Jerusalem, there was also the Temple. The synagogue was where the Jewish community assembled for worship, prayer and study, where they read the Scriptures, explore its meaning, and apply it to life.[20] The home was a place for family living, where a family enjoyed meals in a religious, prayerful atmosphere, especially on the Sabbath. At the beginning, the early Christians participated in the synagogue, and their homes were culturally Jewish, but gradually, they moved out of the synagogue, and the home became the main religious setting.

In the third scene, Jesus moves to the door of the home and ministers to the whole population of the town that gathered outside (1:32-34). In the fourth scene, Jesus went to a desert place to pray, after which he went to other towns and villages throughout Galilee, where he went to their synagogues, preaching and driving out demons (1:35-39). Finally, in the fifth scene, a leper, one who was unclean, an outcast who had to live outside the towns, came to Jesus, and Jesus cured him (1:40-45).

The main focus in the five scenes is actually not on the places or setting but on the people involved. Beginning with those who are related to one another religiously at the synagogue (1:21-28), Jesus

[20] For the relationship of the synagogue to architecture, see Kenneth Atkinson, "On Further Defining the First-Century CE Synagogue: Fact or Fiction? A Rejoinder to H. C. Kee," *New Testament Studies* 43 (1997) 491–502.

moves into the intimate circle of the first disciples (1:29-31), and after that, to the rest of the town (1:32-34). He then goes on to people in other towns (1:35-39), and finally to those who were prevented from approaching the towns because they were ritually unclean (1:40-45). At each point in this centrifugal movement, Jesus reaches out further and further to those who were troubled and sick, bringing them the gospel of God.

Jesus Teaches with Authority (1:21-28)

The beginning of Jesus' ministry in Galilee (1:21-45) opens with two events that occurred on a Sabbath in Capernaum. The first is situated in the synagogue, where Jesus cured someone who had an unclean spirit (1:21-28).[21] The second is situated in the home of Simon and Andrew, where Jesus cured Simon's mother-in-law from a fever (1:29-31).

While proclaiming the gospel of God and after calling the first disciples by the Sea of Galilee, "they came to Capernaum, and on the sabbath he entered the synagogue and taught" (1:21). We recognize the opening verse as an introduction for the story, introducing the personages, situating them in time and place, and presenting the principal theme, Jesus' ministry of teaching. We also notice a shift from the plural to the singular: "they came [eisporeuontai] to Capernaum," but "he entered [eiselthon] the synagogue and taught [edidasken]."

Jesus and his first followers (see 1:16-20) came to Capernaum. After that, the followers seem to disappear. The story has no further mention of the disciples. Most likely, as told in the oral tradition, the story did not include the disciples. It was about Jesus and Jesus' victory over unclean spirits. Mark transformed it into a story of Jesus and his followers. The nucleus of the Church was present and being formed by Jesus, when he silenced the unclean spirit in the synagogue of Capernaum.

The body of the story (1:22-27) focuses on the people's general reaction to Jesus' teaching. "The people were astonished [exeplessonto] at his teaching [didache], for he taught them as one having authority [hos exousian echon] and not as the scribes [hos hoi grammateis]" (1:22).[22] The crowd reacted not so much to what Jesus taught, but to

---

[21] For a redactional and literary analysis of Mark 1:21-28, see Richard J. Dillon, "'As One Having Authority' (Mark 1:22: The Controversial Distinction of Jesus Teaching," *The Catholic Biblical Quarterly* 57/1 (January 1995) 92–113.

[22] Dillon characterizes this statement as "the intriguing sentence which Mark uses as something of a banner heading for this entire account of the public ministry." Ibid., 92.

how he taught "as one having authority." The scribes, the teachers in the synagogues,[23] did not teach as those having authority. In all this, we sense Mark's summarizing tendency.

Jesus' teaching "as one having authority" *(exousia)* referred not so much to his power to teach as to his right to teach.[24] That right flowed from his God-given mission to announce the gospel of God and that the kingdom of God was at hand (1:14-15). Later, the people in the synagogue would describe his authoritative teaching as "new" (1:27). What was new in Jesus' new teaching was its eschatological aspect. With Jesus' mission, the ultimate restoration of creation and the fulfillment of history was beginning.

The general reaction to Jesus seemed to be positive. But among the people in the synagogue, there was a discordant, hostile voice. While Jesus was teaching, a man with an unclean spirit cried out to him in defiance. But Jesus quieted the unclean spirit and expulsed it from the man (1:23-26). Reading the episode, we are impressed by the violence and the power of the unclean spirit, also the greater power of Jesus to subdue and expulse him. Recalling the story, we may have the impression that we were told the event in great detail, but that is only an impression. Actually, the episode is told very schematically.

The man with the unclean spirit cried out, "What have you to do with us, Jesus of Nazareth? Have you come to destroy *[apolesai]* us? I know who you are—the Holy One of God!" (1:23-24). The man with the unclean spirit recognized Jesus and called him by name, "Jesus of Nazareth" (see 1:9). Notice that in the two rhetorical questions, he did not ask Jesus, "What have you to do with me?" and "Have you come to destroy me?" Instead, using the first person plural, he asked, "What have you to do with us?" and "Have you come to destroy us?" The man with the unclean spirit spoke for the whole synagogue.

Identifying with the synagogue, he had a double challenge. First, he rejected that Jesus had anything to do with the synagogue, that is, he defied Jesus' authority over the synagogue. Escalating the challenge, he accused him of coming to destroy *(apolesai)* it. From the Gospel's point of view, Jesus had everything to do with those in the synagogue. He certainly did not come to destroy them. In contrast with the Pharisees, who were conspiring with the Herodians to destroy *(apolesosin)* him (3:6).

---

[23] For the position of the scribes, see Joachim Jeremias, *Jerusalem in the Time of Jesus* (Philadelphia: Fortress Press, 1969) 233–45; Anthony J. Saldarini, "Scribes," *The Anchor Bible Dictionary* 5:1012–1016.

[24] See Dillon, op. cit., 97–102.

Defying Jesus, the man with the unclean spirit was defying the gospel of God. Now, using the first person singular, he cried out, "I know who you are—the Holy One of God!" The man with the unclean spirit knew that Jesus of Nazareth was the Holy One of God. He knew who Jesus was. But he did not know Jesus. To know Jesus, one has to have faith in him. Rejecting Jesus, he rejected the Holy One of God and with him the gospel of God.

In his response, Jesus did not rebuke the man himself, only the unclean spirit, commanding him to be quiet and come out of the man (1:25). "Quiet!" *(phimotheti)*. Jesus would use a similar command to rebuke the wind and the sea: "Quiet! Be still!" (*siopa, pephimoso* 4:39).

Jesus silenced the unclean spirit that both identified him as Jesus of Nazareth and knew that he was the Holy One of God. The unclean spirit was not fit to proclaim Jesus' identity. Only those who follow Jesus, those who have faith in him, have authority to proclaim who Jesus is without distorting the message.

What matters in the episode is Jesus' victory over the unclean spirit. We are not even given the man's reaction after he was cured. Instead, we are given the reaction of the people in the synagogue: "All were amazed and asked one another, 'What is this? A new teaching with authority. He commands even the unclean spirits and they obey him'" (1:27). After Jesus silenced and expulsed the unclean spirit, the story returns to the theme of Jesus' authority (see 1:22). In 1:27, we continue to observe Mark's tendency to summarize and generalize.

In the introduction, we were told that Jesus came to Capernaum (1:21). In the conclusion, Mark says that Jesus' "fame spread everywhere throughout the whole region of Galilee" (1:28). Jesus began his mission in Capernaum, but from Capernaum the good news of God spread throughout Galilee (see 1:14, 39).

Jesus' confrontation with the unclean spirit (1:23-26) is part of a larger story concerning Jesus' teaching as one with authority (1:22, 27). In Mark, the silencing of the unclean spirit illustrates Jesus' authority *(exousia)* to teach. The scribes could not command unclean spirits. They taught, but not as those having authority. Jesus' teaching with authority is part of a larger story about the spread of Jesus' fame from Capernaum throughout Galilee (1:22, 28).

Mention of the scribes (1:22) prepares the series of conflicts with the scribes and the Pharisees told in 2:1–3:6. Jesus' teaching was so new and authoritative that even the unclean spirits obeyed him (1:27). One who is able to command and dismiss unclean spirits has nothing to fear from the scribes.

The Raising of Simon's Mother-in-law (1:29-31)

Leaving the synagogue, Jesus went to the home of Simon and Andrew, accompanied by James and John, the first four who were called by Jesus by the Sea of Galilee (1:16-20). Entering the home, Jesus was immediately told that Simon's mother-in-law was sick with a fever. Today, fever can be very serious, for example, in certain strains of malaria and in typhoid. But usually a fever is not very serious, given modern advances in medicine. In biblical times, however, fever was taken very seriously.[25] Jesus cured her. Grasping her hand, he raised her up *(egeiren),* and the fever left her and she ministered *(diekonei)* to them.

The story's introduction focuses on the change of setting and the personages involved (1:29). Leaving the public setting of the synagogue, Jesus went with James and John to the home of Simon and Andrew (1:29).

In the previous story (1:21-28), Jesus' followers accompanied him to Capernaum (1:21) but did not have a direct role in the body of the story. The entire focus was on Jesus as one who taught with authority. In this second story (1:29-31), the followers have an integral part in the story. After introducing Simon's mother-in-law (1:30a), Mark says that they immediately told Jesus about her fever (1:30b). At the end of the story, Simon's mother-in-law ministers to Jesus and his followers (1:31b).[26]

At the time, Jesus and the four followers constituted the nucleus of what would be the Church. From the point of view of Mark and those for whom he wrote, Simon's mother-in-law ministered to the Church in embryo.

The body of the story (1:30-31) focuses on Simon's mother-in-law. In the Revised New American Bible (RNAB), we read that Jesus "approached, grasped *(kratesas)* her hand, and helped her up *(egeiren)*" (1:31a). We read much the same in The New Jerusalem Bible (NJB) and in the New International Version (NIV): Jesus "helped her up." All three presuppose that Simon's mother-in-law herself got up and Jesus assisted her in getting up.

---

[25] See Max Sussman, "Sickness and Disease" *The Anchor Bible Dictionary* (New York: Doubleday, 1992) 6:6–15, esp. 8–9.

[26] As told by Matthew, the disciples do not have any role in the story (Matt 8:14-15). Luke refers to the home of Simon, but since Simon was not yet a follower or a disciple of Jesus (see Luke 5:1-11), he and the others may have been there but not as disciples (Luke 4:38-39).

In The New Revised Standard Version (NRSV), we read that Jesus "came and took her by the hand and lifted her up." The translation presupposes that Simon's mother-in-law was not able to get up, and Jesus not only helped her to get up, but he lifted her up. In the NRSV, we have a more literal translation of *egeiren*. The literary context of Mark's Gospel, however, demands even more.

The verb *egeiro* (raise) brings to mind two important references to Jesus' resurrection: "But after I have been raised up *[egerthenai]*, I shall go before you to Galilee" (14:28); "Do not be amazed! You seek Jesus of Nazareth, the crucified. He has been raised" *(egerthe)* (16:6). The same word was used in a very early baptismal creed: "that he was raised *[egegertai]* on the third day in accordance with the scriptures" (1 Cor 15:4).

The verb also brings to mind several instances when Jesus heals a paralytic (2:9, 11, 12), someone with a withered hand (3:3), a boy possessed with a mute spirit (9:27), a blind beggar (10:49), or raises a girl to life (5:41). Jesus raises people from illness and from affliction as well as from death. The verb *egeiro* is also associated with the general resurrection of the dead (12:18-27).[27]

Jesus' cure of a sick man (1:21-28) was a tremendous victory over unclean spirits, prefiguring his victory in the passion and resurrection over the powers of evil. His cure of Simon's mother-in-law manifested him as the Lord of life. Symbolically, Jesus raised her from illness and ultimately from death. From the point of view of early baptismal theology (see 10:38-40), the Lord Jesus gave her a share in his risen life. Filled with new life, she set about ministering to Jesus and his first followers.

The Greek verb describing the response of Simon's mother-of-law may be rendered in several ways. We read in the RNAB that "she waited *[diekonei]* on them," and in the NIV, that "she began to wait on them." Both translations suggest an attitude of subservience. In the NRSV and the NJB, we read that "she began to serve them." This translation associated her response to Christian service *(diakonia)*. Her response can also be translated as, "she began to minister to them."

The same verb, *diakoneo*, described the ministry of the angels at the end of Mark's prologue: "He was among wild beasts, and the an-

---

[27] In the early tradition and in Paul's letters, the transitive verb *egeiro* (to raise up), was normally used to refer to resurrection. Later, another verb, *anistemi*, came into normal use for resurrection. In the Pauline letters, it appears only in 1 Thessalonians 4:14, 16 and Ephesians 5:14. In Mark, the verb is associated with Jesus' prophetic announcements of his death and resurrection (8:31; 9:31; 10:34).

gels ministered *[diekonoun]* to him" (1:13). Later, Jesus used the re
lated term *diakonos* (servant) in giving his followers an ideal: "Whoever wishes to be great among you will be your servant" (10:43).
After that, Jesus used it to describe the mission of the Son of Man,
who "did not come to be served *[diakonethenai]* but to serve *[di-
akonesai]* and to give his life as a ransom for many" (10:45). Mark
presents Jesus' life of service as a model for those who aspire to
greatness in the exercise of authority (10:42-44). Still later, the verb
diakoneo refers to the role of the women who followed Jesus in
Galilee: "These women had followed *(ekolouthoun)* him when he
was in Galilee and ministered *(diekonoun)* to him" (15:41).

The story of the raising of Simon's mother-in-law marks the first
mention in Mark's gospel of pastoral ministry, that is, ministry to
the Church itself. After Jesus raised her to life, she ministered to
the nucleus of the Church. Like many stories in Mark's Gospel, the
story of Simon's mother-in-law was probably formed in view of baptismal catechesis. In the early Church, everyone who was baptized
was expected to share in the mission and ministry of the Church.[28]

Pastoral ministry can be distinguished from apostolic ministry, in
which a Christian community reaches beyond itself to a world in
need of salvation. In Mark's Gospel, apostolic ministry is the primary ministry of Jesus and his followers. The purpose of pastoral
ministry is to build up and strengthen a Christian community and
ensure the quality and effectiveness of its apostolic ministry.

Other Cures (1:32-34)

Mark began by telling two particular events, in which Jesus
drove out an unclean spirit (1:21-28) and performed a cure (1:29-31)
on the Sabbath. With sunset, the Sabbath comes to a close, and a
new day, the first of the week, begins (see 16:1-2). Mark emphasizes
that it was evening *(opsias de genomenes)* and after sunset *(hote edu
ho helios)*, leaving no doubt that the Sabbath was over.

He then summarizes the events of that evening in two separate
moments. In the first moment, people brought to Jesus all who were
ill or possessed by demons. The whole city assembled *(episynegmene)*
at the door of the home of Simon and Andrew (1:32-33).

---

[28] In their version of the cure of Simon's mother-in-law, Matthew and
Luke have removed any allusion to Christian baptism. In Matthew, Jesus
"touched her hand, the fever left her" (Matt 8:15). In Luke, Jesus "stood
over her, rebuked the fever, and it left her" (Luke 4:39).

The term "unclean spirits" (1:23, 27) evokes a Jewish, religious context in which people are generally concerned about ritual cleanness and uncleanness (see 1:40-45; 7:1-23). The term "demons" (1:32, 34) evokes a broader Hellenistic context. The verb *episynago* is a compound of *epi* and *synago,* meaning assembling together. The noun *synagoge,* assembly or synagogue, comes from that verb. In the assembly at the synagogue, there was only one man with an unclean spirit. When the city assembled at the door of the home of Simon and Andrew, people brought all who were ill or possessed by demons.

In the second moment, Jesus cured many of the sick who had various diseases and drove out many demons. As in the synagogue, where Jesus silenced the unclean spirit (1:24-25), he did not permit the demons to speak because they knew him (1:34). The demons may have known him, but they had no faith. Only those who know Jesus in faith are able to proclaim who Jesus truly is.

The summary in 1:32-34 shows Jesus exercising the apostolic ministry for which he called the disciples. The pastoral ministry of Simon's mother-in-law helped Jesus to fulfill his apostolic ministry (1:29-31). Together, the two passages may demonstrate the relationship between pastoral and apostolic ministry in the Markan community.

To the Neighboring Villages (1:35-39)

Rising very early before dawn *(proi ennycha lian),* Jesus left *(exelthen)* Capernaum and the home of Simon and Andrew and went *(apelthen)* to a deserted place *(eis eremon topon),* and there he prayed (1:35). The desert *(eremos)* was the place where John fulfilled his mission (1:3-4). It was also the place where Jesus, driven by the Spirit, spent forty days tested by Satan (1:12-13). As one who taught with authority, who expelled unclean spirits, healed the sick, and drove out demons, Jesus needed to pray. For that, he needed some solitude, and that is why he went to a desert place *(eremos topos)* to pray. But as we shall soon see, Jesus had another reason.

Simon and those who were with him *(hoi met' autou),* namely Andrew, James and John (see 1:16-20, 29-31), searched for Jesus and told him that everyone was looking for him (1:36-37). Responding, Jesus invited them to go with him elsewhere *(allachou)* to the neighboring villages where he would also preach (1:38a), proclaiming *(keryxo)* the gospel of God (see 1:14). This was the purpose for which he left *(exelthon)* Capernaum and the home of Simon and Andrew (1:38b; see 1:35) and went to the desert place. The people of Capernaum would have kept him home and restricted his mission.

Jesus then went into the neighboring villages and preached *(kerysson)* in their synagogues throughout Galilee, driving out demons (1:39). Mark does not say, but we are left to assume that Simon and those who were with him followed Jesus to the neighboring villages.

The Cleansing of a Leper (1:40-45)

Such is the context of Jesus' cure of a leper, an event that Mark situated somewhere in Galilee. The beginning of Jesus' ministry in Galilee (1:21-45) opened with an encounter between Jesus and a man with an unclean spirit (1:21-28). It now concludes with a story in which Jesus cures a man who was unclean because of leprosy (1:40-45). Proclaiming the gospel of God, Jesus drove out unclean spirits and made everyone clean (see 7:1-13).

The story of the cleansing of the leper (1:40-45) develops in two parts. The first (1:40-43) presents the event itself. It includes the leper's prayer, begging Jesus to make him clean, and Jesus' response. Curing him, Jesus made him clean and dismissed him with a warning.

The second part (1:44-45) seems to be an addition. After dismissing the one whom he cleansed, Jesus added further instructions, telling him to show himself to the priest and offer the prescribed offering (1:44). The second part ends with the conclusion (1:45) for the story of the leper as well as the whole series of events that began in the synagogue at Capernaum (1:21-45).

The leper's prayer demonstrated great faith: "If you wish, you can make me clean" *(katharisai)* (1:40). In some manuscripts, the leper knelt before Jesus when he prayed. For the leper, there was no question that Jesus was able to cleanse him. The only question he had was whether Jesus was willing.

Jesus was deeply moved by the leper's plea and his heart went out to him. Extending his hand, he touched him, saying: "I do will it. Be made clean" *(katharistheti)* (1:41). Immediately, the leprosy went away from him *(apelthen ap' autou),* and he was made clean *(ekatharisthe).* It is as though Jesus expelled the leprosy from him (1:42), as he had expelled the unclean spirit from the man in the synagogue. On that occasion, the unclean spirit came out of him *(exelthen ex autou,* 1:25-26). Jesus then dismissed the former leper with a stern warning (1:43).

Jesus responded to the leper in deed and word. First, he reached out and touched him. In itself, this was a very significant gesture. According to the law of Moses (see Lev 13:1-46), once it was ascertained by a priest that someone indeed had leprosy, the priest declared the person unclean. From that moment on, the leper went about with his garments rent, his head bare, and he was expected to cover his mouth as he cried out, "Unclean, unclean," warning everyone to stay away. The leper also had to live apart and make his home away from people who were clean.

In touching the leper, Jesus was touching someone who was humanly and religiously untouchable. Jesus could not have reached out any further from the synagogue, from the home, and from the people gathered at the door of the home. Since the kingdom of God was for all, Jesus proclaimed the gospel of God to all.

The story now moves to its second part (1:44-45). At the end of the first, Jesus gave a stern warning while dismissing the leper that had been cleansed (1:43). This may have been the end of the story as handed down in tradition. But Mark expanded the story giving the content of Jesus' warning: "See that you tell no one anything" (1:44a). In doing that, he related the warning to other warnings, when Jesus silenced the unclean spirit (1:25) and did not permit demons to speak (1:34).

After telling him to tell no one anything, Jesus commanded him to show himself to the priest and to offer what Moses prescribed for his cleansing. This would be a witness *(martyrion)* for everyone that he was truly cleansed (1:44b). Since lepers had to be declared unclean by a priest, they also had to be declared clean by a priest, if the leprosy was cured. As the law of Moses prescribed, the leper had to go to the priest, have the cure verified, be declared clean, and present a sacrificial offering (see Lev 14:1-32). Curing the leper, Jesus observed the law of Moses.

Cured of his leprosy, the man ignored Jesus' warning. Instead, going away, he began to proclaim *(keryssein)* many things, and spread the word *(ton logon)* all around (1:45a). Using the term "the word," Mark suggests that he proclaimed the gospel of God as Jesus did (see 2:2; 4:34; 8:32). But now the gospel of God included his cure. When Jesus cured the man with an unclean spirit, his fame spread throughout the region of Galilee (1:28). Later, when he left Capernaum and the home of Simon and Andrew and went to a desert place *(eis eremon topon),* everyone was looking for him (1:35-36). Now, Jesus was no longer able to enter a city openly. Instead, he stayed outside *(exo)* in desert places *(ep' eremois topois),* but people came to him from everywhere (1:45b).

The spread of Jesus' fame (1:28, 45a) and the growing crowds (1:32-33, 36-37, 45b) set the stage for the escalating series of conflicts presented in the second part (2:1–3:6) of the story of Jesus and the first disciples (1:14–3:6).

Mounting Opposition (2:1–3:6)

Our reflection on Jesus and the first disciples (1:14–3:6) began by exploring the story's geographical and temporal setting and its cast of personages. We looked at the three from a literary point of view, sensitive not only to their historical background but to the way Mark presented them in the literary and theological world of the Gospel.

We then examined the story's introduction and saw how Jesus proclaimed the gospel of God (1:14-15) and called disciples to follow him (1:16-20). After this, we took up the story's first part (1:21-45), joining Jesus as he taught with authority and showing his disciples what the mission involved. In that first part, we saw how Jesus met resistance from unclean spirits and demons (1:21-28, 32-34, 39) but emerged victorious.

Seeing Jesus expulsing unclean spirits, the people in the synagogue compared Jesus' teaching with the scribes: "he taught . . . as one having authority and not as the scribes" (1:22). With Jesus' popularity growing steadily, he was bound to come into conflict with the scribes.

The second part (2:1–3:6) complements the first. In the first part (1:21-45), we saw how Jesus of Nazareth, the Holy One of God (see 1:24), came into conflict with unclean spirits. In the second, we see how Jesus, the Son of Man (see 2:10, 28), with his new teaching with authority (1:27) came into conflict with the scribes and the Pharisees.

The second part (2:1–3:6) of the story includes five conflict episodes, each focusing on a particular issue. As in the first part, the disciples, those whom Jesus had called to follow him (1:16-20), were always present, learning from him as he proclaimed the gospel of God (1:14-15). In two of the episodes, it was the disciples' behavior, not that of Jesus, that occasioned the conflict (2:18-22, 23-28).

Each of the five stories is related to the one that follows or precedes it.[29] The first deals with Jesus' authority *(exousia)* as the Son of Man to forgive sins (2:1-12). The second also deals with the forgiveness of sins, but in the context of a meal Jesus shared with tax collectors and sinners (2:13-17). The third moves away from the issue of forgiveness, but continues the theme of eating and fasting (2:18-22). The fourth also is about eating, but this time the concern is eating food gathered on the Sabbath (2:23-28). The fifth and final story moves away from the issue of gathering food on the Sabbath

---

[29] See Joanna Dewey, *Markan Public Debate, Literary Techniques, Concentric Structure, and Theology in Mark 2:1–3:6* (Chico, Calif.: Scholars Press, 1980).

and comes to grips with the more basic issue of doing good and saving life on the Sabbath (3:1-6).

The interlocking pattern gives this second part a strong sense of forward movement, with each story adding to the mounting conflict. Step by step, the negative reaction to Jesus and his new teaching escalates until it reaches the definitive conflict, culminating with plans to destroy him. As the section closes, the Pharisees take counsel with the Herodians to find a way to put him to death (3:6). With this, the Gospel leaves us on the threshold of the passion and resurrection, pondering what the death of the Son of Man (2:1–3:6) has to do with the victory of the Son of the Most High over unclean spirits (1:21-45).

Authority to Forgive Sins (2:1-12)[30]

After some days, Jesus returned (*eiselthon palin,* see 1:21) to Capernaum and people heard that he was at home *(en oiko).* Mark uses the adverb *palin* (again) to associate an event with a previous event.[31] The first episode (2:1-12) is situated at Capernaum, where Jesus had begun his mission (see 1:21-28), but not in the synagogue. The setting for the story is the home of Simon and Andrew, where Jesus had raised Simon's mother-in-law from a state of illness to a life of service (see 1:29-31). The home of Simon and Andrew had become Jesus' home (2:1). That home, which already had witnessed many cures (see 1:32-34) would now become the setting for the dramatic healing or raising of a paralytic (2:9-12).

The day and time of the event are not given. For Mark, it sufficed to distinguish the new event from those told in the previous section (1:21-28). After some days *(di' hemeron),* Jesus again entered Capernaum. This temporal indefiniteness aside, no other story in this section is told with such detail. Until now, we observed Mark's tendency to generalize and summarize. Now, we see him as a very engaging story-teller.

Having heard that Jesus was at home (2:1), the crowd *(polloi)* gathered so that there was no longer room for anyone else, not even at the door *(pros ten thyran,* see 1:33). Jesus spoke *(elalei)* the word *(ton logon)* to them (2:2), as he proclaimed the gospel of God throughout

---

[30] For the authority to forgive sins (2:1-12), see Richard Dillon, "'As One Having Authority' (Mark 1:22): The Controversial Distinction of Jesus' Teaching," *The Catholic Biblical Quarterly* 57/1 (January 1995) 103–06.

[31] For Mark's usage of the adverb *palin* in Mark's Gospel, see David Barrett Peabody, *Mark as Composer,* New Gospel Studies 1 (Macon, Ga.: Mercer University Press, 1987) 115–58.

Galilee (see 1:14-15, 39). For Mark, "the word" is the gospel of God as proclaimed by Jesus.

Later, Mark uses the same expression, "he spoke the word" *(elalei . . . ton logon),* with reference to Jesus' parables (4:33) and to his prophetic announcement of the passion and the resurrection of the Son of Man (8:32). Here, the expression refers to Jesus' entire gospel message. Like John and Luke, Mark also has a theology of the word.

Such was the setting for the event: the home at Capernaum, the overflowing crowd, and Jesus proclaiming the word (2:1-2). All is in place for the story of Jesus and the cure of the paralytic.

Until now, Mark has shown how the crowd could be either an opportunity, facilitating the ministry of Jesus (1:32-34), or a hindrance, preventing Jesus from reaching out to others (1:45). This time, Mark shows how the crowd could hinder others from approaching Jesus. Neither hindrance was absolute, but it did test the ingenuity of those concerned.

In this story, four men come carrying a paralytic to Jesus. Since they could not get near to Jesus because of the crowd, they opened the roof above Jesus. Having broken through, they lowered the mat on which the paralytic was lying in front of Jesus (2:3-4). In those days, a roof for a home in Capernaum was made of poles holding up a kind of thatch. Elsewhere, a roof could be made of loose tiles without mortar. Mark does not indicate the kind of roof he was thinking of. Either way, it was simple enough to make an opening in the roof and close it afterwards.

The effort and the remarkable ingenuity of the four and the presence of the paralytic lying on the mat before Jesus, was a clear demonstration of faith *(pistis).* Seeing their faith *(ten pistin),* Jesus addressed the paralytic, "Child, your sins are forgiven" (2:5).

In general, the word of Jesus (2:2) was the gospel of God (1:14), announcing that the time *(ho kairos)* was fulfilled, that the kingdom of God was near, calling for repentance and faith in the gospel (1:14). To the paralytic, the word of Jesus, the gospel of God, was that his sins were forgiven. The paralytic and those with him had repented and had faith. That his sins were forgiven manifested the time of fulfillment and the proximity of the kingdom of God.

The Greek word for child, *teknon,* does not refer to the age of a little child. For that, Greek has the another word, *paidion. Teknon* refers to the child's relationship to its parents and others who in different ways gave life to the child. A child outgrows being a *paidion,* but even as an adult, he or she is still *teknon* in relation to the parents. In the vocative, *teknon* may be used as an expression of warmth and loving familiarity. Jesus recognizes the paralytic as his *teknon.*

In itself, the declaration, "Child, your sins are forgiven," does not necessarily imply that Jesus is the one who has forgiven his sins. Expressed in the passive, it can also mean that God has forgiven the sins of the paralytic. Later, responding to the scribes (2:10), Jesus would further specify the meaning. God forgave the paralytic through his beloved Son. As the Son of Man, Jesus forgave the sins of the paralytic in response to his faith (2:5a).

So far, there has been no hint of a conflict or controversy. However, some scribes were there, sitting among the crowd, listening to Jesus. When Jesus forgave the sins of the paralytic, they reacted inwardly, asking themselves: "Why does this man *(houtos)* speak *(lalei)* that way." For them, Jesus was blaspheming: "Who but God alone *(heis ho theos)* can forgive sins?" (2:6-7). The scribes had not repented and did not believe in the word of Jesus and his gospel of God.

The scribes formed a class of learned teachers and many of them were Pharisees (see 2:16). Mark referred to the scribes earlier in the Gospel, but this is the first time they play an active role. Jesus' teaching contrasted with theirs. Jesus taught as one having authority *(hos exousian echon),* not like the scribes (1:22). Now Jesus is about to manifest his teaching as one with authority.

Without the presence of the scribes, the story would have been one of simple faith, gracious forgiveness, and wondrous healing, a manifestation of the time of fulfillment (2:1-5, 11-12). With the scribes (2:6-10), it becomes a story of resistance, conflict and rejection as well as a powerful demonstration of Jesus' identity as the Son of Man, one who exercises heavenly authority and power *(exousia)* on earth to forgive sins.[32]

Throughout the controversy (2:6-10) the story focuses on the reaction of the scribes and Jesus' response, but the scribes remain eloquently silent. The question which arises in their hearts *(en tais kardiais auton)* is not a real question but a judgment: Jesus has blasphemed! At the end of the section, Jesus would grieve at the hardness of their heart *(epi te porosei tes kardias auton,* 3:5). The accusation of blasphemy, associated with Jesus' claim to be the Son of Man, would one day resurface and lead to Jesus' condemnation and death (14:61-64).

---

[32] The structure of the story of the paralytic (2:1-12) parallels that of the cure of the demoniac (1:21-28), where the story of Jesus' teaching in the synagogue as one having authority (1:21-22, 27-28) is interrupted by a conflict with a demoniac (1:23-26).

Knowing what was going on in the minds of the scribes, Jesus challenged them with a real question: "Why are you thinking such things in your hearts *[en tais kardiais]*? Which is easier, to say to the paralytic, 'Your sins are forgiven,' or to say, 'Rise pick up your mat and walk?'" (2:8-9). Still speaking to the scribes, but with Mark's readers in mind, Jesus proceeds to answer his question: "But that you may know that the Son of Man has authority *[exousian]* to forgive sins on earth . . ." (2:10a). With that, the role of the scribes is over.

Shifting mid-sentence, Jesus addresses the paralytic directly: "I say to you, rise *[egeire]*, pick up your mat, and go home" (2:10b-11). The paralytic rose *(egerthe)* and immediately took his mat and went away in front of everyone (2:12a). The previous time Jesus was at home, he grasped the hand of Simon's mother-in-law and raised *(egeiren)* her up (1:31). This time, Jesus commands the paralytic to rise, showing the power *(exousian)* of his word and the gospel of God. The raising of the paralytic manifests the authority and the power *(exousian)* of the Son of Man to forgive sins on earth.

Like the story of the demoniac (1:21-28), that of the paralytic says nothing about his personal reaction. Instead the story focuses on the reaction of those present. Astounded, everyone glorified God, saying, "We have never seen anything like this" (2:12b).

Within their stories, the demoniac and the paralytic were the principal beneficiaries of Jesus' exorcising and healing power, but their stories were told for the benefit of those who would read them as gospel. For Mark's readers, the reaction of those present was more important than the reaction of those who were cured. In baptism, they had also been cured and their sins had been forgiven. Reading or listening to the story in Mark's Gospel, they should recall their own response when they were catechized and baptized. Now, identifying with the crowd, they should glorify God.

Calling Sinners to Repentance (2:13-17)

The first conflict episode was over Jesus' authority to forgive sins as he healed a paralytic at the home of Simon and Andrew (2:1-12). The second is over Jesus' authority to call sinners to repentance when he dines with tax collectors and sinners at the home of Levi (2:13-17).

This second conflict has two distinct settings. First, Jesus is along the Sea of Galilee, where he calls Levi to follow him (2:13-14). Second, Jesus is at the home of Levi, where many tax collectors and sinners join him at table (2:15-17).

The story opens by recalling the previous time Jesus was by the sea: "Once again *[palin]* he went out along the sea" (2:13a). The first time Jesus passed by the sea, he called Simon and his brother Andrew to come after him (1:16-18). Going a little farther, he also called James and his brother John (1:19-20). Using the same literary pattern and many of the same terms, Mark now tells how Jesus called Levi, a tax collector, to follow him.

This is the second time Mark uses the adverb "again" *(palin)* to associate a story with a previous story. He connected the healing of a paralytic (2:1-12) to the cure of a demoniac (1:21-28): "When Jesus returned *[eiselthon palin]* to Capernaum" (2:1a; see 1:21). Now he associates the call of Levi with the call of the first disciples.

Jesus had called Simon and his brother when they were casting their nets in the sea. He had called the sons of Zebedee when they were mending their nets in the boat. Now he calls Levi, the son of Alphaeus, while he was sitting at the customs post: "Follow me" *(akolouthei moi)*.

Jesus had called Simon and Andrew to come after him, "Come after me" *(deute opiso mou)*, evoking how Jesus had come after *(opiso)* John the Baptist (see 1:7). Recall that coming after Jesus is another expression for following Jesus. Simon and Andrew left their nets and followed *(ekolouthesan)* Jesus. James and John came after him *(apelthon opisou autou)*. Levi now left the customs post: "he got up and followed *[ekolouthesen]* him." Both expressions, following Jesus and coming after Jesus, play an important role in Mark's theology of the following of Christ.

Like the first disciples, Levi did not ask where Jesus was going. The personal relationship between Jesus and the disciples is at the heart of the following of Jesus. For now, where Jesus was going and where they would follow him is quite secondary. The main concern is to be with Jesus wherever he goes. Later, in the second part of the Gospel (8:22–16:8), going to Jerusalem for Jesus' passion and resurrection would be primary.

One of the finest expressions of what it means to follow Jesus is the response of Ruth, the Moabite, to Naomi, her Judean mother-in-law: "Wherever you go I will go, wherever you lodge I will lodge, your people shall be my people and your God my God. Wherever you die I will die, and there be buried" (Ruth 1:16-17).

In itself, the commitment to follow Jesus, to be with him, and take up his mission was quite extraordinary but even more in the case of a tax collector. As a class, tax collectors were regarded as religious outcasts and sinners.[33] Part of the reason for this may have

---

[33] For tax collecting as a despised trade among Jews, see Joachim Jeremias, *Jerusalem in the Time of Jesus* (Philadelphia: Fortress Press, 1969) 303–12.

been their propensity to collect more than what was prescribed (see Luke 3:13), a practice especially burdensome for the poor who had no legal recourse or personal influence.

When he called Levi, Jesus was teaching *(edidasken)* the whole crowd *(pas ho ochlos)* that had come to him. Mark integrated the story of the call of Levi in the general flow of this section of the Gospel, where the growth of the crowd (1:33, 37, 45; 2:4) and Jesus' teaching ministry (1:21, 22, 27) are both emphasized.

Important as it is, the call of Levi (2:13-14) is merely an introduction for the meal at Levi's home (2:15-17). Together, the call of Levi and the meal at Levi's home show how the setting for evangelization became the Christian meal. Inviting people to dine with Jesus was a call to repent and believe in the gospel (see 1:15). Accepting the invitation was a sign of repentance.

After the simple statement that Levi got up and followed Jesus, the setting abruptly shifts from the shore of the sea to the home of Levi, where many *(polloi)* tax collectors and sinners were reclining at table with Jesus and his disciples. Grammatically, Mark's statement is ambiguous. It could mean that Jesus was reclining at table in his own home, that is, at the home of Simon and Andrew (see 1:29; 2:1). The context, however, points rather to the home of Levi. As a follower of Jesus, Levi invited other tax collectors and sinners to follow Jesus.

Up to now, Mark indicated that Jesus had five followers or disciples, the first four and Levi. Now he adds that there were many *(polloi)* disciples, including some scribes among the Pharisees, who also followed him (2:15-16a). Grammatically, Mark includes some scribes among Jesus' followers,[34] introducing an element of tension among those who followed Jesus.[35]

Jesus and his disciples were reclining at a dinner in the home of a tax collector together with many tax collectors and sinners. Of itself, this was an extraordinary event for the participants as well as

---

[34] For a discussion, see Vincent Taylor, *The Gospel According to St. Mark* (London: MacMillan, 1963) 205, and Henry Barclay Swete, *The Gospel According to St. Mark* (London: MacMillan, 1909) 41.

[35] We should remember that Saul Paul was a Pharisee (Acts 23:6). Introducing the "council of Jerusalem," Luke refers to Pharisees who had become believers: "But some from the party of the Pharisees who had become believers stood up and said, 'It is necessary to circumcise them and direct them to observe the Mosaic law'" (Acts 15:5). In Luke's presentation, some of the Pharisees could have been scribes.

for all who witnessed it. Joining at the same table was a powerful symbol of mutual respect and commitment among the participants.

A meal could seal a new relationship. It could also bring about reconciliation. Those who shared in a meal welcomed one another in peace and extended their family unit even beyond the ordinary extended family. The meal transformed strangers and outsiders into friends. It also extended a community, incorporating new members. At table with Jesus, tax collectors and sinners joined those who heard the gospel and did the will of God. Later, Jesus would declare all such people to be his true relatives (3:20, 31-35).

It is not clear that the scribes who followed Jesus were reclining at table at the home of Levi. It could be that the scribes observed Jesus eating regularly with tax collectors and sinners, and at one point they asked his disciples: "Why does he eat with tax collectors and sinners?" (2:16).[36] The question presupposes that they did not view Jesus or themselves as sinners. They disassociated themselves from tax collectors and sinners, and they could not understand or accept that Jesus did not do the same.

From a historical point of view, it is very unlikely that some scribes who were Pharisees would have joined Jesus and his disciples for a dinner at Levi's home with other tax collectors and sinners. But as described by Mark, the meal at Levi's home seems to reflect a conflict situation in the early Christian community. If so, "the scribes" refer to a segment of the Christian community. As such, the scribes could have been there. It would seem that some distinguished between those who were sinners and those who were righteous, objecting to the presence of "tax collectors and sinners" at the community table. In that, they did not recognize the "tax collectors and sinners" as followers of Jesus, as they themselves were.

Jesus responded with a saying and a statement about his mission. The saying, "Those who are well do not need a physician, but the sick do" (2:17a), like all sayings, can apply to a variety of situations. Here the saying responds to the scribes' objection. Like the sick, the tax collectors and sinners need Jesus' ministry. It also implies that those who are not sinners have no need of his ministry.

---

[36] In Mark's Gospel the scribes ask why Jesus was eating with tax collectors and sinners (see also Matt 9:11). In Luke's Gospel the Pharisees and their scribes ask why Jesus' disciples ate and drank with tax collectors and sinners (Luke 5:30). In Mark's story, the emphasis is on christology, while in Luke, the emphasis is on ecclesiology.

In conclusion, Jesus adds that his mission is not to call (*kalesai,* see 1:19) the righteous but sinners (2:17b), indirectly asking the scribes to recognize that they too were sinners. The meal is consequently a setting where Jesus calls disciples to follow him. The call of Levi, which took place by the sea (2:13-14) is thus transposed to the table of Levi (2:15-17) and the table of the Lord. The early Christians were being challenged to live the Lord's Supper as a moment of evangelization.

Those whom Jesus calls are sinners. Those who think themselves righteous have no need to being called and reconciled, but then no one is righteous. Ultimately, the problem of the scribes is that they considered themselves righteous, whereas they were sinners like tax collectors.

The New and the Old (2:18-22)

The first and second conflict episodes showed how Jesus' new teaching contrasted with the old teaching of the scribes. Jesus, who had authority to forgive sins (2:1-12) and called sinners to repentance (2:13-17). The second episode unfolded when Jesus and his disciples were reclining at table at the home of Levi, a former tax collector, but now a follower of Jesus. The third conflict episode continues the theme of eating. Focusing on feasting and fasting, it again contrasts Jesus' new teaching with the old or prevalent teaching.

The story begins with an observation: "The disciples of John and of the Pharisees were accustomed to fast" (2:18a). In the previous story, we saw that Jesus and his disciples ate at the home of Levi. Those who now object are not named, but their objection is in the spirit of the scribes (2:6-7) and the scribes of the Pharisees (2:16), who questioned Jesus' authority in the two previous stories. Nor does the story have a particular setting. The entire focus is on eating and fasting.

The objection is simple. Whereas the disciples of John and those of the Pharisees fast, the disciples of Jesus do not (2:18b). At the home of Levi, the scribes addressed Jesus' disciples about his behavior. Now they challenge Jesus about their behavior. From their point of view, the disciples of Jesus could and should be classed with observant Jews such as the disciples of John and of the Pharisees.

In the previous two stories, Jesus' own behavior challenged the scribes, but we saw how both stories reflected situations in the early Christian communities. In the present story and the next, attention shifts to the behavior of Jesus' disciples. As usual, Jesus responds to the challenge, addressing important concerns in the communities at the time of Mark.

Jesus' response is considerably longer than in the two previous and two following episodes. Jesus responds with a short parable discourse (2:19-22), preparing us for the much longer parable discourse (4:1-34) in the next section of the Gospel (3:7–6:6a). The discourse consists of three parables, all of which remain quite enigmatic apart from its context in the Gospel and its relation to Mark's readers.

The first parable deals explicitly with feasting and fasting (2:19-20). In the parable, Jesus evokes the setting of a wedding feast, well-known to all from their popular culture and from Scripture, where it is associated with the presence of the Lord and Israel's intimate relationship with the Lord. At wedding feasts, the guests do not fast. All fasting is suspended until the bridegroom departs. Only then they will fast.

The little parable compares Jesus' life with his disciples to a wedding feast. It also compares Jesus' passion to the departure of the bridegroom. Jesus, the bridegroom, was the presence of God, the Lord, among them (see 1:24; 2:6-12). So long as he remained with them, it was time to feast. It was not time to fast. Jesus' first parable was an effective response only for those who recognized the presence of God in the person of Jesus. For others, it would not have been very meaningful.

The parable addressed the life of the early Christian communities in the time of Mark. In this context, its purpose was not so much to explain why the disciples did not fast while Jesus was with them, but why they fasted when he entered his passion. The very wording of the parable speaks not simply of the bridegroom's departure but of his being taken away from them *(aparthe ap' auton)*. Evoking the fourth song of the suffering servant of the Lord (Isa 53:8), the expression refers to the passion and death of Jesus.

For the disciples, the passion and death of Jesus was a time of fasting. Mark's readers needed to recognize, accept, and understand the passion in their own lives in relation to the passion of Jesus. For them, it was a time of fasting, in preparation for the coming of the kingdom and the return of the Son of Man in glory. Then, at the banquet of the eternal wedding feast, all fasting would be set aside.

The second parable tells what happens if someone repairs an old cloak with a piece of unshrunken cloth. The new piece shrinks, and it is torn away from the cloak, and the tear gets worse (2:21). The second parable gives the basis for understanding the first parable.

Jesus' way of life is new, a radical departure from the disciples' former way of life. This applies to the time of feasting but also to the time of fasting as a preparation for the great feast that will accompany the coming of the Son of Man (see 13:24-27; 14:62). Mark continues to develop the theme introduced in the story of the cure of the demoniac (1:21-28), when all were amazed at Jesus' new teaching as one having authority (1:27), unlike the teaching of the scribes (1:22).

The third parable tells what happens if someone pours new wine into old wineskins (2:22). As the new wine ferments, the pressure in the wineskin increases. A new wineskin would expand, but the old wineskin bursts. The wine is spilled, and the wineskin is ruined.

The third parable goes one step further than the second. In the parable of the new piece of cloth, the tear gets worse. In the parable of the new wine, everything is lost. Jesus' teaching is not a patchwork of the new and the old. His disciples need to put on a new garment, the symbol of their new identity in Christ.

Jesus' teaching is like new wine. The old wineskins of John and the Pharisees would not be able to contain it. The new wine of Jesus' teaching requires new wineskins. For the same reason, Jesus would warn his disciples against the leaven of the Pharisees and the leaven of Herod (8:15). The table of Jesus requires unleavened bread (14:12), that is, bread made entirely from the new harvest. The disciples of Jesus have embarked on a whole new way of life.

Lord of the Sabbath (2:23-28)

In the synagogue at Capernaum, Jesus had cured a demoniac on the Sabbath (1:21-28). Later on the same day, he went to the home of Simon and Andrew and cured Simon's mother-in-law (1:29-31). At that point, the observance of the Sabbath was not the issue. In the fourth and fifth conflict episodes, it is.

The first and second conflict episodes showed how Jesus, the Son of Man, had authority to forgive sins (2:1-12) and to call sinners (2:13-17). That is why he came. He did not come to call the righteous but sinners to follow him. Those who are well have no need of a physician (see 2:17). As the people in the synagogue had realized, Jesus' teaching was very new, "a new teaching with authority" (1:27; see 1:22). In the third episode, Jesus showed how his teaching had to be completely new. Jesus' teaching was not a mixture of the new and the old (2:18-22).

The fourth conflict shows how Jesus, the Son of Man, has authority even over the sabbath. Following the literary pattern of the third, it first presents a concrete situation involving the disciples: as Jesus was going through a field of grain on the sabbath, his disciples were clearing a way *(hodos)* while picking heads of grain (2:23). When the Pharisees objected (2:24), Jesus responded with a mini-discourse (2:25-28), as he did in the previous conflict.

The Pharisees addressed Jesus about his disciples' behavior: "Look, why are they doing what is unlawful on the sabbath?" (2:24). On any other day, what the disciples did would have been lawful (Deut 23:25). Jesus' response gives the basic rationale for the Christian stance on sabbath observance.

First, Jesus recalls an event from the biblical story of David (2:25-26). When David and his companions were hungry, their need superceded the law (see 1 Sam 21:2-7), which forbade anyone but a priest to enter the house of God and eat the bread of offering (see Lev 24:9).

In Mark's context, the point is not that David set a precedent for breaking the sabbath. The sabbath had nothing to do with the incident in David's story as told in 1 Samuel, nor with the law in the book of Leviticus regarding eating the bread of offering. Again, the point is not that the disciples of Jesus were hungry like David and his companions. Jesus' response addresses a broader issue in the life of the early Church. By analogy with what David did, it may be legitimate not to observe the sabbath, just as it may be legitimate not to observe other laws, depending on the circumstances. Witness the example of David. Later, Jesus would address the "the tradition of the elders" in a similar way, especially the laws regarding defilement and purification (7:1-23) as well as the laws governing marriage and divorce (10:1-12) in a similar way.

After recalling an event in David's life, Jesus adds a saying, placing the Sabbath observance in perspective: "The sabbath was made for man, not man for the sabbath" (2:27). The institution of the sabbath was associated with God's work of creation (Gen 2:1-3) and with the Lord God's historic liberation of Israel from Egypt (Exod 20:2, 8-11; Deut 5:6, 12-15).

Created in the image and likeness of God to be God's co-creators (1:1-31), the human couple would observe the sabbath as God, the Creator, did. Once the people of God were slaves, but God had led them out of bondage into freedom. Freed by God, they would observe the sabbath. The sabbath was clearly made for human beings and the people of God, and not the other way around.[37]

---

[37] See E. LaVerdiere, "The Origins of Sunday in the New Testament," *Sunday Morning: A Time for Worship,* edited by Mark Searle, (Collegeville, Minnesota: The Liturgical Press, 1982) 11–27, esp. 21–24.

In conclusion, Jesus clinches the entire argument with a Christological claim: "That is why the Son of Man is lord even of the sabbath" (2:28). It may be legitimate not to observe the sabbath, as it was legitimate for David not to observe other laws (2:25-26), especially since the sabbath was made for human beings (2:27). What David could do, *a fortiori,* Jesus can do. Ultimately, everything depends on who Jesus is. As the Son of Man, Jesus was able to forgive sins on earth (2:10). Great as David was, Jesus, the Son of Man, is lord even of the sabbath (2:28).

Saving Life on the Sabbath (3:1-6)

The series of five conflict episodes reaches its climax when Jesus again *(palin)* entered the synagogue and cured a man with a withered hand (3:1-6). With the adverb "again" *(palin),* Mark associates this final conflict with the first time Jesus entered the synagogue and cured a man with an unclean spirit (1:21-28).[38] Both cures took place on the Sabbath (3:2; see 1:21)

Like the fourth conflict, which also took place on the sabbath, this final conflict begins by describing the situation. There was a man with a withered hand in the synagogue (3:1). They were observing Jesus closely. If Jesus cured the man with the withered hand on the sabbath they would accuse him (3:2). The vague subject "they," in the opening clause, "they watched him closely," evokes all those who protested the behavior of Jesus and his disciples in the four previous episodes.

Knowing their unspoken thoughts, Jesus addressed the man: "Come up here before us" (3:3). Already tense (3:2), the setting becomes even tenser, when Jesus dramatically calls the man to come up before everyone. With the man standing there, Jesus then addressed the people in the synagogue: "Is it lawful to do good on the sabbath rather than to do evil, to save life rather than to destroy it?" (3:4a). His question was met with silence.

In the previous conflict, the focus was very general: the sabbath was made for human beings (2:27). This time, the focus is more specific, showing why the sabbath was made for human beings. The purpose of the sabbath is to do good, not evil, to save *(sosai)* life, not to destroy it (3:4a).

---

[38] Previously, Mark associated Jesus' return *(palin)* to Capernaum and the cure of the paralytic (2:1-12) with the first time Jesus came to Capernaum and cured a demoniac (1:21-28). He also associated the story of the call of Levi when he again *(palin)* went along the sea (2:13-17) with the first time he passed by the sea and called his first followers (1:16-20).

Looking around the synagogue, Jesus became angry and grieved at their hardness of heart (3:5a). This is the first time Mark refers to "hardness of heart" (*porosis tes kardias,* see 6:52; 8:17), a very striking expression describing someone's resistance to the mission of Jesus and the gospel of God. Later, Mark will use an alternative expression, "the sclerosis of the heart" (*sklerokardia,* 10:5; see also 16:14). The expression recalls an Old Testament exhortation:

> Oh, that today you would hear his voice:
>> Do not harden your hearts (*me sklerynete tas kardias hymon*)
>>> as at Meribah,
>> as on the day of Massah in the desert (Ps 95:8 [LXX 94:8]).[39]

In a final dramatic moment, Jesus said to the man with the withered hand, "Stretch out your hand." Before this, his hand was crippled and he could not stretch it out. At Jesus' command, he stretched out his hand, and his hand was restored (3:5b).

Jesus had asked if it was lawful to do good on the sabbath rather than do evil, if it was lawful to save life rather destroy it (3:4). His question had many ramifications for this story. First, it develops the saying at the end of the previous story: the sabbath was made for human beings, not the other way around (2:27). Second, it points an accusing finger at those who have hardened their hearts and are plotting on the sabbath how they might put Jesus to death (3:5a, 6).

The question also recalls the cure of the paralytic (2:1-12). On that occasion, Jesus' asked, "Which is easier, to say to the paralytic, 'Your sins are forgiven,' or to say 'Rise, pick up your mat and walk?'" (2:9). By curing the paralytic Jesus had revealed his power and authority as the Son of Man to forgive sins. Now, healing the man with the withered hand, he demonstrated his power and authority to do good and save life on the sabbath.

As in the previous stories, we are not told anything regarding the man's reaction to the cure. Everything focuses on Jesus, the people in the synagogue, especially the Pharisees. Silenced by Jesus' question and the manifestation of Jesus' power and authority, they resort to violence. The only way they could silence the one who silenced them was to destroy him. To do that, they left the synagogue and went to take counsel with the Herodians against Jesus in order to put him to death.

---

[39] See Psalms 106:32 and 81:8-9. For the story of what happened in Meribah, see Exodus 17:1-7 and Numbers 20:2-13.

With that, the series of five conflict episodes (2:1–3:6), indeed the whole of Jesus' ministry in Galilee (1:14–3:6) brought the Gospel to the very threshold of the passion. The next verse could very well be the opening verse of the passion: "The Passover and the Feast of Unleavened Bread were to take place in two days' time" (14:1a). But this was only the first section (1:14–3:6) of "the beginning of the gospel of Jesus Christ [the Son of God]" (1:1). For Mark, the story of Jesus and the first disciples led to the next section, the story of Jesus and the Twelve (3:7–6:6a).

The story of Jesus has only begun. As the Son of Man, Jesus had authority to forgive sins. He had authority even over the sabbath. As such, the Son of Man would be handed over and put to death and rise after three days (see 8:31; 9:31; 10:33-34), but his authority would be fully revealed when the Son of Man comes in the clouds in great power and glory (13:26; 14:62).

V

❧ Section II ❧

Jesus and the Twelve

Mark 3:7–6:6a

The first section of the Gospel told how Jesus came into Galilee proclaiming the gospel of God and how he called and formed a group of disciples to follow him (1:14–3:6). The section began with a summary of Jesus' preaching ministry in Galilee: "This is the time of fulfillment. The kingdom of God is at hand. Repent, and believe in the gospel" (1:15). It ended with a story showing how the Pharisees hardened their hearts against Jesus and the gospel of God. Refusing to repent, the Pharisees took counsel with the Herodians seeking to put Jesus to death (3:5-6).

Those who accepted Jesus' call to follow him could expect the same reaction. The day would come when they too would meet persecution and rejection. For Mark's community, that day had arrived (see 10:30; 13:9-13).

At the beginning, everything seemed hopeful as Jesus taught in the synagogue at Capernaum (1:21-28) and then at the home of Simon and Andrew (1:29-34). People were amazed at his new teaching with authority. But even then, a man with an unclean spirit challenged Jesus, "What have you to do with us, Jesus of Nazareth? Have you come to destroy us? I know who you are—the Holy One of God!" (1:24). The storm was gathering. As Jesus continued to manifest his authority (*exousia*) as the Son of Man, opposition mounted from many sides. The thunder was coming nearer and nearer. By the end of the section, the sky was very dark and ominous, as the Pharisees began to plot Jesus' death (3:6).

But this was only the first section of Mark's story. Now, as the Gospel moves into its second section (3:7–6:6a), the story leaves the Pharisees to their plotting. Every so often, we will hear rumblings in the distance, but the storm is not about to break. In one sense, the Gospel has reached the threshold of the passion. In another sense, the Gospel has only begun.

The Pharisees would return only in the third section (6:6b–7:21), questioning Jesus about his disciples who did not observe "the tradition of the elders" (7:1-23). In the same section, Herod himself enters the Gospel in relation to the identity of Jesus (6:14-16) and the death of John the Baptist (6:17-29).

An Overview

The first section began with a double introduction, including a summary of Jesus' mission and ministry (1:14-15) and the call of the first disciples (1:16-20). The body was divided into two parts, including the beginning of Jesus' ministry in Galilee (1:21-45) and a series of conflict, or controversy episodes showing mounting opposition to Jesus and his message (2:1–3:6).

The pattern for the second section (3:7–6:6a) is very similar, also beginning with a double introduction. Like the first, the second includes a summary of Jesus' mission and ministry (3:7-12) and a passage concerning the disciples (3:13-19). As in the first section, the introduction announces the basic theme of the entire section. This second section can be appropriately entitled "Jesus and the Twelve" or "Jesus and the New Israel."

The body of the section is framed by one of the Gospel's key issues, Jesus' relationship to his family and relatives (3:20-35; 6:1-6a). In the first section, we saw how Jesus and his new teaching transcended the synagogue and the Sabbath. In this second section, we see how Jesus and his new teaching also transcended family ties as well as the people of his place of origin. Transcending blood ties, Jesus also transcended Judaism itself and the people of Israel.

The second section ends with a rejection scene at the synagogue in Nazareth (6:1-6a), paralleling Jesus' rejection at the synagogue in Capernaum at the end of the first section (3:1-6). Like the Pharisees, the people of Jesus' native place were unable to repent and believe in the gospel. They too rejected Jesus. They may not have hardened their hearts as the Pharisees did (see 3:5), but they showed amazing lack of faith (6:6a).

As in the first section, the body can be divided into two parts. The first presents the continuation of Jesus' ministry in Galilee

(3:20–4:34). It includes a discourse of Jesus in which he used parables to show the meaning and the purpose of his teaching in parables (4:1-34). The first part prepares the second, where Jesus and his disciples cross the sea to the other side. Leaving the Jewish shore, they crossed over to the Gentile territory of the Gerasenes, and later returned to the Jewish shore, eventually ending up in Nazareth (4:35–6:6a).

The importance of this first sea journey cannot be overestimated. Crossing from the Jewish shore to the Gentile shore was very perilous (4:35-41) but it was required for the kingdom of God. The kingdom of God was at hand, not only for the Jewish people, but also for all peoples. The kingdom of God transcended the distinction between Jew and Gentile. Hence the sea journey to the other shore.

A number of elements in the first section prepared this symbolic expression of the universal mission of Jesus. There was Jesus' preaching that the kingdom of God was at hand (1:15). There were the christological titles, Holy One of the God (1:24) and Son of Man (2:10, 28). There was also the emphasis on Jesus' new teaching, as one having authority and as one who was lord even over the Sabbath (2:28).

But in the first section, the story focused mainly on how Jesus' teaching transcended the teaching of the scribes and the Pharisees, the synagogue, and the sabbath. As such, Jesus' teaching could have been understood as a reform movement within Judaism, a prophetic movement akin to that of John the Baptist. It was not yet clear that Jesus' coming to Galilee and the call of his first disciples were in view of a new creation and a new exodus, that would cut across ethnic boundaries, including the one that separates the Jews from the Gentiles.

Setting and *Dramatis Personae*

As we did in the first section (1:14–3:6), we begin our reflections on Jesus and the Twelve (3:7–6:6a) by examining the geographical and temporal settings and the personages who play a role in the story.

In the second section, geography and specific places continue to be extremely significant. In the first section, we saw that the geographical setting was symbolic and integral to the theological significance of the events. In the second, we see that the geographical movement across the sea, from the Jewish shore to the Gentile shore, supports the theological development of the Gospel.

The section's geography is also much more extensive, including a Gentile region as well as Jewish regions. Accordingly, the personages in the second part are more diverse, as people come to Jesus from outside Galilee, and Jesus himself leaves Galilee for the first time, accompanied by the Twelve (4:35-41). Temporal indications, however, are minimal.

Geographical Setting: Jesus and the Sea

The physical and geographical setting for the first section filled the reader's imagination. There was Galilee and the Sea of Galilee, casting nets in the sea, Capernaum, its synagogue, the home of Simon and Andrew, desert places, other villages in Galilee, and a field of grain ready for harvest.

The setting for the second section is even more extraordinary. Again, there is the sea. As in the first section, Jesus withdrew toward the sea (3:7) and taught by the sea (4:1). But in this section Jesus does not merely pass by the sea (1:16; 2:13). He got into a boat and sat down on the sea (4:1b), crossed the sea with his disciples and calmed a great storm threatening the boat (4:35-41). Very significant are the two shores of the sea, the Gentile shore (5:1-20) and the Jewish shore (5:21-43), as well as the wonders that Jesus performed on each shore.

There is also the home of Simon and Andrew, which became the home of Jesus. The home had been the setting for Jesus' ministry and the ministry of Simon's mother-in-law (1:29-34) and the cure of a paralytic (2:1-12). It now becomes the setting for Jesus' true family (3:20-35). In the first section, Jesus dined at the home of Levi, the tax collector (2:13-17). In the second, he goes to the home of Jairus, the synagogue official, to raise his daughter to life (5:38-43).

For the first time, there is also the mountain, on whose heights Jesus appointed the Twelve as the foundations of a new Israel (3:19-19). In Mark's Gospel, "the mountain" does not refer to a particular mountain on the map of Galilee. "The mountain" is the mountain of God, evoking Mount Sinai and Mount Horeb. Later, Jesus would heal a demoniac on the mountain (5:5, 11) on the Gentile shore of the sea (5:1-20).

Finally, there is the synagogue of Nazareth, Jesus' native place (see 1:9), where people thought they knew him but could not see that Jesus was much more than one of them (6:1-6a). In Mark's Gospel, this is the last time Jesus teaches in a synagogue. In the first section, Jesus left Capernaum and a desert place to preach in the synagogues in neighboring villages (1:38-39). Here, he simply "went around the villages in the vicinity teaching" (6:6b). There is no mention of synagogues.

Temporal Setting: As Evening Drew On

The temporal setting in the second section has less importance than in the first. There are but two specific temporal indications, "On that day, as evening drew on" (4:35; see 1:32), and "when the sabbath came" (6:2). The next and last time the sabbath is mentioned in the Gospel, is in relation to the women's visit to the tomb of Jesus (16:1). In the evening, the day before the sabbath (15:42), the women watched where Jesus was laid (15:47). Then they waited until the sabbath was over to buy spices to anoint Jesus (16:1). They went to the tomb the day after the sabbath, that is, "on the first day of the week" (*te mia ton sabbaton,* 16:2; see also 16:9, *prote sabbatou*).

In general, Mark is much more interested in situational time, that is, the experience of time, than in the measured time itself. Accordingly, every other temporal reference is relative to the circumstances surrounding Jesus:

> On another occasion he began to teach (4:1);
> And when he was alone (4:10);
> When he got out of the boat, at once a man from the tombs (5:2);
> When Jesus had crossed again [in the boat] to the other side (5:21);
> While he was still speaking (5:35).

Mark does not only tell when something happened. He shows it.

Dramatis Personae

Many of the principal personages in the first section appear in the second, as their role continues to develop. Of course, there is Jesus, the Gospel's principal personage, and the unclean spirits, his principal antagonists (3:11). The crowds continue to grow, but their composition is much more diversified, and Mark indicates the regions where they came from, not only from Galilee and Judea, but also from Jerusalem, Idumea, Transjordan, and the surroundings of Tyre and Sidon (3:7-8).

In the first section, Jesus called Simon and his brother Andrew, and James and his brother John to come after him. In the second, eight others join them, when Jesus constitutes the Twelve (3:13-19). Notice, Levi is not among them.[1] The importance of the Twelve cannot be

---

[1] Matthew would replace Levi by Matthew, the tax collector, in the traditional story of the call of Levi (Matt 9:9; see Mark 2:13-17; Luke 5:27-32). In the list of the Twelve, Matthew also included Matthew, the tax collector (Matt 10:2-4).

underestimated. Together with Jesus, they would dominate the rest of the Gospel. It also becomes very clear that three of them, Peter, James, and John, the brother of James, would have a special role among the twelve apostles (5:37; see also 9:1; 14:33). Andrew joins the three on the Mount of Olives for Jesus' eschatological discourse (13:3).

Then there are the family and the relatives of Jesus (3:21, 31-35), the scribes from Jerusalem (3:22-30), and the townspeople of Jesus' native place (6:1-6a), all of whom appear in the Gospel for the first time. Besides the scribes from Jerusalem, the scribes from Galilee have no role in the story of Jesus and the Twelve (3:7–6:6a), nor do the Pharisees.

Finally, Mark introduces a number of particular people, whose stories are told in considerable detail. There is a man with an unclean spirit, who dwelt among the tombs, and some swineherds (5:1-20); a synagogue official named Jairus, his twelve-year old girl, and some mourners (5:21-24, 35-43), and a woman who had been hemorrhaging for twelve years (5:25-34). Apart from Jairus, the rest remain nameless, as was the case in the first section with the man with an unclean spirit (1:21-28), the leper (1:40-45), the paralytic (2:1-12), and the man with the withered hand (3:1-6). As such, they represent everyone who needs Jesus' exorcising and healing ministry, indeed, everyone who needs the new life that Jesus gives.

Jesus the Healer (3:7-12)

Like the first section (1:14–3:6), the second (3:7–6:6a) opens with a general summary of Jesus' mission and ministry (3:7-12). In the first, the summary presented Jesus as a proclaimer of the gospel of God. The second presents him as a healer. The emphasis in the first summary was on Jesus' proclamation. The second emphasizes the crowd that came to him from far and wide, wanting to be healed.

It is not that Jesus had two different missions, one proclaiming the gospel of God, the other healing the people who came to him. Jesus had only one mission, but this mission can be viewed from different angles. From one angle, Jesus' mission can be described as the proclamation of the gospel of God. From the other, it could be seen as a healing mission. Jesus proclaimed the gospel in word and deed. For Jesus, proclaiming the gospel meant healing those who heard him, and in healing them he proclaimed the gospel of God.

When Jesus called the first disciples (1:16-20) and again when he called Levi (2:13-17), Jesus was passing by the sea. Now, for the third time, Jesus withdrew with his disciples toward the sea, where a large crowd followed him (3:7; see 2:13b).

The summary places great emphasis on the growth of the crowd, continuing the theme from the first section, but this time, the focus is on the crowd's provenance. A large number *(poly plethos)* followed *(ekolouthesen)* Jesus from Galilee, but also from Judea, and from Jerusalem, and from Idumea, and from across the Jordan and the surroundings of Tyre and Sidon, a great crowd *(plethos poly)*. They had heard what he was doing and came to him (3:7b-8). We are reminded of Luke's description of the crowd in Jerusalem who heard the apostles on Pentecost (Acts 2:5-12). In terms of Luke-Acts, the crowds in the Markan summary were preparing the crowds at Pentecost.

People came to John the Baptist from the whole of Judea, also from Jerusalem when he was baptizing by the Jordan (1:5). Jesus also came from Nazareth of Galilee (1:9). In the first section, we saw how large crowds came to Jesus from the whole of Galilee, where his ministry was centered. But now, large numbers are also coming to him from Judea and Jerusalem, and well beyond.

Idumea, ancient Edom, is the Gentile territory south of Judea, stretching from the Dead Sea and the Arabah to the Mediterranean Sea. Today, the territory would include the Negev in Israel and the region of Gaza in Palestine. Herod the Great (37–4 B.C.) came from an aristocratic Idumean family converted to Judaism a few decades before he was born.[2]

The territory described as "across the Jordan" *(peran tou Iordanou,* see also 10:1), corresponds roughly to ancient Moab and Ammon. It refers to Gentile lands across the Dead Sea and the lower Jordan River. Today, the territory would be included in the western part of the Hashemite Kingdom of Jordan.[3]

The environs of Tyre and Sidon refer to the Gentile territories north of Galilee in the Mediterranean coastal areas of ancient Phoenicia, in New Testament times, Syro-Phoenicia. In the next section, Jesus would go to the district of Tyre and drive out a demon from a daughter of a Syrophoenician woman (7:24-30). The journey would eventually bring him to the Decapolis via Sidon (7:31). Today, the territory would correspond to the southern part of Lebanon.[4]

[2] See Ulrich Hubner, "Idumea," *The Anchor Bible Dictionary* (New York: Doubleday, 1992) 3:382–83.

[3] See Henry O. Thompson, "Transjordan," *The Anchor Bible Dictionary* (New York: Doubleday, 1992) 6:642–43.

[4] For Tyre, see H. J. Hatzenstein and Douglas R. Edwards, "Tyre," *The Anchor Bible Dictionary* (New York: Doubleday, 1992) 6:686–92; for Sidon, see Philip C. Schmitz, "Sidon," *The Anchor Bible Dictionary* (New York: Doubleday, 1992) 6:17–18.

Whereas the preposition "from" *(apo)* is repeated for Galilee, Judea, and Jerusalem, it is used only once to govern the crowds that came from all the Gentile territories. Mark viewed these diverse territories as one. For him, they represented the Gentile world.

Great crowds from all those regions, Jewish and Gentile, followed *(ekolouthesen)* Jesus (3:7; see 1:18; 2:14, 15). They came to him because they heard what he did (3:8). To avoid being crushed by the crowd, Jesus asked his disciples to prepare a little boat for him (3:9). This "little boat" *(ploiarion),* henceforth referred to as "the boat" *(ploion),* plays a great role throughout this section of the Gospel and the next, beginning with the discourse on parables (4:1-34).

After giving the setting (3:7a) and describing the crowd of Jesus' followers (3:7b-9), the summary focuses on Jesus' healing activity. Jesus healed all the sick who were pressing upon him trying to touch him (3:10), making no distinctions between those who came from Jewish regions and those who came from Gentile regions.

Already in the first section, Jesus' healing activity was quite prominent. Jesus cured a demoniac (1:21-28), Simon's mother-in-law from a fever (1:29-31), many people from the town of Capernaum (1:32-34; 2:1-12; 3:1-6), indeed from the whole of Galilee (1:39, 40-45). Now he cures people who came from both Jewish and Gentile lands, announcing the mission to the Gentiles.

Later in this second section, Mark tells the story of how Jesus went across the sea and healed a man with an unclean spirit in the Gentile territory of the Gerasenes (5:1-20). Returning to the Jewish side of the sea, Jesus then healed a woman with a hemorrhage (5:25-34) and even raised a daughter of a synagogue official from the dead (5:21-24, 35-43).

The summary concludes with Jesus' confrontations with unclean spirits (3:11-12). When the unclean spirits saw Jesus, they would fall down before him in mock worship and proclaim, "You are the Son of God." Each time, Jesus would warn them not to make him known, as he did in the first section (1:23-26, 34, 39). The summary's mention of the unclean spirits prepares us for the story of Jesus' great confrontation with unclean spirits in the region of the Gerasenes (5:1-20).

We saw that Jesus' healing mission coincided with his evangelizing mission. When Jesus healed someone, he was proclaiming the gospel of God, and when Jesus proclaimed the gospel, he was healing people of their afflictions. Both were also direct confrontations with unclean spirits, who needed to be silenced and driven away. As a proclaimer of the gospel and as a healer, Jesus was also an exorcist.

The unclean spirits knew who Jesus was and shouted: "You are the Son of God," but they were not among the followers of Jesus. The unclean spirits had no faith in Jesus, and their proclamation would have distorted who Jesus was as the Son of God. Accordingly, Jesus forbade them to tell anyone who he was.

Jesus Constitutes the Twelve (3:13-19)

After summarizing the mission of Jesus as a proclaimer of the gospel of God (1:14-15), Mark showed how Jesus called his first disciples (1:16-20). Jesus called (*ekalesen,* 1:20; *kalesai,* 2:17) disciples to come after him or follow him (1:16-20; 2:13-14). Eventually, those who followed him became quite numerous (2:15).

After summarizing the mission of Jesus as a healer (3:7-12), Mark shows how Jesus called *(proskaleitai)* those he wanted to be the Twelve (3:13-19). For the initial call to be a follower, Mark used the verb *kaleo* ("to call"). For a more specific role in the following of Jesus, Mark now uses the verb *proskaleo* ("to summon").

The appointing, or more accurately, the making or the creation *(epoiesen)* of the Twelve[5] evokes Genesis' first account of creation, "when God created *[epoiesen]* the heavens and the earth" (Gen 1:1). In Luke, Jesus chose twelve apostles among his disciples (see Luke 6:12-16). In Mark, Jesus created the Twelve.[6]

After Jesus ascended the mountain *(eis to oros),* he called those he wanted, and they came to him (3:13). The mountain does not refer to a particular mountain, one that could be localized on a map with precise geographical coordinates. As Moses did (see Exod 19:3), Jesus went up the mountain of God, the mountain of awesome manifestations, great revelations, and historic commissions. The mountain evokes Mount Sinai and Mount Horeb, where the twelve tribes of Israel were formed into the people of God (see Exod 19:1–24:18). Now, the mountain is where Jesus creates the Twelve and a new people of God.[7]

The Twelve evokes the twelve sons of Jacob or Israel (see Gen 32:29), the ancestral heads of the ancient tribes that God united as a people of God (Exod 24:1-11). Here in Mark 3:13-19, the Greek for

---

[5] See Joseph Cardinal Ratzinger, *Called to Communion, Understanding the Church Today* (San Francisco: Ignatius Press, 1996) 24–25.

[6] In comparison with Mark, Luke and Matthew are more historical. Like John, Mark is more symbolic.

[7] From a Christian point of view, the Israelites formed a first stage in the development of the people of God. The Christians, including Jews and Gentiles, form a second and definitive stage in the development of the people of God.

"the Twelve" *(dodeka),* is without the definite article. As such, it is a theological designation, a title, for the universal Church. To refer to the particular individuals that made up the Twelve, Mark uses the term "apostles" (3:14a; see 6:30). Jesus created *(epoiesen)* the Twelve, and he named *(onomasen)* them "apostles" *(apostolous,* 3:14).

Jesus created the Twelve. As apostles, their names were "Simon, whom he named Peter; James, son of Zebedee, and John the brother of James, whom he named Boanerges, that is, sons of thunder; Andrew, Philip, Bartholomew, Matthew, Thomas, James the son of Alphaeus; Thaddeus, Simon the Cananean, and Judas Iscariot who betrayed him" (3:16-19).

Aside from those named at the head of the list, Simon, James, John, and Andrew (3:16-18a) and the one named at the end the list, Judas Iscariot who betrayed Jesus (3:19), we know little or nothing about them (3:18).[8] As individual apostles, seven of them have no role in the Gospel of Mark.

At the time Mark wrote his Gospel, the designation "the Twelve" already had a long history, especially in the church at Antioch and in the churches that had sprung from the Pauline missions from Antioch (see Acts 13:1-3; 15:36-41). "The Twelve" was mentioned in a traditional creed that Paul cited in 1 Corinthians, this time with the definite article:

> I handed on to you as of first importance what I also received:
> that Christ died for our sins in accordance to the scriptures;
> that he was buried;
> that he was raised on the third day in accordance with the scriptures;
> that he appeared to Cephas, then to the Twelve
> *(hoi dodeka)* (1 Cor 15:3-5).

In that creed, "the Twelve" was not accompanied by a list of those who made up the Twelve. It was enough to refer to the Twelve. There had been the Twelve of Jacob or Israel, gathering twelve disparate tribes into one people of God. Now there was the Twelve of Christ, gathering all peoples into one people of God. Such would be their mission of the Twelve and the mission of the Church down the ages.

It is important not to reduce the theological notion of the Twelve into a list of twelve individual apostles. Paul gives no indication

---

[8] From John's Gospel, we also know about Philip (John 1:43-51; 12:20-22), Nathaniel (John 1:43-51; 21:2), and Thomas (John 20:24-29; 21:2). Mark's list of the apostles does not include Nathaniel.

that he knew of a list of twelve apostles. Adding a traditional list of twelve apostles, Mark personalized the theological notion of the Twelve, giving the Twelve individual names. At the same time, he related a group of the twelve apostles to the theological notion of the Twelve.[9]

While creating the Twelve, Jesus gave Simon a new name, Peter *(Petros)*. The name was based on a Greek word for rock *(petra)*. Since *petra* was a feminine word, it was given a masculine ending *(os)* when it became Simon's apostolic name. Simon was the very first to bear the name Peter *(Petros)*.

At the end of the Gospel in the story of the empty tomb (16:1-8), a young man who commissioned the women referred to the disciples and singled out Peter by name: "But go and tell his disciples and Peter" (16:7). Shaken by the events of the passion (14:27-31; 66-72), Peter had come through the ordeal. Standing firm, he was indeed the Rock, ready to follow the risen Lord in Galilee where he would see him as Jesus had promised (14:28).

Like "the Twelve," "Peter" was a symbolic name, and it too had long been part of the faith language of the Church, especially at Antioch and in the many Churches that shared its tradition. In the early years of the tradition, the name was given in its Aramaic original, *Kephas* (1 Cor 15:5; 1:12; 3:22; 9:5; Gal 1:18). A reference to Kephas or Peter spoke of the emerging Church and its solid foundations in Peter's normative experience of the risen Lord.[10]

Jesus also gave a new Aramaic name to James and John, *Boanerges,* which Mark translated into Greek as *Huioi Brontes,* meaning "Sons of Thunder." Many in the Markan Church still appreciated traditional expressions in the old language. But Mark could not count that all in the Church would understand the expression. For the benefit of his Greek-speaking readers, Mark translated all the Hebrew and Aramaic words and expressions that appear in his Gospel.

---

[9] The list of the twelve apostles also underlines a very significant difference between the Twelve of Israel and the Twelve of Christ. In Genesis, the Twelve of Israel were presented as the sons of Jacob or Israel. As such, they were brothers. The Twelve of Christ included two sets of brothers, but the others were not related to one another. They were called and created to be the Twelve. The list of the apostles shows how the Church is not based on birth or ethnicity.

[10] For a theological reflection on Peter's normative experience and its implications for the Church, see E. LaVerdiere, "The Teaching Authority of the Church: Origins in the Early New Testament Period," *Chicago Studies* 17, 2 (Summer, 1978) 172–87.

None of the other apostles, including Judas, was given a new name. Mark did note, however, that Judas was the one who would betray Jesus (3:19). In this section the Gospel focuses on the nature and scope of the Church as a new people of God. This focus does not allow us to forget the passion. The Pharisees and the Herodians are already plotting behind the scenes to put Jesus to death (3:6), and now we learn how their plot (14:1-2) would succeed (3:19; see 14:10-11).

The Gospel's second great passage on the disciples also announces the mission of the Twelve (3:14-15). Jesus created the Twelve "[whom he also named apostles] that they might be with him *(met' autou)*, and he might send them forth to preach," as he himself preached (1:14), "and to have authority to drive out demons," just as Jesus did (1:27, 34, 39). Jesus created the Twelve, the foundation of the new Israel, in view of the universal mission of the Church.

Later, Jesus would send the Twelve on mission (6:7-13). The new Israel, the people of God, was to continue to proclaim the gospel of God, to announce that the kingdom of God was at hand, and to call people to repent and believe in the gospel. The Church, founded on the Twelve, was also to pursue Jesus' decisive confrontation with unclean spirits and the demonic world.

The Continuation of Jesus' Ministry in Galilee (3:20–4:34)

Like the first section of the Gospel (1:14–3:6), the second opens with a summary of Jesus' mission and ministry (3:7-12; see 1:14-15) and a major passage concerning the disciples, also a kind of summary (3:13-19; see 1:16-20). The summary emphasized the growth and diversity of the crowds, which came from Gentile as well as Jewish regions. The passage on the disciples showed how Jesus called some and made the Twelve, thereby transforming the community of disciples into a new Israel, open to both Jews and Gentiles.[11]

After setting out the sections' basic issues in summary form, Mark develops them in story form. The first part of the story, the continuation of Jesus' ministry in Galilee (3:20–4:34), presents Jesus' message for the new Israel. The meaning and implications of the new Israel had to be clarified. This was done by showing its relationship to Jesus' family and relatives (3:21, 31-35), to the scribes from Jeru-

---

[11] From a Christian point of view, we could also describe the new Israel as the fulfillment of Israel. The people of God began with the Twelve of Israel. Its fulfillment is in the Twelve of Christ.

salem (3:22-30), to the crowds (4:1-9, 26-34), to the Twelve, and all those who share their life and commitment (4:10-25).

Most of Jesus' teaching in this section is in the form of parables (3:23-27; 4:2-9, 21-25, 26-29, 31-32), or directly related to parables. It applies the parables to Jesus' listeners (3:28-30), and interprets the parable of the sower (4:3-9) for the benefit of the Twelve (4:13-20).

One of the major concerns in 3:20–4:34 is the very nature and purpose of Jesus' parables in relation to his mission and message (4:10-12, 33-34). Jesus' parables had been spoken in the course of his historical life in a Jewish setting. How were Christians to understand them now in the post-Easter context of the new Israel? Why did so many find Jesus' parables enigmatic or totally incomprehensible? These questions underlie the whole section, but especially 4:1-34.

The teaching of Jesus (3:20–4:34) is presented in two large sub-units, each with its own special setting. The first unfolds at the home (3:20-35), the second by the sea (4:1-34). The general structure of the two sub-units is identical. After describing the setting and context (3:20; 4:1), Mark presents a Markan sandwich or intercalation, a literary device in which a particular story is interrupted and another is inserted within it.

In the first Markan sandwich, the story of the relatives of Jesus (3:21) barely begins when it is interrupted by the story of the scribes from Jerusalem (3:22-30). After the story of the scribes, that of the relatives continues (3:31-35).

In the second sandwich, Jesus' teaching to the crowds (4:2-9) is interrupted by his teaching to the Twelve and those who were with them (4:10-25). Once Jesus has completed his teaching to the Twelve, he proceeds with his teaching to the crowds (4:26-34).

Jesus Teaching at Home (3:20-35)

Jesus came home *(eis oikon)*.[12] This is the fourth time in Mark's Gospel that Jesus' teaching and ministry has a domestic setting.[13]

First, Jesus entered the home of Simon and Andrew upon leaving the synagogue at Capernaum (1:29-31). His ministry on that occasion extended to the whole town that gathered at the door (1:32-34).

---

[12] For the theme of the home in Mark's Gospel, see F. Manns, "Le thème de la maison dans l'évangile de Marc," *Revue des Sciences Religieuses* 66, 1–2 (January–April 1992) 1–17.

[13] For an analysis of Mark 3:20-21 and its relationship to 3:31-35, see Ernest Best, "Mark iii. 20, 21, 31–35," *New Testament Studies* 22 (1976) 309–19.

Second, Jesus returned home, healed a paralytic who was lowered before him through an opening in the roof because of the crowds, and declared that his sins were forgiven (2:1-12). At this, the crowds glorified God in their astonishment, but the scribes thought that he was a blasphemer.

Third, Jesus dined in the home of Levi the tax collector, transforming a home of a sinner who became his follower into his own home. On that occasion, some scribes who were Pharisees objected that Jesus dined with tax collectors and sinners (2:15-17).

On each of those occasions, the home was defined primarily by the personal presence of Jesus. When Jesus entered the home of Simon and Andrew and the home of Levi, their homes became home to him. Now Jesus has come home for the fourth time (4:20). Presumably, the home that is referred to is that of Simon and Andrew, but what matters is that their home is now the home of Jesus. Earlier, Jesus had entered that home as one who called forth disciples to be his followers. He now came home as one who constituted the Twelve, the new Israel, a new reality that completely transformed the nature of the home.

Jesus and the Crowd (3:20). When Jesus came home, again the crowd gathered again *(palin)* at the home. Using the adverb "again" *(palin),* Mark associates the event with the previous time when the crowd gathered by the sea (3:7-8).[14] The same crowd now gathered at Jesus' home.

The home of Simon and Andrew and any other home Jesus made his own has become the hearth of the new Israel. Jesus' home was open to the townspeople (1:32-34), the huge crowds (2:1-12), as well as tax collectors, sinners, scribes and Pharisees (2:13-17). Now it is open to crowds that came even from the Gentile lands of Idumea, Transjordan, the region of Tyre and Sidon, as well as from Galilee, Judea and Jerusalem (3:7-8).

The crowd that now gathered at Jesus' home was not the same crowd that gathered after he healed Simon's mother-in-law (1:32-34) and healed the paralytic (2:1-12). This time, the crowd was much greater. More significantly, the crowd was much more diversified, including people from Jewish lands as well as from Gentile lands, representing both Jews and Gentiles.

---

[14] This is the fourth time Mark uses the adverb *palin* (again) to connect a new event with a previous event (3:20; see 2:1, 13; 3:1), and to integrate a new event with the greater story of the Gospel. To understand the new event, its relationship to the previous event is essential.

By welcoming such a crowd, Jesus broke with "the tradition of the elders" (see 7:1-23) and what was expected of a devout, observant Jew. Jews did not go to Gentile homes. They would have to accept their hospitality, including something to eat. They did not go even to a Jewish home that welcomed Gentiles. They would have been defiled. The crowd's presence at the home of Jesus challenged all those who were humanly related to him as family or religiously related to him as Jews. For them, Jesus' home, once a Jewish family home, had become a stranger's home. It was no longer their home.

Besides, the crowd was so great and so diversified that it was impossible for them even to eat bread *(arton phagein),* that is, to have a meal (see also 6:31). With this brief statement, Mark introduces the theme of bread and meals that will dominate the next section of the Gospel (6:6b–8:21).

The very notion of home was intimately associated with meals. When someone came home or when visitors were welcomed at someone's home, culture and custom required that a meal be served (see 1:31; 2:15-17). Meals, whether simple or elaborate, were an integral part of home life and hospitality.

But now, the crowd that gathered at Jesus' home was so great that the ordinary requirements of hospitality could not be observed. For observant Jews, the composition of the crowd, including both Jews and Gentiles, made it impossible to eat.

The Relatives of Jesus (3:21). Two groups of people, for very different reasons, were most profoundly challenged by the making of the Twelve and the creation of the new Israel, the relatives of Jesus and the scribes from Jerusalem.[15]

The new Israel called for a new understanding of the most basic human relationships, those that spring from birth. In the new Israel, a person's relationship to Jesus was not determined by kinship. Among Christians, blood ties in themselves were not significant or at most only a secondary consideration. The new Israel thus struck at the very heart of Jewish identity, which was intimately associated with a person's birth, family, and genealogy.

Jesus' relatives rejected the challenge of the new Israel. They went out to seize him saying that he was out of his mind (3:21). The same word, "to seize" *(kratesai),* a very strong word, is used several times in Mark, notably in the story of the arrest or seizing of Jesus

---

[15] For Mark 3:20-21, 31-35, see Ernest Best, "Mark iii, 20, 21, 31–35," *New Testament Studies* 22 (1976) 309–19.

and a young follower in the garden of Gethsemane (14:44, 46, 49, 51). With that, Jesus' relatives *(hoi par' autou),* who once had been insiders, became outsiders *(exo,* 3:31, 32). As "those outside" *(ekeinoi de hoi exo),* they were among those who did not receive the mystery of the kingdom of God (4:11).

Mark's statement about Jesus' relatives could lend itself to a very negative interpretation, one that would be unduly harsh. It was not retained by Matthew and Luke (see Matt 12:12-32; Luke 11:14-23). However, the statement is quite in keeping with Mark's hyperbolic style (see, for example, 9:42-48; 10:25; 11:23). Its intent is more rhetorical than historical. It addresses and challenges all who view their Christian identity in terms of family, tribe, ethnic or background. To read it as a historical statement about Jesus' relatives is to miss the point.

The Scribes from Jerusalem (3:22). The story of Jesus' relatives has barely been introduced (3:21) when it is interrupted by the story of the scribes from Jerusalem (3:22-30).

The scribes have already played a major role in the Gospel. Like Jesus, the scribes were teachers, but unlike Jesus, they did not teach as having authority (1:22). When Jesus cured a paralytic and pronounced that his sins were forgiven, they accused him of blasphemy (2:6-7). Later, some scribes who were Pharisees objected to Jesus' eating with tax collectors and sinners (2:16). Their accusation now goes much further. The scribes from Jerusalem accused Jesus of being possessed by Beelzebul. As such, he drove out demons by the prince of demons (3:22).

The family of Jesus and the scribes from Jerusalem were challenged by the new Israel, but in different ways. The family was humanly challenged. The scribes were religiously challenged. Jesus already had angered the scribes by his extraordinary manifestation of teaching authority. The new Israel, gathered at Jesus' home, invited them to rethink their religious role as teachers in the synagogue.

In the new Israel, they would have to be teachers for all peoples, both Jews and Gentiles. Their interpretation of Scripture and tradition in the limited Jewish setting, to which they were accustomed, would no longer be adequate. In effect, Jesus was challenging the role of the scribes, the synagogue, the local center of Jewish life, and Jerusalem itself, the ancient center of Jewish authority and teaching. Hence the explicit mention of the fact that the scribes had come from Jerusalem. These were not ordinary scribes invested with ordinary authority. Challenging them, Jesus was challenging the highest scribal authority in Judaism.

Like the relatives of Jesus, the scribes also rejected the new Israel. For the relatives, who were humanly challenged, Jesus was humanly out of his mind. For the scribes, who were challenged as religious teachers, Jesus was demonically possessed. Others may have been possessed by ordinary demons, but the scribes accused Jesus of being possessed by the prince of demons. The scribes from Jerusalem saw their authority and power challenged. In response, they challenged not only Jesus' authority and power, but the very source of his authority and power, that is, the holy Spirit (3:29; see 1:10, 12-13).

Jesus and the Scribes from Jerusalem (3:23-30). After showing how the scribes from Jerusalem responded to Jesus' mission and the new Israel, Mark shows how Jesus answered them. Jesus spoke to the scribes in parables (*en parabolais,* 3:23a). Although Jesus had taught in parables earlier in the Gospel (2:19-22), it is at this point that the expression "in parables" and the word "parable" itself enter the Gospel for the first time.

There is no doubt that Jesus employed many parables in his teaching. His parables consisted of graphic comparisons, some of which were in story form, while others consisted of paradoxes, and still others were bold but simple images. Whatever their form, all of Jesus' parables were both revelatory and challenging. Their purpose was to make matters and situations plain, so plain that Jesus' listeners could not avoid understanding and responding to them. Mark's Gospel focused on the confrontational aspect of Jesus' parables. Matthew emphasized their revelatory aspect, and Luke shows how they illustrated proper Christian attitudes and behavior.

With three short parabolic statements, Jesus begins by responding to the second charge made by the scribes, namely, that Jesus drove out demons by the prince of demons. He introduces the parabolic statements with a question: "How can Satan drive out Satan?" (3:23b). Is not that a contradiction in terms? Jesus responds to the question with three conditional statements, of which the third focuses on the figure of Satan. A kingdom divided against itself cannot stand, nor a house divided against itself, nor Satan when he rises against himself (3:24-26).

The image of the kingdom evokes the core of Jesus' proclamation, the kingdom of God (see 1:14-15). The house calls to mind the royal house that rules over the kingdom. It is in this sense, for example, that both the Old and the New Testament spoke of the house of David ruling over the kingdom of David. The image of the house also evokes the home of Jesus and the hearth of the New Israel, which is intimately connected with the kingdom of God. It is not that the parabolic statements refer directly to them, but the literary context of Mark must surely have influenced the choice of these images.

A fourth parable follows. No one can enter and plunder a strong man's house unless he first binds the strong man (3:27). The parable may well be a reference to Isaiah 49:24-25, which speaks of taking captives from the strong and rescuing prey from the tyrant.

In Mark's context, the fourth parable tends toward allegory. The strong or mighty one *(ho ischyros)* is Satan. Jesus, the mightier one *(ho ischyroteros,* 1:7) has bound Satan and plundered his house. Jesus is certainly not driving out demons by the prince of demons. Satan's house has fallen. Jesus' house stands with its doors open to welcome both Jew and Gentile.

Jesus then takes up the scribes' first charge, that he was possessed by Beelzebul (3:22a). He does so with a solemn utterance (3:38-29), introduced by "Amen, I say to you." The utterance is not in the form of parable, but its two parallel statements constitute a bold paradox, inviting the listener or reader to ponder the possibilities.

The first statement is a generalization: "All sins and all blasphemies that people utter will be forgiven them" (3:28). The affirmation seems to allow no exception. But the second statement presents a clear exception: "But whoever blasphemes against the holy Spirit will never have forgiveness, but is guilty of an everlasting sin" (3:29). The two statements appear to contradict one another.

Anyone who attributes the work of Jesus to Satan capitulates to Satan and is doomed. Those who blaspheme against the holy Spirit are bound and their authority nullified, just as Satan, the mighty one, was bound and his power was destroyed by Jesus, the mightier one (3:26).

Jesus' short discourse in parables had been mounting to this climax, where a literary paradox demands reflection and rhetorical hyperbole jolts the listener into full awareness of what is at stake. Very simply, the choice is between Jesus, endowed with the Spirit of holiness, and Satan, who embodies the spirit of evil.

Jesus' discourse has come to an end. Lest anyone miss the reason for the harsh words against the scribes from Jerusalem, Mark adds, "For they had said, 'He has an unclean spirit'" (3:30; see 3:22).

Jesus and His Family (3:31-35)

The story of Jesus' relatives *(hoi par' autou)* began when they came to seize Jesus because they thought he was out of his mind (3:21). As the story resumes, his mother and his brothers arrive, and staying outside *(exo),* they send for him (3:31).

Since this is the first time Mark refers to Jesus' mother and brothers, it is very striking that he did not identify them by name. This omission is very likely intentional. It is also very significant. Mark knew their names. Later in the gospel, he refers to Jesus as the carpenter, "the son of Mary, and the brother of James and Joses[16] and Judas and Simon" (6:3).

Normally, the Gospel would have identified them the first time they were mentioned. Such was the case for Simon and his brother Andrew, James and his brother John (1:16-20). But at this point in the story, the name and personal identity of the mother of Jesus and his brothers were not important. What was important was their relationship to Jesus. Later, when Jesus came to Nazareth (6:1-6a), it would be the reverse. Then, what will be important is Jesus' relationship to them.

The Gospel places all the emphasis on the relationship itself, that is, being Jesus' mother and his brothers. As such, it focuses on those who were related to Jesus by blood through family, extended family, and ethnic ties. But this does not mean that the precise nature of the blood relationship was a concern. The concern was the blood relationship as such.

Once again, the crowd from Jewish and Gentile lands enters the story (3:32; see 3:7-8, 21). This time, the crowd was seated around Jesus *(peri auton)* and told Jesus that his mother and his brothers— some manuscripts add "his sisters"—were outside *(exo)* looking for him. To whom does Jesus belong, to the crowd seated as disciples around him *(peri auton),* or to his blood relatives outside *(exo)*? How would Jesus respond? The new Israel was at stake.

Jesus' response begins with a question. But the question is not about those to whom he belonged, but about those who belonged to him: "Who are my mother and [my] brothers? (3:33)." "Brothers" in that question could be qualified by "my" as we find it in some

---

[16] The Gospel refers to Jesus as the brother of James and Joses and not to Mary as the mother of James and Joses. At the crucifixion, mark refers to another Mary as the mother of the younger James and Joses (15:40; see also 15:47; 16:1). John also refers to Jesus' mother and his mother's sister, Mary, the wife of Clopas, and Mary of Magdala (John 19:25). If Mary, the wife of Clopas (John 19:25) was the mother of James and Joses (Mark 15:40, 47; 16:1), James and Joses would have been Jesus' cousins (Mark 6:3). But even if James and Joses had been close neighbors and childhood friends of Jesus, they would have been thought of as the brothers of Jesus.

ancient manuscripts. But if it is not so qualified, the reference to "my mother and brothers" with the one possessive pronoun would emphasize the blood relationship itself rather than the specific relationship of being a mother or a brother.

Jesus' question was rhetorical, and Jesus proceeded to answer it. Looking at those seated in a circle around him *(peri auton),* Jesus asserted that these were his mother and my brothers, that is, his true relatives (3:34). The purpose of the story, then, is to contrast Jesus' true relatives with those who were merely blood relatives. This contrast makes sense only after Jesus' passion and resurrection.

Jesus concludes with a generalization: "[For] whoever does the will of God is my brother and sister and mother" (3:35). Again the single pronoun "my" qualifying "brother and sister and mother" emphasizes the generic blood relationship and not the specific relationship of being a brother or a sister or a mother.

The order we found in 3:32, "your mother and your brothers [and your sisters]" is reversed in the generalization, as "my brother and sister and mother" (3:35). It was more appropriate to describe a true relative of Jesus as his brother and sister rather than his mother.

Mention of "sister" in the generalization (see also 6:3) is significant in view of the role of women in Mark's Gospel. Already we have seen Simon's mother-in-law, who was raised from illness and ministered to the nucleus of the Church (1:29-31). Women play a decisive role in the development of the Church, which began as a Jewish, male community and became one that included both Jews and Gentiles as well as men and women. But Mark cannot tell everything at once.

In the new Israel, the crowd replaces Jesus' blood relatives. Of course, the blood relatives are not excluded from discipleship. They too can join those who do the will of God and sit in the circle gathered around Jesus. For that they would have to enter the house. The same contrast between blood relatives and faith relatives will be applied to the disciples themselves (see 10:29-31). They too would have to learn who were their true relatives.

Jesus' response to the scribes from Jerusalem and to the crowd gathered around him speaks to key concerns regarding the nature of the kingdom of God. It also speaks very eloquently to basic issues that the Markan communities had to face.

As the Gospel unfolds, it becomes progressively clearer that Mark tells the story of Jesus on two levels. We hear the story of Jesus and his disciples, but we also hear the story of the Christ, the risen Lord, and his Christian followers.

The implications of the kingdom of God continued to emerge as the early Church focused on its identity as a new Israel. There were many issues to sort out, including the relationship between Jews and Gentiles, and the roles of men and women in the Church. While telling the story of Jesus and his disciples, Mark also presents the history of the early Church from Jesus' passion and resurrection until the Roman siege of Jerusalem, if not its destruction.

Jesus' Teaching by the Sea (4:1-34)

The first part of Jesus' teaching for the new Israel took place at home (3:20-35). Surrounded by great crowds coming from both Jewish and Gentiles lands, Jesus responded to accusations made by the scribes from Jerusalem. Then, with his family standing outside calling for him, he defined his true family as all who do the will of God, that is, those who repent and believe in the gospel (1:15).

For the second part, the setting shifts from Jesus' home to the seashore for the Gospel's first great discourse (4:1-34). Mark's Gospel contains many small discourses of Jesus. One of the small discourses presented Jesus as teaching in parables (3:23-30), setting the stage for the first great discourse, in which Jesus also teaches in parables.[17]

Besides the discourse on the tradition of the elders (7:1-23), the only other great discourse in Mark is the eschatological discourse on the Mount of Olives (13:1-37). In that later discourse, which immediately precedes the passion-resurrection, the Gospel deals with apocalyptic fears and false messianic expectations. The discourse uses apocalyptic language and refers to apocalyptic events, but it also shows how Mark's readers should understand them.

In the discourse in parables, the Gospel deals with the difficulty or inability that many experienced in understanding Jesus' teaching in parables. It presents some of Jesus' teaching in parables and interprets it for Christians living in the new Israel years after Jesus' passion-resurrection.

Literary Discourses. As a teacher, Jesus must have spoken many discourses, short and long, at least from time to time, along with stories, sayings, and simple parables. However, the Gospels do

---

[17] For the discourse in and on parables, see John Paul Heil, "Reader-Response and the Narrative Context of the Parables about Growing Seed in Mark 4:1-34," *The Catholic Biblical Quarterly* 54/2 (April 1992) 271–86; Marcus Joel, *The Mystery of the Kingdom of God* (Atlanta: Scholars Press, 1986); Freg Fay, "Introduction to Incomprehension: The Literary Structure of Mark 4:1-34," *The Catholic Biblical Quarterly* 51/1 (January 1989) 65–81.

not present these directly or word for word. They draw from Jesus' discourses, surely, but with the intention of responding to the new situations in the Christian communities and to the new issues they had to face. The literary discourses in the Gospels were composed by the evangelists who wrote the Gospels and not by the people to whom they are attributed.

There is a difference between a historical discourse, which marks a historical event, and a literary discourse, which refers to the same event. This is particularly true of farewell discourses, such as Jesus' great discourse at the Last Supper in John 14-17 and Luke 22:14-38 and Paul's discourse to the elders of Ephesus gathered at Miletus in Acts 20:17-38.[18] The discourse in John is actually several successive discourses, of which the first clearly ends at 14:31 when Jesus says, "Get up, let us go."

The difference between a historical and a literary discourse applies not only to farewell discourses but also to all the other discourses in the Gospels. Unlike the farewell discourses, however, ordinary literary discourses do not attempt a comprehensive synthesis of Jesus' teaching for a new situation.

Following the literary canons of the time, those that composed the discourses in the Gospels enjoyed great flexibility and freedom of expression. Historically, a discourse must have been delivered in one place, at one time, and for a particular audience. Literarily, however, an author could rise above the historical context. A discourse could start in one place and time and then, with little or no transition, it could jump to another place and time, freeing the ancient discourse to speak with a new voice for a new people confronting challenges of their own. Such is the case with Mark 4:1-34.[19]

Overview of the Discourse. The beginning of the discourse is fairly simple. There is an introduction. Jesus spoke to a large crowd

---

[18] See E. LaVerdiere, "A Discourse at the Last Supper," *The Bible Today* (March 1974) 1540–48.

[19] The difference between a historical and a literary discourse sheds light on many discourses in the New Testament. Consider Jesus' discourse in John's Gospel after he nourished the 5,000 (6:25-71). At the beginning of the discourse, Jesus speaks to the crowd of 5,000 (see 6:10, 22-24), but at one point the narrator says that Jesus said these things "while teaching in the synagogue in Capernaum" (6:59). The synagogue could accommodate just a few people, certainly not 5,000. The discourse also has two audiences, beginning with the crowd (6:25-59), ending with the disciples (6:60-71).

by the sea, and he spoke to them in parables (4:1-2).[20] The discourse then presents one, and only one, of the many parables Jesus spoke to the crowd (see 4:2b, 33), the parable of the sower (4:3-9).

After the parable, the audience changes. With a stroke of the pen, the crowd disappears, and Jesus is alone with those who were around him with the Twelve. His message to them unfolds in three parts. First, Jesus explained why he spoke in parables (4:10-12). Second, he interpreted for them the parable of the sower (4:13-20). Third, he concluded by speaking to them further about parables and their purpose (4:21-25).

With no explicit indication, the discourse then returns to its original audience. Throughout 4:10-25, Jesus had been speaking to those who were around him with the Twelve. He now presented two further parables to the crowd, both of them concerning the kingdom of God (4:26-32).

The discourse ends with a conclusion reaffirming the distinction between Jesus' teaching to the crowds, which was done with many such parables, and his teaching to his own disciples, which included private explanations (4:33-34).

From this short overview of the discourse, it is quite clear that Mark, while referring to a discourse Jesus had given, has no intention of presenting that discourse. Instead, he uses the setting of Jesus' discourse to present a discourse of his own in the name of Jesus.

In the discourse, Jesus has two distinct audiences, the crowd (*ho ochlos,* 4:1) and those who were around him with the Twelve (*hoi peri auton syn tois dodeka,* 4:10), that is, his own disciples (*hoi idioi mathetai,* 4:34). In the previous unit (3:20-35), Mark referred to those who were around Jesus *(peri auton)*. Now, the crowd is around him *(peri auton)*. At the same time, the crowd was with the Twelve *(syn tois dodeka)*.

---

[20] For Jesus' parables in general, see Joachim Jeremias, *The Parables of Jesus,* Second Revised Edition (New York: Charles Scribner's Sons, 1963); C. H. Dodd, *The Parables of the Kingdom* (New York: Charles Scribner's Sons, 1961); Dan Otto Via, Jr., *The Parables* (Philadelphia: Fortress Press, 1967); Madeleine I. Boucher, *The Parables,* New Testament Message 7, Revised Edition (Wilmington: Michael Glazier, Inc., 1983); John R. Donahue, S.J., *The Gospel in Parable* (Philadelphia: Fortress Press, 1988).

For the parables in Mark, see especially Jan Lambrecht, *Once More Astonished, The Parables of Jesus* (New York: Crossroad, 1981) 85–145; and John R. Donahue, S.J., *The Gospel in Parable* Philadelphia: Fortress Press, 1988) 28–62.

In the narrator's introduction (4:1-2) and the conclusion (4:33-34), as well as in Jesus' message to his disciples (4:10-12), the Gospel says that Jesus addressed the two audiences differently. He spoke publicly to the crowds in parables but he explained the parables in private only to his disciples, that is, those who were around him with the Twelve.

With these distinctions, we can see how Mark has built a bridge between the time of Jesus, when the parables were quite clear, and his own time, when they required some explanation. Once explained, the parables once again became clear, but only for those who gathered around Jesus with the Twelve.

The discourse includes yet another important distinction, that between those who were around Jesus (*peri auton,* 4:10; see 3:32) with the Twelve and those who were outside (*hoi exo,* 4:11; see 3:32). For those who were outside, not only did the parables remain obscure, but no explanation would suffice to clarify them (4:12). To understand the parables, one had to be a follower of Jesus and associated with the Twelve in the new Israel.[21]

With this final distinction, we can see how Mark accounted for the abyss separating those who stood in continuity with the original teaching of Jesus, albeit in a new era, and those who disassociated themselves completely from the community.

Those who were in continuity represented the community that Mark envisioned. He wrote his Gospel, including this discourse, to strengthen or form such a community.

Those who disassociated themselves represented the scribes from Jerusalem, who capitulated to Satan (3:22, 28-29), and the relatives of Jesus, who remained outside the household of Jesus and were not with the Twelve (3:21, 31-35). The scribes from Jerusalem and the relatives of Jesus must have reflected tendencies Mark observed among the Christians. He also wrote his Gospel to counter those tendencies. The scribes and the relatives did not have the ears to hear the parables Jesus had taught (4:9). They had not been granted the mystery of the kingdom of God (4:11).

---

[21] In 1 Corinthians 1:18-19, Paul has a similar theology concerning the paradox of the cross: "The message of the cross is foolishness to those who are perishing, but to us who are being saved it is the power of God. For it is written: 'I will destroy the wisdom of the wise, / and the learning of the learned I will set aside.'" Mark based this theology on Isaiah 6:9. Paul based his theology on Isaiah 29:14. 1 Corinthians 1:20-25 further develops Paul's reflections on the paradox of the cross.

Jesus and the Crowd (4:1). Jesus again *(palin)* went to teach by the sea, and a very large crowd gathered. He got into a boat and sat on the sea, while the crowd stayed by the sea on the land. Such was the physical setting for Jesus' great discourse in parables.

In the first section of the Gospel (1:14–3:6), two closely related events were situated by the sea. The first time Jesus went by the sea *(para ten thalassan),* he called Simon and Andrew, James and John to follow him (1:16-20). The second time, he went by the sea *(para ten thalassan),* he taught the crowd and called Levi to follow him (2:13-17). The second event recalled the first. It was not only that Jesus went by the sea but that he went again *(palin)* by the sea (2:13).

At the beginning of the second section (3:7–6:6a), Jesus returned to the sea *(pros ten thalassan)* with his disciples, those whom he had called by the sea (1:16-20; 2:13-14), and great crowds followed (3:7-8). This was the third time Jesus went by the sea.

Now, Jesus went to teach by the sea *(para ten thalassan)* for the fourth time. Mark could have said simply that Jesus went by the sea. Instead, he said that Jesus went again *(palin).*[22] As in the first section (see 2:13), when Jesus returned by the sea, the Gospel recalls the previous time and invites us to think of the new event in light of the previous event.

Mark also invites us to think of the events by the sea as a body. They are the events that took place by the sea. In the same way, Mark situates events that took place in the home, on the mountain, in the desert, and on the way.

Referring to the previous time that Jesus went by the sea, the parable discourse recalls the introductory summary for this whole section of the Gospel (3:7-12). The previous summary situated Jesus in Galilee (1:14-15). In the second major summary, Jesus withdrew toward the sea. The summary also described the crowd that gathered to be healed. They came from all of Galilee and Judea, even Jerusalem. They also came from neighboring Gentile lands, including Idumea, Transjordan, and the region of Tyre and Sidon (3:9).

We noted that Jesus had asked his disciples to have a boat ready for him to avoid being crushed by the crowd (3:9). At the time, this appeared somewhat strange, since Jesus did not used the boat but went up the mountain (3:13), and when he came down from the mountain he went home (3:20).

---

[22] This is also the fifth time Mark uses the adverb *palin* (again) to associate a new event with a previous event. This time, he uses *palin* to connect Jesus' teaching in parables (4:1-34) to his healing ministry by the sea (3:7-12).

The making of the Twelve, which took place on the mountain (3:13-19), and the subsequent teaching at home (3:20-35) were very important theologically and literarily, but they interrupted Jesus' teaching by the sea. The Gospel consequently establishes a fresh link between 3:7-12 and 4:1-34. The boat had already been prepared (3:9), and now as the huge crowd gathered, Jesus had only to get into it.

Everyone was wonderfully positioned for the discourse. The setting constituted a natural amphitheater. The water separating Jesus and the crowd provided natural amplification. The crowd was by the sea on the land *(epi tes ges)*. Jesus was in the boat *(eis ploion)* seated on the sea *(kathesthai en te thalassa,* 4:1).

The crowd was on land but on the very edge of chaos, as symbolized by the sea. Jesus was in the boat in the teacher's seated position dominating the chaos. After the discourse, Jesus would remain in the boat and cross the sea with his disciples. He would rebuke and quiet a violent storm and bring on a great calm (4:35-41). Later yet, in another crossing he would even walk out to his disciples on the sea (6:45-52). For the discourse in parables, he merely sat on the sea in the boat. But the story of Jesus and the new Israel has barely begun.

Teaching in Parables (4:2). Jesus taught the crowd in parables *(en parabolais)*. This is the second time Jesus is said to have taught in parables (see 3:23). Saying that Jesus taught "in parables" is not the same as saying that Jesus told parables. This second expression, telling parables, describes the content of Jesus' teaching in relation to its rhetorical or literary form. The first, teaching "in parables," describes the method of teaching and implies that this method was chosen for a special purpose.

The parable discourse speaks of how Jesus taught in parables, and of the purpose of the parables. It also speaks of how the parables fulfilled their purpose and why in many cases they did not. The discourse also speaks of the role of the disciples regarding the parables and their purpose.

The expression, "teaching in parables," usually implied that several parables were presented, and as a matter of fact, the Gospel states that Jesus spoke with many parables on this occasion (4:33). At this point, however, only one of those parables is presented, that of the sower and the seed.

The Sower and the Seed (4:3-9). The parable of the sower and the seed was part of Jesus' teaching to the large crowd that had gathered by the sea. To get the crowd's full attention, Jesus gave the parable a one-word preface: "Hear this" (*akouete,* listen). Then he drew his listeners into the parable with an introductory "look" (*idou,* see) as he launched into the parable, "a sower went out to sow" (4:3).

The basic elements of a parable can be developed in different ways. In this case, the parable could easily have focused on the sower and the act of sowing, but it did not. The sower and the sowing merely provide a setting for the seed and the kinds of ground on which it fell, as well as what subsequently happened to it (4:4-8). Even here, the parable focuses far more on the path, the rocky ground, the thorns, and the rich soil. The seed was the same in each case. What differed was the ground, and what happened to the seed depended entirely on the place where it fell.

It is easy to misinterpret a parable. In this case, the temptation is to transform the parable into a allegory, associating the different kinds of ground with distinct categories of people, with some being the path, others the rocky ground, still others the thorns, and others yet the rich soil. Instead, the parable should be read as a challenge to each of Jesus' listeners, inviting one and all to reflect on how they were responding to Jesus' ministry of the word and holding their response up to the ideal of the rich soil which yielded an abundant harvest.

A brief epilogue, "Whoever has ears to hear *[akouein]* ought to hear *[akoueto]*" (4:9), recalls the one-word preface "Hear this" (*akouete,* listen 4:3). It may be that in Jesus' original telling of the parable, the focus was on the sower and the seed, that is, on Jesus himself and his work on behalf of the kingdom. But in Mark's retelling of the parable the accent is on the ground on which the seed fell, that is, on those whom Jesus was addressing.

The preface, "Hear this," and the epilogue, with their emphasis on hearing, make the parable a good introduction for the remainder of the discourse, which deals with the problem of truly hearing and understanding the parables.

The Purpose of the Parables (4:10-12). After the parable and Jesus' challenge to hear (4:3-9), the crowd disappears. As the discourse continues, Jesus is alone with those around him *(peri auton),* those who with the Twelve *(syn tois dodeka),* that is, those who were committed to the new Israel. The emphasis here is not on the Twelve, but on all those who associated themselves with the Twelve as opposed to those who were not with the Twelve.[23]

---

[23] For Mark 4:10-12 and its literary and historical context, see Michael D. Goulder, "Those Outside (Mk 4:10-12)," *Novum Testamentum* XXXIII, 4 (1991)

Those gathered around Jesus while he was alone *(kata monas)* questioned him about the parables.[24] The Gospel consequently assumes that they had been present as Jesus spoke to the crowd at length in parables (4:2). Jesus began by explaining why they were able to understand the parables while those outside were unable to understand.[25]

Those who were with the Twelve had been granted the mystery *(mysterion)* of the kingdom of God (see 1:14-15). As part of the new Israel Jews and Gentiles had the faith that allowed them to understand. What was hidden in the past and even now from others was thus being revealed to them.

In reading the passage, it is better to avoid using the term "secret" as a translation for *mysterion* (mystery). The word "secret" draws attention to a secret's content, whereas the word mystery is much broader. It evokes the faith experience which underlies the content and its formulation (see Col 1:24-29; Eph 1:8-10; 3:1-6).

Those who remained outside had not received the mystery of the kingdom of God, in which all human beings were called to participate in the new Israel. For them, Jesus' teaching in parables remained opaque. They lacked the experience of faith and commitment that would have allowed them to understand. As a result, the very purpose of the parables was defeated. The parables should have brought perception and understanding. In their case, it did the opposite.

Translating an Aramaic rendering (a Targum) of Isaiah 6:9-10 into Greek, the Gospel says that even what they saw and heard would lose its former meaning lest they be converted and forgiven. An era had ended. The conversion and forgiveness associated with

---

289–302. Goulder has good insights concerning "those outside," as he responds to interpretations based on the distinction between tradition and redaction. But unfortunately, he did not distinguish the literary discourse, addressing Mark's contemporaries, from a historical discourse, addressing Jesus' contemporaries.

[24] For a discussion of Mark's theology regarding the parables, see Madeleine I. Boucher, *The Parables,* New Testament Message 7, Revised Edition (Wilmington, Del.: Michael Glazier, Inc., 1983) 44–53.

[25] For Mark 4:10-12 and its context, see Michael D. Goulder, "Those Outside (Mk. 4:10-12)," *Novum Testamentum* XXXIII, 4 (1991) 289–302. Goulder has good insights and suggestions concerning "those outside," but unfortunately he does not distinguish between Mark's literary discourse, addressed to the Church, and the historical discourse, attributed to Jesus, addressing his contemporaries.

the old era, even the conversion and forgiveness that John the Baptist preached (1:4), no longer sufficed.

A new era had begun, that of the new Israel, ushering in the universal kingdom of God. For those who did not enter into the new era, the old religious circuits, which had fed the old era, had been short-circuited. For those who had capitulated to Satan and blasphemed against the holy Spirit, there could be no forgiveness (3:29).

The Sower and the Seed, a New Interpretation (4:13-20). After explaining the purpose of the parables in general (4:10-12; see 4:2), Jesus interpreted the one parable he told while he was addressing the whole crowd (4:3-9). If the disciples did not understand this parable, how could they understand any of the others (4:13)? The parable of the sower and the seed had not been selected at random. Understanding this particular parable provided the key for understanding all the others.

In his interpretation, Jesus identified the seed as the word *(ho logos),* that is, the gospel (see 2:2). He then showed what happened to the word that fell on the path, on rocky ground, among thorns and on the rich soil. In the first telling of the parable (4:3-9), emphasis lay on the seed and the ground on which it fell, and the parable climaxed in the rich ground which contrasted with the other three kinds of ground.

In its new interpretation, the emphasis shifts from the seed and the ground on which it fell to the various kinds of ground and what subsequently happened to the seed. The rich ground, which had been the climax of the first telling, the ideal against which one could measure oneself, is mentioned again but without additional development, whereas the other kinds of ground and what happened to the seed that fell on them receives a new and imaginative treatment.

The development is quite similar to some of the parabolic and allegorical teachings found in the Mishnah in the tractate called the Fathers *(Aboth)*.[26] In that format, it would read as follows.

> There are three kinds of disciples in whom the word is sown, and there is a fourth kind:

---

[26] Herbert Danby, *The Mishnah* (New York: Oxford University Press, 1933) 446–61. The tractate entitled *Aboth* ("The Fathers"), also called *Pirke Aboth* is part of the Fourth Division: *Nezikim* ("Damages"). The tractate includes sayings and maxims handed down between 300 B.C. to A.D. 200. See especially the fifth chapter.

- the path, from whom the word is immediately snatched away by Satan—they hardly even hear the word;
- the rocky ground, in whom the word is joyfully received, but has no roots—they hear the word but fall away when tribulation or persecution comes because of the word;
- the thorns, in whom the word is choked by worldly anxiety, the lure of riches, or craving for other things—they hear the word, but it bears no fruit;
- and the rich soil—they not only hear the word but accept it, and it bears fruit, thirty, sixty, and a hundredfold.

The first telling of the parable held up an ideal. The second aimed at moral formation. In presenting the interpretation, Mark may have meant to evoke the disciples' baptismal catechesis. This is suggested by two themes, that of the sowing of the word and that of bearing fruit (see Col 1:5-6, 9-10; 1 Pet 1:22-25; Jas 1:21-25).

As he evoked the baptismal catechesis, Mark also held it up to the challenges faced by the early Christians, including his readers, who experienced tribulation, persecution (4:17; see 2:20; 10:30; 13:5-23), worldly anxiety, the lure of riches, and other cravings (4:19; see 10:13-26; 42-44; 12:38-40).

Parables for the Disciples (4:21-25). Jesus' teaching to the disciples now turns to their mission regarding the mystery of the kingdom of God as well as the meaning of Jesus' teaching in parables. For this, Mark presents two short parables, that of the lamp and that of the measure, along with their interpretation (4:21-25).

A lamp is not placed under a basket or under a bed, but on a lampstand. Why? Because nothing is hidden *(krypton)* or secret *(apokryphon)* except to be brought to light (4:21-22).[27] The parables are meant to enlighten, and for this their meaning must be made plain for those who have been granted the mystery of the kingdom of God (see 4:11-12).

The little parable of the lamp and its interpretation has a brief epilogue very similar to the one that followed the parable of the sower and the seed (4:9): "Anyone who has ears to hear ought to hear" (4:23). This time, however, it is addressed not to the crowd but to the disciples, who should not take their hearing for granted. Jesus had just shown this in his interpretation of the sower and the seed (4:13-20). Not everyone who received the word received it the same way, and not everyone persevered.

---

[27] Compare Jesus' parable of the lamp in Mark with Jesus' teaching in the Sermon of the Mount (Matt 5:14-16).

The theme of hearing also introduces the second little parable, that of the measure: "Take care what you hear. The measure with which you measure will be measured out to you, and still more will be given to you" (4:24). Today, we probably would use the word "scale," which refers to weight, rather than "measure," which refers to quantity.

"To the one who has, more will be given; from the one who has not, even what he has will be taken away" (4:25). "The one who has" is the one who was granted the mystery of the kingdom (4:11a) and will receive new understanding because of it (4:13-20). "The one who has not" is the one who was not granted the mystery of the kingdom. Those who have not are not with the Twelve. Remaining outside, they will lose even that sight and hearing they had once enjoyed. Everything will become opaque to them (4:12b). The words of Isaiah apply not only to those who stayed outside. Mark also directed them as a warning to those who received the word on the path, on rocky ground, or in thorns.

Parables of the Kingdom of God (4:26-32). Jesus' special teaching for the disciples is over. The crowd reappears on the seashore, and Jesus is once again teaching from the boat on the sea (see 4:33-34). The discourse concludes with two parables, further developing the image of the seed.

The first parable draws attention to the seed's growth, which proceeds mysteriously, inexorably, and independently of human effort once it is sown. The seed grows and matures all the way to the harvest (4:26-29). The parable enables Jesus' listeners to see how the seed of the kingdom continues to grow without fanfare.

It also evokes Jesus' own life and mission. Jesus planted the word, which then grows and develops in the course of history. When it is fulfilled in the kingdom of God, Jesus will return for the harvest (see 13:24-37).

The discourse concludes with the parable of the mustard seed, the tiniest of all seeds. This time the parable does not concern the mystery of the seed's growth. Rather, it describes the way an extraordinary plant with great branches comes from practically nothing (4:30-32). So it is with the kingdom of God whose beginnings are extremely modest but which will eventually grow into God's universal dominion.

Both parables are meant to reassure a Christian community concerning the reality (4:26-29) and the value (4:30-32) of their commitment to follow Christ in the new Israel. Once planted the seed continues to grow, from a modest beginning to full maturity.

Concluding Comments (4:33-34). With that last parable of the mustard seed, the discourse comes to an end, but Mark adds a few summarizing comments. We learn again that Jesus' discourse included far more parables than Mark presented in 4:3-32, and that he taught the crowd in parables in such a way that all could hear *(akouein),* that is, understand (4:33).

The parables are referred to as "the word" *(ho logos),* an early Christian term for the gospel. In Mark, the term first appears in the healing of the paralytic when Jesus was preaching the word to the crowd that gathered in his home (2:2). In the interpretation of the parable of the sower and the seed, the word is the seed (4:14-20). In 4:33, the word is presented in parables. In 8:31-32 (see also 9:31; 10:32-34), the word is the passion and resurrection of Jesus.

Jesus also had to explain the parables for his own disciples that they might hear them in the context of the new Israel. This he did in private *(kat' idian,* 4:34; see also 13:3), since others would not be able to understand (4:10-12). Hopefully, his disciples would have the ears to hear (4:23).

Going to the Other Side (4:35–6:6a)

Mark opened this section of the Gospel (3:7–6:6a) with a summary describing Jesus' ministry by the sea (3:7-12). For the first time, the crowd that came to him included people from Gentile as well as Jewish territories (3:7-12). To meet this challenge, Jesus made the Twelve and established the new Israel, which would be open to both Jews and Gentiles (3:13-19).

We then listened to Jesus as he taught first at home and then by the sea (3:20–4:34). We heard Jesus redefine the meaning of home, family, and relationships among his followers. He also redefined religious authority (3:20-35). We then heard him give a great discourse, presenting and interpreting parables and explaining his purpose for teaching in parables. He showed how parables remained opaque to those who were not with him and with the Twelve, even after his explanation. But the same parables could be made clear to those who were with him and the Twelve in the context of the new Israel (4:1-34).

In the section's second phase (4:35–6:6a), Jesus and those who were him crossed from the Jewish to the Gentile shore. Since the crowds came to him from Gentile lands (see 3:7-12), Jesus and the Twelve had to go to them and minister to them in their own territory. They now were included among his brothers and sisters (3:31-

35). Although the journey proved to be very stormy, Jesus was always in control (4:35-41).

On the Gentile shore, Jesus cast unclean spirits out of a man who lived among the tombs, that is, among the dead. So doing, he cast them even out of the Gentile territory itself. He left the man there to be a forerunner for his mission and the mission of the Twelve among the Gentiles (5:1-20).

Jesus and the disciples then returned to the Jewish shore where he had earlier ministered and performed two important miracles (5:21-43) before appearing in the synagogue at Nazareth, where the whole section ends (6:1-6b). The new Israel was for the Jews as well as for the Gentiles.

A Storm at Sea (4:35-41)

While Jesus was teaching by the sea, he gave the great discourse in parables (4:1-2). Because of the large crowd, he had gotten into the boat the disciples had prepared for him (see 3:9). As the discourse comes to an end (4:1-34), Mark reminds us of the setting: "On that day, as evening drew on, he said to them, 'Let us cross to the other side'" (4:35).

Still in the boat, Jesus invited the disciples, that is, the Twelve, to cross to the Gentile side. At this point, Mark transforms the story. Until now, the story was mainly about Jesus. For the crossing of the sea, the story is mainly about the Twelve: "Leaving the crowd, they took him with them in the boat just as he was" (4:36a; see also 5:1). It is as though, instead of Jesus, the Twelve were in the boat, and they took Jesus "just as he was," that is, as the risen Lord, with them to the other side. Mark thus told the story of the crossing of the sea as a story of the Twelve, that is, the Church, with the risen Lord. With the risen Lord, the Twelve took the other boats that were "with him *(met' autou)*" (4:36).

In Mark's Gospel, the evening is a time for new challenges. As reckoned by the Jews, the day went from sundown to sundown. As such, evening came at the end of the day and announced a new day. In 1:32, it marked the beginning of Jesus' ministry for the many that gathered at the door of the home of Simon and Andrew. Much later in the Gospel, the evening announced the day of Jesus' passion and death (14:17) as well as the day of burial (15:42). Here in 4:35, it signaled the start of a great sea journey.

Until now, Jesus had confronted his relatives and the scribes from Jerusalem with the implications of the new Israel (3:20-35). He had also taught the crowds and those who were gathered around him with the Twelve concerning hearing the word and how it was with the kingdom of God (4:1-34). However, it was not enough for the Gentiles to come to Jesus. Jesus had to go personally to the Gentiles. Jesus had spent the whole day teaching on the Jewish shore. Now, at the close of the day, he asked the Twelve to cross to the other side (4:35).

Leaving the great crowd on the Jewish shore, the Twelve would take Jesus to the Gentile shore (4:36a), more specifically to the territory of the Gerasenes (5:1). From there Jesus' deeds would be proclaimed throughout the Decapolis, that is, the region of Ten Greek Cities (5:20). Bringing Jesus to the other shore, the Twelve were bridging the sea, joining the Gentile shore with Jewish shore. They were forming the new Israel that would be universal in its welcome (3:7–4:34) as well as in its mission (4:35–6:6a).

There were other boats "with him" (4:36b). Since the story tells how the disciples took Jesus with them in the boat, it would have been normal to say that there were other boats "with them," but the story very pointedly says that the boats were "with him." Many others joined Jesus in the crossing to the Gentile shore. Being with Jesus meant sharing the same vision and commitment.

The crossing was extremely difficult. A great windstorm arose and the waves pounded into the boat, filling it up very quickly. Through it all, Jesus was in the stern, quietly sleeping on the helmsman's seat-cushion (4:37-38a). The contrast between the storm's violence and Jesus' peaceful attitude could not be more striking.

Storms are not uncommon on the Sea of Galilee. They can sweep down quite suddenly from the heights of the Golan that dominate the sea from the east. In this story, however, the storm is not only a natural phenomenon. It is symbolic of another kind of storm. For the young Church, the transition from its Jewish origins to the new Israel was extremely stormy. For Jesus, the crossing was calm, but not for the disciples who saw their pilot asleep.

They raised Jesus from sleep *(egeirousin),* asking him if he did not care that they were perishing (4:38). With that, Jesus rose *(diegertheis,* 4:38b-39a). The meaning of the verbs *egeiro* and *diegeiro* (to rise) is "to awaken," but they also evoke Jesus' resurrection. For the first time in Mark's Gospel, Jesus is addressed as "teacher" *(didaskale),* a title which may witness to the story's origins and development in early Christian catechesis.

As risen Lord, Jesus rebuked the wind and commanded the sea to be silent (4:39a). At his command, the wind stopped and there came a great calm (4:39b). Earlier, at the synagogue of Capernaum, he had rebuked the unclean spirit and ordered it to be silent (1:25).

Jesus commands the forces of chaos just as he commands unclean spirits and the forces of evil, and they obey him (1:27, 34, 39). In the Old Testament, the sea was often personified as a great threatening monster that only God could restrain.

As the mightier one (*ho ischyroteros,* 1:7), Jesus had bound Satan, the mighty one (*ho ischyros,* 3:27) and plundered his house. As the Lord of creation, he commanded the sea and it obeyed him. His action evokes many passages from the Old Testament, especially from the wisdom literature. One of the most striking is from the book of Job:

> And who shut within doors the sea,
>   when it burst forth from the womb;
> When I made the clouds its garments
>   and thick darkness its swaddling hands?
> When I set limits for it
>   and fastened the bar of its door,
> And said, "Thus far shall you come but no farther,
>   and here shall your proud waves be stilled!" (Job 38:8-11).

And then there is this passage in praise of wisdom from the Book of Proverbs:

> When he established the heavens I was there,
>   when he marked out the vault over the face of the deep . . .
> When he set for the sea its limit,
>   so that the waters should not transgress his command (Prov 8:27-29).

The storm was over, and Jesus, the teacher, asked the disciples why they were afraid. Had they no faith? The disciples, we are told, were overwhelmed with awe. The expression that describes their fear, *ephobethesan phobon megan* (literally, "they were fearing a great fear"), appears only twice in the Septuagint, where it describes the fear of the sailors in the story of Jonah (Jonah 1:10, 16).

In Jonah's story, the Lord hurled a violent wind upon the sea. In their fright, the sailors prayed each to his god, but Jonah, who was fleeing from the Lord, went to sleep in the hold. When the sailors finally cast Jonah into the sea, "that the sea might be stilled," the storm abated, and they were filled with a great fear of the Lord (Jonah 1:4-16).

Unlike Jonah, Jesus was not fleeing his mission but fulfilling it. Still, for the disciples, who did not yet know who Jesus really was, this was not apparent. As the story ends, we are left with their question: "Who then is this whom even wind and sea obey?" (4:41).

Jonah was a figure for Jesus in early Christian tradition (see Luke 11:29-32; Matt 12:38-41). In Matthew, the "sign of Jonah," is an image of Jesus' death and resurrection. Something akin to it may underlie the disciples' reaction in Mark 4:35-41). Their fear could have come from the prospect of Jesus' death and resurrection, an event in which they themselves would participate through baptism (10:38-39). If so, a likely origin for the story would be early baptismal catechesis familiar to Mark's readers.

In the Land of the Gerasenes (5:1-20)

They now arrived on the other side of the sea (*eis to peran tes thalasses,* 5:1; see 4:35) into the Gentile territory of the Gerasenes. Gentiles from Idumea, Transjordan, and the region of Tyre and Sidon (see 3:7-12) had come to Jesus while he was teaching at home (3:20-35) and on the Jewish shore of the sea (4:1-34). But this was the first time Jesus himself went into a Gentile territory.

The story of the crossing of the sea (4:35-41) was principally about the Twelve. Now its focus is once again on Jesus. Now in the land of the Gerasenes the focus is on Jesus, as it was earlier at the home (3:20-35) and beside the sea (4:1-34). The next time the disciples are mentioned would be only toward the end of the section when Jesus allows only Peter, James, and John to accompany him inside the home of Jairus (5:37).

After the Twelve and Jesus arrive on the other side of the sea (5:1), the story describes a man living among the tombs (5:2-5) and his encounter with Jesus (5:6-10). It then focuses on a herd of swine, the swineherd and the people of the district (5:11-17) before returning to the man Jesus had just cured (5:18-20).

Among the Tombs (5:2-5). When Jesus got out of the boat, someone *(anthropos)* from the tombs who had an unclean spirit confronted him (5:2). The encounter is the most highly developed story in Mark's Gospel to this point. It is also unique from several points of view.

The story's introduction is interrupted after 5:2 by a long parenthesis describing the man from the tombs in considerable detail (5:3-5). The story then resumes in 5:6. Until now, Mark's stories have not focused on the reaction or response of those who were healed, but on those who witnessed the event.

Mark introduced the Gerasene demoniac as coming from the tombs. This point is repeated at the beginning and at the end of the parenthesis: "The man had been dwelling among the tombs" (5:3); "night and day among the tombs" (5:5). In fact, everything in the man's description is related to the tombs. The tombs are where he had his home *(ten katoikesin eichen)* and every effort to restrain *(desai)* him had been fruitless (5:3). No one was strong *(ischyen)* enough to restrain *(damasai)* him (5:4).

This first part of the description recalls one of Jesus' sayings, "But no one can enter a strong man's house *[ten oikian]* to plunder his property unless he first ties up *[dese]* the strong man *[ton ischyron]*" (3:27). The saying was used in Jesus' response to the scribes from Jerusalem with reference to Satan. Satan was strong, but Jesus, who was stronger, bound him and took over his domain. The same would happen to the unclean spirit in the man who lived among the tombs.

The description of the man continues with another reference to the tombs. All night long and day after day, he was among the tombs and on the hillsides crying out and bruising himself with stones (5:5). Everything about this man spoke of death, the overwhelming evil, and self-destruction.

The Encounter (5:6-10). After the long parenthesis (5:3-5), the story returns to the main point of the introduction, that is, the meeting or encounter of Jesus and the man with the unclean spirit (5:2b). In 5:2b, Mark did not say that the man simply "met" Jesus. The verb he selected, *hypantao,* is very strong, meaning "to meet against someone," "to oppose," and "to fight in battle."

In 5:6, Mark tells us more about his confrontation. The man had actually seen Jesus from a distance *(apo makrothen),*[28] had run up to him and prostrated himself *(prosekynesen)* before him. The gesture, which normally expresses worship, merely shows his recognition of Jesus' superior strength. For the reader, however, the gesture injects a note of irony. Is the man with the unclean spirit worshipping Jesus? What no one else had been able to restrain would not be a problem for Jesus.

This is the second story in which Jesus banishes an unclean spirit from someone (see 1:21-28). In the first, the unclean spirit had greeted Jesus as follows: "What have you to do with us, Jesus of Nazareth? Have you come to destroy us? I know who you are—the Holy One of God" (1:24). In the second story, the unclean spirit cries out in a loud voice: "What have you to do with me, Jesus, Son of the Most High God? I adjure you by God, do not torment me!" (5:7).

---

[28] Mark used the same expression *(apo makrothen)* after Jesus was seized at Gethsemane, when Peter followed him at a distance to the palace of the high priest (14:54).

The two different titles, "the Holy One of God" and "Son of the Most High God" correspond to the settings in which the two stories unfold. "The Holy One of God" is a title one would expect in the synagogue and the Jewish setting of Capernaum. "Son of the Most High God," on the other hand, is well suited to the Gentile context of the Gerasene territory. In the pagan Hellenistic world, the title, "Most High" *(hypsistos)* was very often attributed to Zeus. Since the title *hypsistos* could also render an ancient Hebrew title for God, "Most High," it also appears quite frequently in the Septuagint and in synagogue inscriptions in the Egyptian diaspora.

In the first story, Jesus had immediately ordered the unclean spirit out of the man (1:26). In this second story, there is an oblique reference to the fact that Jesus had been saying, "Unclean spirit, come out of the man!" (5:8). Then Jesus asks the unclean spirit a question, "What is your name?" (5:9a).

Jesus had asked questions in two of the healing stories (2:8-10; 3:4), but the questions were rhetorical questions. They were addressed to those who would witness the healing, not to the one about to be healed. In those stories, no answer was expected, and none was given. This time, Jesus asked a real question and he addressed it to the unclean spirit. The unclean spirit knew Jesus' name: "Jesus, Son of the Most High God," and Jesus wanted to know the unclean spirit's name.

The unclean spirit replied, "Legion is my name," adding "There are many of us" (5:9b). He then pleaded not to be driven away from the territory *(exo tes choras,* 5:10). Note that Legion did not beg to remain in the man but to remain in the territory, namely, that of the Gerasenes (5:1). The story began by telling about a man who was possessed. Now, widening the perspective, it tells about a territory that was possessed. To enter the new Israel, the Gentile world needed to be exorcised.

A Herd of Swine (5:11-17). The story now takes an unexpected twist. The unclean spirits presuppose that Jesus will order them out of the possessed man and beg to be cast into a herd of swine feeding on the hillside (5:11-12). That way they could continue to dwell in the territory (see 5:10). For the Jews, swine were unclean animals, not to be eaten or even touched when dead (see Lev 11:1-8). Their presence in the territory of Gerasa highlights the Gentile nature of the Gerasene territory. The irony that the unclean spirits asked to be cast into unclean animals was surely not lost on Mark's readers, who were not so very far from Christianity's Jewish origins.

Jesus did not actually order them to enter into the swine. He allowed them to go, and they went: "the herd of about two thousand rushed down a steep bank into the sea *[eis ten thalassan]*, where *[en te thalasse]* they were drowned" (5:13). The sea is mentioned twice in succession, emphasizing the place. Filled with unclean spirits, the unclean animals plunged into the depths of chaos where they belonged.

The unclean spirits had gone from the man living in the tombs and from the territory of the Gerasenes to the chaos of the sea, but even there Jesus' power extended (see 4:35-41). They were indeed strong (5:3-5), but no match for Jesus, who even allowed them to choose the means of their own destruction.

Until now, the swineherds had not even been mentioned. Their role in the story is minimal. They enter the story only to run away and report the event in the town and in the countryside. As a result, people came to see what actually had occurred (5:14).

The story now focuses on the people who heard the news and how they reacted to Jesus. Mark says, first of all, that the people came to Jesus. They did not come to the tombs, to the person who had been cured, nor to the steep bank and the water's edge where the swine disappeared. They came to Jesus.

On coming to Jesus, they saw the one who had been possessed by Legion. He was seated, clothed, and self-possessed (5:15). Earlier he had been unrestrainable, crying out, and bruising himself with stones (5:3-5). Now he was calmly seated, and no one needed to restrain him. He was clothed, a person among other persons. We assume that among the tombs he had been naked (see Luke 8:27), that is, with no personal identity. Now he was clothed like other human beings.

In ancient cultures, as in many cultures today, clothing does more than protect someone from the elements. It expresses a person's identity (see 1:6; 2:21). That is why Paul was able to refer to Christians as people who have clothed themselves with Christ. Christians have a new identity that makes them one in Christ (see Gal 3:26-28). Awareness of the significance of clothing will prove very helpful for understanding many of the stories yet to be told in Mark's Gospel.

Upon seeing the man who had been possessed by unclean spirits so self-possessed, the people were seized with fear. When those who witnessed the event told them what happened to the possessed man and the swine, they started asking Jesus to leave their territory (5:16). Note that the economic loss incurred by the destruction of the swine, a concern frequently voiced in the modern world, is not even alluded to.

The people of the territory had come to Jesus (5:15), but were not prepared to be with him or for him to be with them. Not so the man whom Jesus had cured of the unclean spirits.

The Response of the Gerasene (5:18-20). The first time Jesus cured someone of an unclean spirit, we were told absolutely nothing of the persons' subsequent relation to Jesus (1:21-28). The same was true of the other cures Jesus performed (1:40-45; 2:1-12; 3:1-6), except for Simon's mother-in-law (1:29-31). This time, however, the man who had made his home among the tombs wanted to accompany Jesus and be with him. The expression, being "with him" *(met' autou),* refers to being a follower and a disciple, one who was committed to the person of Jesus, and ready to follow him wherever he might go (see 3:14; 4:10, 36).

For the person just cured, who was a Gentile, this would have meant accompanying Jesus in the boat back to the Jewish shore. This was not to be. Gentiles were not required to become Jewish in order to be Christian. Christianity would transcend the distinction between Jews and Gentiles.

Jesus consequently told the man to return to his home *(eis ton oikon)* and to his people *(pros tous sous).* He was to announce *(apaggeilon)* to them all that the Lord *(ho kyrios)* in his mercy had done for him (5:19). He was to be the Lord's forerunner for the mission among the Gentiles, whose story will be told later in the third section of the Gospel (6:6b–8:21).

John the baptizer, a Jew, had prepared the way for Jesus' mission among the Jews. The Gerasene, a Gentile, would prepare the way for his mission among the Gentiles. So it is that the former demoniac went off to proclaim *(keryssein)* what the Lord had done for him in the Decapolis, the Ten (Greek) Cities and their territories (5:20a).

Earlier the people who had come to Jesus and seen the former demoniac were filled with fear *(ephobethesan,* 5:15) just as those in the boat with Jesus had been filled with fear when Jesus calmed the storm (4:41). However, all those in the Decapolis who heard the forerunner's proclamation were filled with wonder *(ethaumazon,* 5:20b). Everything was now ready for the Gentile mission.

Back on the Jewish Shore (5:21-43)

For the time being, Jesus had completed his work on the Gentile side of the sea. After a stormy crossing to the other shore (4:35-41), Jesus had expelled a legion of unclean spirits from a demoniac, indeed from the territory of the Gerasenes. Preparing to leave, he also appointed the man he had cured to prepare the Christian mission among the Gentiles (5:1-20). The story shows how Jesus' mission transcended the distinction between Jews and Gentiles. Both would take part in the new Israel. As the community of the Twelve, the Church had to be universal in its outreach and in its welcome.

But there remained yet another distinction, that between men and women. It too had to be dealt with. The new Israel would include Jews and Gentiles as well as men and women. The mission to the Gentiles was based on faith in Jesus' person (see 4:40-41). So would be the inclusion of the women (5:34, 36).

So it is that Jesus then returned *(palin)*[29] to the other side *(eis to peran),* that is, back to the Jewish shore (5:21), where earlier he had left the crowd (see 4:35-36). Once again, Jesus was beside the sea *(para ten thalassan,* 5:21; see 1:16; 2:13; 4:1), and a great crowd *(ochlos polys)* gathered around him (see 4:1, 36).

It is there in Jewish territory while Jesus was beside the sea that two extraordinary events took place. One involved a young Jewish girl of twelve who died from a sickness. Jesus raised her to life (5:22-24a, 35-43). The other involved a Jewish woman who had been hemorrhaging for twelve years. She touched Jesus in faith and was cured of her affliction (5:24b-34).

The healing of the woman and the raising of the young girl introduced them into the community of faith and salvation. Giving them life, Jesus abolished the distinction between men and women regarding membership in the new Israel. As the community of the Twelve, the Church would reach out to women and welcome them in the community.

Each of the two events has its own story, but in typical Markan fashion one is sandwiched within the other, and the two are told as one. As the story begins, a synagogue official *(archisynagogos)* named Jairus comes to Jesus and intercedes on behalf of his sick daughter (5:22-24). When Jesus leaves and accompanies Jairus to his home, this first story is interrupted, and the second, that of the woman with a hemorrhage is introduced (5:25-34). After curing the woman, Jesus dismisses her in peace, and the first story resumes (5:35-43).[30]

---

[29] This is the sixth time Mark uses the adverb *palin* (again) to associate a new event with a previous event. This time, *palin* connects the events on the Jewish side of the sea (5:21-43) with the events on the Gentile side (5:1-20).

[30] See James R. Edwards, "Markan Sandwiches, The Significance of Interpolations in Markan Narratives," *Novum Testamentum* XXXI, 5 (1989) 203–05. As Edwards concluded, "The woman's faith forms the center of the

The same pattern, which invites us to see each event in light of the other, has already been observed in 3:21-35 (3:21 [22-30] 31-35) and 4:2-34 (4:2-9 [10-25] 26-34). In each case, the two events were also provided with a common introductory setting (3:20; 4:1; 5:21).

Jairus and Jesus (5:22-24). In the first part of the story of Jairus' daughter (5:22-24), attention focuses almost entirely on Jairus and Jesus. Jairus refers to his daughter (5:23b), but her role does not begin until the second part (5:35-43), and even then it remains minimal (5:42a). Her personal response is not noted.

Jairus was an officer of the synagogue *(archisynagogos)*. The general context of Mark's Gospel might lead us to assume that he was an official of the synagogue at Capernaum (see 1:21; 2:1; 3:1), but the immediate context makes this very unlikely. The story introduces Jairus as "one of the synagogue officials" *(heis ton archisynagogos)*. This does not mean that he was one of several officers in the same synagogue, but that he was the officer of one of the synagogues (see 1:39). Each synagogue had but one elected leader (see Luke 8:41, *archon tes synagoges*).

Jairus could have been the officer of the synagogue at Capernaum, but Mark emphasized his position as an officer of the synagogue, not the particular synagogue in which he served. As an *archisynagogos,* a title widely used in the Greco-Roman diaspora from the first century on, Jairus was the synagogue's president, its highest officer. He was the head of the assembly, responsible for maintaining order in the assembly and appointing particular members for various functions.

The story's focus on Jairus precisely as the head of the synagogue is further sharpened by the way Jairus is introduced. Mark describes the one who comes to Jesus not as, "Jairus, one of the officials of the synagogue," but as "one of the officials of the synagogue, named Jairus" *(onomati 'Iaïros)*. Even Jairus' personal name and identity were secondary to his position at the synagogue.

When Jairus saw Jesus, he threw himself *(auton piptein)* at his feet. The gesture of respect, all the more extraordinary since it came from of the head of a synagogue, acknowledged Jesus' power over illness.[31] For the cure of his daughter, the head of the synagogue did not

---

sandwich and is the key to its interpretation. Through her Mark shows how faith in Jesus can transform fear and despair into hope and salvation. It is a powerful lesson for Jairus, as well as for Mark's readers." (205)

[31] Unlike the Gerasene, who prostrated *(prosekynesen)* before Jesus, Jairus' gesture did not imply worship.

turn to the synagogue. Instead, he fell pleading at the feet of Jesus, confident that Jesus could and would accept his request. Jairus' attitude contrasts sharply with that of the scribes and the Pharisees, who refused to recognize Jesus' authority and even attributed his power to the prince of demons (see 2:6-7, 16-17, 24; 3:6, 22).

Jairus asked Jesus to come and lay his hands on his daughter that she might be saved and live (*hina sothe kai zese*, 5:23). His request was quite unusual for a Jew living in the time of Jesus. The purpose of laying on hands for the purpose of healing is not found in the Old Testament and in early rabbinical writings. It appears, but only once, in the sectarian writings found among the Dead Sea Scrolls. The New Testament refers fairly frequently to the laying on hands as a practice of Jesus (for Mark, see 6:5; 7:32-35; 8:23-25), but Jesus rarely seems to actually do it (see 8:25). Instead he takes someone by the hand (5:41; see also 1:31; 9:27) or puts his finger into someone's ears, spits, and touches the person's tongue (7:33).

Only later, among the early Christians, and particularly among those of Hellenistic culture and Gentile background (see 16:18; Luke 4:40; 13:13; Acts 9:12, 17-18; 28:8), does laying on of hands become widespread. The Christians of Jewish origin had another practice. Instead of laying on hands, they prayed over the sick and anointed them with oil (see Jas 5:14). For Mark's readers, the head of the synagogue was consequently asking Jesus to perform a Christian symbolic gesture, and they heard his plea as a Christian prayer.

The reason the head of the synagogue begged Jesus to lay his hands on his daughter was that she might be saved (*sothe*) and live (*zese*, 5:23). Again the official used terms that had become extremely meaningful among the Christians. "To be saved" can mean to be made physically well, but it is used throughout the New Testament to refer to salvation in Christ. As such, "to be saved" includes personal and spiritual health as well as physical (see 2:1-11; see also Jas 5:14-15). "To live" can refer to being preserved from physical death, but the New Testament uses it to speak of eternal life. For Mark's readers, the head of the synagogue was thus asking Jesus to lay his hands on his daughter that she might be saved and have eternal life.

In response, Jesus went away with him, leaving the large crowd that had gathered around him by the sea (5:21). But the large crowd followed him (*ekolouthe auto*) and pressed upon him (5:24). With that the story of the head of the synagogue and Jesus is interrupted.

A Woman in the Crowd (5:25-34). Jesus had the crowd pressing upon him as he accompanied the head of the synagogue to cure his stricken daughter. Such is the setting for the extraordinary event that takes place along the way. It involves a woman in the crowd who had been hemorrhaging for twelve years. Unlike Jairus' daughter, the woman with the hemorrhage has the central role in this second encounter with Jesus.

In the biblical contexts of the Old and New Testaments, blood *(haima)* meant life. So it is, for example, that at Sinai a life-relationship between and the people of Israel was established by the sprinkling of blood (Exod 24:3-8). Or again, in the memorial of Jesus' gift of life, the early Christians spoke of his blood as the blood of the covenant that would be poured out for many (14:24). Saying that the woman was suffering from a twelve-year flow of blood was saying that life itself had been draining from her for twelve years.

But there is more. As one who was hemorrhaging, she was personally unclean (see Lev 15:25). Her presence in the midst of the crowd, where all not only touched but pressed against one another, would have made many in the crowd unclean. By touching Jesus, she would normally have made him unclean as well.

To understand the situation, it is good to review the law in Leviticus that covers such uncleanness:

> When a woman is afflicted with a flow of blood for several days outside her menstrual period, or when her flow continues beyond the ordinary period, as long as she suffers this unclean flow she shall be unclean, just as during her menstrual period (Lev 15:25).

Such was the case with the woman who came in the crowd from behind and touched Jesus. Her flow had continued beyond the ordinary period for twelve years.

The law goes on to say that as during her menstruation, any bed on which she lay and any article of furniture on which she sat would also become unclean (Lev 15:26). Finally, the law states that anyone who touched her, her bed, or her furniture also became personally unclean (15:27).

In its richness of descriptive detail, Mark's presentation of the afflicted woman is second only to that of the man living among the tombs (5:3-5). The woman had suffered from many doctors and had spent all she had, but instead of recovering she had only gotten worse (5:25-26). All the doctors had been unable to stop the flow of blood that made her personally unclean. Her plight brings to mind that of the poor widow who had been exploited by the scribes and reduced to penury (see 12:38-44). Having spent all she had, the woman with the hemorrhage could have been subjected to permanent uncleanness.

However, the woman had heard "about Jesus" *(peri tou Iesou),* and so she came from behind in the crowd and touched his cloak, saying to herself: "If I but touch his clothes, I shall be cured" *(sothesomai)* (5:28). Like the head of the synagogue, she used a Christian term to express her hope. The ordinary verbs to speak of curing were *therapeuo* (see 3:10) and *iaomai* (see 5:29). Instead, she used the verb *sozo* ("to save," see also 5:23, 34), which by Mark's time had become almost synonymous with Christian salvation. The many doctors had not been able to cure the woman so that she once again would be clean. Jesus the healer would do much more. He would grant her salvation.

The woman expressed the desire to touch Jesus' garments *(himatia),* and when she touched his cloak *(himation),* her bleeding stopped instantly *(euthys).* In her very body, she knew she was healed of her ailment (5:27-29). Some may wonder why she did not want to touch Jesus himself. Why did she want to touch only his clothing? And how is it that she was healed upon doing so?

In the cultural world of the Bible, as in so many cultures today, a person's clothing was an important expression of identity as well as a means of protection from the elements. Clothing was a personal symbol, just as someone's name was a personal word. As we pointed out earlier, that is why early tradition and St. Paul could speak of baptism and becoming a Christian as putting on or clothing oneself with Christ (see Gal 3:27). In Mark's Gospel clothing was used to identify John the Baptist as a new Elijah (1:6), to emphasize the radical newness of Jesus' message and way of life (2:21), and to speak of the new-found identity of the man who had been living naked among the tombs (5:15).

Jesus' garments were a wonderful symbolic expression of his very person. By touching his garments, one could come in touch with him.

As soon as *(euthys)* she was healed, the woman knew in her body *(egno to somati)* that she was freed from her affliction. In the same instant *(euthys),* Jesus knew himself *(epignous en auto)* that power went forth from him. Since the woman had approached him from behind, Jesus had not seen her, and so, turning around in the crowd (see 5:21, 24), he asked, "Who has touched my clothes?" (5:29-30).

Jesus' question prompted a further question from his incredulous disciples: "You see how the crowd is pressing upon you (see 5:24; 3:9-10), and yet you ask, 'Who touched me?'" (5:31). For the disciples, the question, "Who touched me?" was equivalent to, "Who touched my clothes?"

We are reminded of the disciples' reaction during the stormy crossing of the sea while Jesus was sleeping, "Teacher, do you not care that we are perishing?" (4:38). The disciples had found the crossing from the Jewish to the Gentile shore very difficult (4:35-41). Now back on the Jewish shore, given the huge crowd pressing against Jesus, they could not imagine that Jesus could be aware of a particular person touching him.

Ignoring the disciples' question, Jesus looked around to see who had touched him. The woman, fearful and trembling *(phobetheisa kai tremousa)*,[32] aware of what had happened to her, came, fell down *(prosepesen)* before Jesus, and told him the whole truth (5:32-33). We are left to assume that she told him of her hemorrhage and how she was cured. Possibly, she also acknowledged how she had exposed everyone to her uncleanness.

Her falling down before Jesus recalls how Jairus also fell at his feet (5:22). Jairus fell at Jesus' feet in supplication, recognizing Jesus' power and authority over life. Cured of her hemorrhage, the woman, filled with fear and trembling, acknowledged her personal debt to Jesus even as she begged for forgiveness.

Jesus then addressed the woman: "Daughter, your faith has saved *[sesoken]* you" (5:34; see 5:24, 28). The law of uncleanness had included a warning to the Israelites, "Lest by defiling my [God's] Dwelling, which is in your midst, their uncleanness be the cause of their death" (Lev 15:31). Because of her faith, the woman's uncleanness came to naught. Instead of death, she found life. In the new Israel, where salvation reigns, no one is personally unclean.

The disciples had not realized that there were many ways of touching Jesus. When the crowd pressed against Jesus, it did not draw power from him, but the woman did when she touched his garment in faith and with the hope of salvation (see 5:28). Her salvation came from Jesus, but only when she reached out to him in faith. With that Jesus sent her forth in peace on the way of salvation: "Go in peace and be cured of your affliction" (5:34b). She had been cleansed of her ritual impurity.[33]

Jesus and the Daughter of Jairus (5:35-43). The first part of the story of Jesus and Jairus (5:21-24) provided the setting for the story of the woman with the hemorrhage who came out of the crowd, touched Jesus' cloak, and was healed (5:25-34). The story of the woman and the way she was cured and saved has now become

[32] In Paul's letters, we find a similar expression with the words *phobos* (fear) and *tromos* (trembling). See 1 Corinthians 2:3; 2 Corinthians 7:15; Philippians 2:12; Ephesians 6:5.

[33] This is the second time Mark's Gospel deals with ritual impurity. The previous time was when Jesus cleansed a leper (1:40-45). Jesus would deal at length with ritual impurity as such later in a special discourse (7:1-23).

part of the setting for the second part of the story of Jesus and Jairus (5:35-43).[34]

While Jesus was still speaking to the woman, some people came from the synagogue official's home and said: "Your daughter has died; why trouble the teacher any longer?" (5:35). Their assumption is that Jesus could do nothing about the girl's death. We recall, however, that Jairus had asked Jesus to give his sick daughter *(thygater)* salvation and life (5:23). Besides, at that very moment, Jesus was pronouncing a woman—also called daughter *(thygater)*—healed and saved (5:35). Was it too much to expect that faith would also bring life to the daughter who had died?

Jesus disregarded the message from the official's home and spoke to him directly: "Do not be afraid; just have faith" (5:36). The woman with the hemorrhage also had been afraid. But by reaching out to Jesus in faith, this other daughter had found salvation.

Continuing toward the official's home, Jesus did not allow anyone with him *(met' autou)* to follow *(synakolouthesai)* except Peter, James, and John the brother of James (5:37). Many were with him *(met' autou),* but some were selected to be with him in a very special way (see 5:40). All three were among the first four to be called (1:16-20, 29). They were also the first three named in the list of the Twelve and the only ones in the list to whom Jesus gave a new name (3:16-17). The same circle of three would be present at the transfiguration (9:2) and in Gethsemane (14:33).

Andrew, Simon's brother, was not part of that inner circle. However, he was present with the other three on the Mount of Olives for Jesus' great eschatological discourse (13:3).

As they arrived at the synagogue official's home, Jesus could see the commotion. Inside, everyone was crying and wailing. Upon entering, Jesus asked why they were so upset: "Why this commotion and weeping? The child is not dead but asleep" (5:39).

In ancient times, death was frequently referred to as sleep. There is ample witness for this in Greek literature, including the Septuagint (see, for example, Gen 47:30; Deut 31:16; 1 Kgs 2:10). Paul too spoke of those who died as having fallen asleep *(alla katheudei,* see especially 1 Thess 4:13-18; 5:10; 1 Cor 15:18, 20, 51). And that is the way Luke described the dramatic death of Stephen: "Then he fell to his knees and cried out in a loud voice, 'Lord, do not hold this sin against them'; and when he said this, he fell asleep" (Acts 7:60).

---

[34] As James Edwards observed, "The middle story provides the hermeneutical key for the understanding of the whole," op. cit., 200.

For the early Christians, "falling asleep" had a special meaning. Those who died apart from Christ, slept the sleep of death. But those who died in Christ, slept in Christ awaiting resurrection in Christ. When Jesus referred to the child as asleep, he was not merely drawing on a common image for death. He was speaking in Christian terms. That is why those who were weeping and wailing, people without faith, laughed at him. They understood that he was not describing death as sleep, but contrasting sleep with death.

Jesus then put everybody out. Taking the father of the child, and the mother, as well as those who were with him *(met' autou),* Peter, James and John, he entered the room where the child was (5:40b). The little journey had finally reached its term. It had begun by the sea with a large crowd and had started out toward the home of the official of the synagogue. Along the way a woman of faith was saved. Messengers came out to meet them saying there was no point in continuing. Still Jesus proceeded, leaving the crowd behind, taking only Peter, James, and John. Finally they had approached the home, entered it, dismissed the unbelieving mourners, and gone into the girl's room.

The great moment had arrived. Jesus took hold of the girl's hand, as he had done for Simon's mother-in-law (1:31) and said to her in Aramaic, *"Talitha koum,"* which means, "Little girl, I say to you, arise!" (5:41). The tone of Mark's Greek translation corresponds to what one would expect of a liturgical formula. The Greek verb, *egeiro* (to rise), the same that was used in the raising of Simon's mother-in-law (1:31) and in the raising of the paralytic (2:11, 12), is associated with Jesus' own resurrection in the story of his passion-resurrection (14:28; 16:6).

The girl, who was twelve years old, rose *(aneste)* immediately and began to walk around (5:42a). This time the Greek verb for rising is *anistemi,* which appears in Jesus' prophetic announcements of his passion-resurrection (8:31; 9:31;10:34).[35]

Those present were beside themselves with amazement (*exestesan ekstasis megale,* 5:42b). The same verb had been used when Jesus' relatives thought he was out of his mind (*exeste,* 3:21). He was not, as we saw. Jesus was quite in control when he welcomed Gentiles as well as Jews to his home. Now he had given life to a young Jewish girl. It is those who accompanied him who were overwhelmed.

Jesus insisted that no one should know this (5:43a). He had not silenced the man from Gerasa (see 5:19-20). But then the man had

---

[35] See also 9:9-10 and 12:18-27, where both *anistemi* and *egeiro* are used.

wanted to be with him (*met' autou,* 5:18). Nor had Jesus silenced the woman healed of her hemorrhage. She had faith (5:39). This time, however, people did not have the faith that would have enabled them to know what truly happened.

Everyone could see, of course, that the girl who had been dead was now alive and well. But they would not be able to know that Jesus had not merely restored her to the life she had already enjoyed. He had given her new life, that is, a share in his own risen life. That is why Jesus asked that the girl be given to eat (*dothenai phagein,* 5:43b). In the context of the girl's new life in Christ, giving her to eat was more than providing her with natural sustenance. It meant giving her a place at the Lord's Supper (see 6:37).

Jesus in His Native Place (6:1-6a)

The story of Jesus and the New Israel reaches its climax in his native place, where Jesus and his disciples came after leaving the shores of the Sea of Galilee (6:1; see 5:21). This was the first time Jesus came to his "native place" (*patris*) since the beginning of his ministry.

We assume that the native place refers to Nazareth (see 1:9), but the Gospel does not give the name of the town. For Mark's story, what is important is not Jesus' relationship to Nazareth, a town in the hills of lower Galilee, but his relationship to his native place, the place where Jesus had grown up and was well-known. In his native place, people knew Jesus' family and had certain expectations regarding him and his behavior.

Those expectations had nothing to do with Jesus' extraordinary mission. Fulfilling his mission, Jesus called disciples to a profound renewal of Israel (1:14–3:6). He also called Israel to transcend itself and become a new Israel, based not on family, or ethnicity, or even on a long history of shared spiritual experiences (3:7–6:6a).

On the Sabbath, Jesus taught in the synagogue of his native place (6:2). We are not told what he taught there, but from the astonished reaction of those present we must assume that he presented his message of the new Israel and how it transcended family ties, as we saw earlier in this section (3:20-35). We are not surprised then to see that Jesus' family is precisely the issue at which the synagogue community blocks.

Many in the assembly were astonished at Jesus' teaching. They could not account for his wisdom and mighty deeds, both of which were very obvious (6:2b). Jesus' wisdom (*sophia*) and mighty deeds (*dynameis*) refer to all we have read in the gospel. We are not told how the people of Nazareth came to know of these things, but from a literary point of view that does not matter. If suffices that the readers know by reading or hearing the gospel.

Local Expectations (6:3-4). What Jesus said and did raised questions about his identity. For the people of his native place, Jesus was a carpenter, or at least a craftsman, and they expected him to speak and act like a carpenter *(tekton)*. He belonged to a particular family, and they expected him to speak and act like other members of his family. Was he not the son of Mary and the brother of four men they knew, James, Joses, Judas, and Simon? Did he not have sisters, whom they also know and who lived among them (6:3)?

Local expectations were based entirely on the trade Jesus had once practiced and on what they knew, or thought they knew, of his family. Hearing Jesus, they thought they knew him from knowing his occupation and family. In effect, they reduced his identity to those who surrounded him as he grew up. They could not see that Jesus was more than one of them. They could not see that Jesus' association with them called them to transcend their own identity and join him in a new relationship, based not on family, but on doing the will of God (see 3:35).

Those who thought they knew Jesus could not see him with eyes of faith, and so they were scandalized over him (6:3b), that is, they found him an obstacle and they stumbled over him.

Jesus responded with a saying about prophets, who are not without honor, that is, who are honored, except in their native place, among their relatives and in their own home (6:4). The saying points to the most basic issue concerning Jesus' identity and those who are associated with him. As in the case of other prophets, those who knew Jesus through any other relationship had the greatest difficulty recognizing him as prophet.

Lack of Faith (6:5-6a). Because the people of Jesus' native place were unable to receive him as a prophet, he was unable to perform any mighty deed *(dynamis)* there (6:5a). Throughout the Gospel, we see how Jesus cured many, but Jesus attributed the cure to their faith. We see this most clearly in Jesus' response to the woman whom he cured of a long-standing hemorrhage: "Daughter, your faith has saved you" (5:34). Jesus is able to cure, but his curing gesture is part of a faith dialogue. It calls for openness in faith on the part of others. Without faith, Jesus' power has no effect.

In his native place, Jesus did cure a few who were sick by laying hands on them (6:5b; see 5:23). The story had already allowed for this by limiting those who were scandalized to "many" *(polloi),* not all. The unit and the whole section on the New Israel ends with the statement that Jesus was amazed at their lack of faith *(apistia,* 6:6a). Faith is what would have made the difference. It is also what makes all the difference for anyone who encounters the person of Jesus.

The questions remain: "Is he not the carpenter, the son of Mary, the brother of four brothers and several sisters?" Faith alone allows us to see that Jesus is more than the carpenter, and that family ties tell us nothing of Jesus' true identity. In this context, the question whether Jesus actually had brothers and sisters, even when we interpret these as cousins, is a distraction from the real issue. Jesus is not defined by his natural historical relationships. Others are defined by their relationship to him.

With that, the second section with its story of the constitution of the Twelve and its implications for Jesus' relatives, the Jewish people, as well as for the Gentiles comes to an end (3:7–6:6a). The first section (1:14–3:6) ended with the Pharisees seeking out the Herodians to find a way to destroy Jesus (3:6). The second section ends with Jesus' amazement at the lack of faith among people in his native place (6:6a). Again, the next verse could very well be the opening line of the passion: "The Passover and the Feast of Unleavened Bread were to take place in two days' time" (14:1a).

But this was only the second section (3:7–6:6b) of "the beginning of the gospel of Jesus Christ [the Son of God]" (1:1). For Mark, the story of Jesus and the Twelve led the next section, the story of Jesus and the mission of the Twelve (6:6b–8:21). Called to follow Jesus, and constituted as the Twelve, the Twelve are now sent on mission to both Jews and Gentiles.

VI

❦ Section III ❧

Jesus and the Mission of the Twelve

Mark 6:6b–8:21

The first section (1:14–3:6) began with a summary of Jesus' mission and ministry. After John was handed over, "Jesus came to Galilee proclaiming the gospel of God" (1:14). The summary also included what Jesus proclaimed: "This is the time of fulfillment. The kingdom of God is at hand. Repent, and believe in the gospel" (1:15). The section ended with the Pharisees taking counsel with the Herodians on how to put Jesus to death (3:6). For his part, Jesus grieved at their hardness of heart (3:5).

The second section (3:7–6:6a) also began with a summary of Jesus' mission and ministry. Jesus was by the sea, and large crowds came to him from Jewish and Gentile territories (3:7-12). The section ended with the people of Jesus' native place taking offense at him (6:3). For his part, Jesus was amazed at their lack of faith (6:6a).

With that, the Gospel again stands at the threshold of the passion (see 3:6). As in 3:6, however, the Gospel has barely begun. By creating the Twelve (3:13-19), Jesus established the parameters of the new Israel. Now, Jesus would send the Twelve on mission. As we leave the synagogue of Nazareth, the Gospel moves on to its third section, telling about Jesus and the mission of the Twelve (6:6b–8:21).

An Overview

Like the first and section sections, the third begins with a double introduction, including a short summary of Jesus' ministry (6:6b;

see 1:14-15; 3:7-12) and an important new development concerning the disciples. Called (1:16-20) and constituted as the Twelve (3:13-19), the Twelve are now sent on mission (see 6:7-30). They would be Jesus' apostles.

In the first and second sections, the summary of Jesus' ministry and the story of the disciples received equal or nearly equal emphasis. In the third section, most of the emphasis is placed on the mission of the Twelve. In his instructions to the Twelve, Jesus highlights the similarities and the differences between their mission journey and the epic journey of Israel to the land of promise. Together, the two units (6:6b, 7-30) introduce the basic themes of the Gospel's third section.

The body of the section (6:31–8:21) is framed by the fundamental theme of the breaking of the bread (6:34-44; 8:1-9). The Gospel has already shown how Jesus transcended the synagogue, scribal authority, and the sabbath (1:21-31; 2:23–3:6) and how the Church as a new Israel transcended one's natural family, place of origin, and the Israel of old (3:20-35; 6:1-6a). In this third section, we see how the apostolic mission of the Twelve had to reach out to all peoples— Jews and Gentiles, men and women—and gather them in the family of Jesus (see 3:31-35).

As in the previous two sections, the body is divided into two parts. The first presents the beginnings of the apostolic mission among the Jews (6:31–7:23). It focuses on the difficulties experienced by the apostolic community, their lack of understanding (6:52), and on the opposition coming from the Pharisees and the scribes from Jerusalem (7:1-23). This first part is dominated by an extraordinary event, in which Jesus nourishes five thousand men with five loaves and two fish and the Twelve gather twelve baskets of the fragments left over (6:34-44).

The second part shows how the apostolic mission spread from Jewish men to Gentile men and women (7:24–8:21). Like the first part, it emphasizes the apostles' lack of understanding. This second part is dominated by another extraordinary event, in which Jesus nourishes four thousand people with seven loaves and some fish, and how his disciples gathered seven baskets of fragments left over (8:1-9).

Like the first and second sections, the third also ends with the theme of rejection. In their hardness of heart (*porosis tes kardias,* 3:5), the Pharisees took counsel with the Herodians against Jesus (3:1-6). In their lack of faith (*apistia,* 6:6a), the people of Jesus' native place took offense at him (6:1-6a). Both refused to repent and believe in the gospel (1:15).

Now, the apostles fail to understand who Jesus is and how their mission was for all peoples. They still did not understand about the bread (see 6:52). Were their hearts also hardened (see 3:5)? Did they also lack faith (see 6:6a)? Jesus challenged them with their lack of understanding (8:14-21).

With the third section, the first part of the gospel (1:14–8:21) dramatically comes to an end, as Jesus asks the apostles, "Do you still not understand?" (8:21)

Setting and *Dramatis Personae*

As we did in the first and second sections (1:14–3:6; 3:7–6:6a), we begin by examining the geographical and temporal settings, and the personages who play a role in the third section.

In the third section, geography and specific places continue to be very significant. As in the first and second sections, the geographical setting is symbolic and supports the development of Mark's theology.

We also have a few temporal indications, some of which are symbolic. In this section, Mark introduces the theme of "three days" (8:2) that will be extremely significant in the second part of the Gospel (8:22–16:8).

We also meet new personages, including Gentiles. Like the geographical and temporal indications, the personages have a symbolic role in the development of the mission of the Church.

Geographical Setting: Images of the Exodus

As in the first and second sections, the setting for the third is wonderfully suited to its literary themes and development. The first section with its story of Jesus and the call of the first disciples (1:14–3:6) unfolded exclusively in Galilee, especially by the sea, at Capernaum, in the synagogue, in the homes of Simon and Andrew and Levi, in the desert, and in other villages and synagogues of Galilee. There was also a field of grain ready for harvesting.

In the second section, where Jesus created the Twelve as the foundation for the new Israel (3:7–6:6a), much of the setting remains the same. But for the first time, Jesus went beyond Galilee to the land of the Gerasenes, where he cured a man who would become his forerunner in the Decapolis. Again, much of the action takes place by the sea, now a violent personification of evil threatening the foundations of the new Israel. There was also the mountain, where Jesus made the Twelve.

The third section is similar to the first and second, but again we discover striking new developments. Jesus does more than walk by the sea, teach from a boat on the sea, and command its waves to be still. He actually walks on the sea while his disciples in the boat were struggling against the wind, making little headway (6:45-52). The section includes four sea journeys. Two are mentioned briefly (6:31-33; 8:10). The other two are major events told with considerable detail (5:45-52; 8:13-21).

Until now, very little of the Gospel has unfolded in the desert, surprisingly after the role it played in the prologue (1:3, 4, 12-13) and in the first section (1:35, 45). In the third section, the desert is the setting for two of Jesus' great wonders, in which Jesus nourished five thousand men with five loaves and four thousand with seven loaves. The first event (6:34-44) took place on the Jewish side of the sea, the second on the Gentile side (8:1-9).

The expression used to evoke the desert and the great desert experiences of ancient Israel is "desert place" *(eremos topos)*. In this section, it refers to a place away from the crowd where one can find rest and nourishment (6:31-32) but also where one can be pursued (6:33; see 1:4-5, 35-37). For the disciples, it was impossible to nourish the crowd in the desert (6:35-36; 8:4). For Jesus, it was the perfect place to nourish them.

Capernaum, its synagogue, the home of Simon and Andrew and the home of Levi are not mentioned in this section. Neither does the synagogue of Jesus' native place or any other synagogue. There is a reference to going home *(eis oikon,* 7:17). Earlier in the Gospel, this could have referred to the home of Simon and Andrew, but at this point it refers to the home of Jesus and his disciples, wherever that might be. The home is defined by the presence of Jesus, not by its location.

There is another home in this section, in the district of Tyre, where a Greek woman approached Jesus requesting a cure for her daughter (7:24-30). In the first section of the Gospel, Jesus entered the home of Simon and Andrew (1:29-34) and the home of Levi, the tax collector (2:13-17). In the second section, he welcomed to his home large crowds coming from both Jewish and Gentile territories (3:20-35). Now, he himself goes to a home in the Gentile region of Tyre where he ministers to Gentiles.

Finally, there are the villages (6:6b; see 1:38) and a wide range of places and districts, both Jewish and Gentile, where the mission unfolds. There is Bethsaida (6:45; see 8:22), Gennesaret (6:53), the districts of Tyre (7:24), Sidon (7:31), and the Decapolis (7:31), and the region of Dalmanutha (8:10).

Until now, crowds had come to Jesus from the regions of Tyre and Sidon (3:8), but he himself had never been there. He had been to the territory of the Gerasenes (5:1), but no further. He had sent a Gentile forerunner to prepare his way in the Decapolis (5:20). Now Jesus came to the Decapolis personally.

Temporal Setting: Approaching the Third Day

There are only six temporal indications in this section, each one important. Two of them are in the first story of the breaking of the bread (6:34-44). Mark emphasized that it was late, first through the narrator, "by now it was already late" *(ede horas polles genomenes),* and then through the disciples, who came to Jesus and said, "It is already very late" *(ede hora polle)* (6:35).

Later, in the story of the crossing of the sea, Mark again emphasizes it was late. "When it was evening" *(opsias genomenes)* (6:47), the disciples were far out on the sea, and Jesus came to them "about the fourth watch of the night" *(peri tetarten phylaken tes nyktos)* (6:48), that is, between 3:00 and 6:00. Outside the passion and resurrection, the Gospel does not usually indicate the time of day, or night, when something happened.

Mark also introduces the second story of the breaking of the bread (8:1-9) with a general temporal reference, "In those days" *(en ekeinais tais hemerais)* (8:1). Then, Jesus tells the disciples that the crowd had been with him "now for three days" *(ede hemerai treis)* (8:2). As we shall see, Christian tradition associated the third day with Jesus' resurrection as the day of salvation.

Dramatis Personae

The cast of characters in the third section includes Jesus and the disciples, the crowds, the Pharisees and the scribes, Herod and his company, and two special people, each with a story of personal need.

Jesus remains a key figure, but there is a difference. The first and second sections focused directly on Jesus. Once called (1:16-20) and constituted as the Twelve (3:13-19), the disciples were always present, but the spotlight was on Jesus, who taught and formed the disciples as he went about his own ministry. The disciples stayed in the shadows, more often than not, even for entire episodes (see, for example, 2:1-12; 5:1-20).

In the third section, the Gospel's main focus is on the disciples. Emerging from the shadows, the disciples stand at the center together with Jesus, who challenges and encourages them in their universal mission. As the Twelve of Christ (6:7) and Jesus' apostles (6:30), they still do not understand even essential matters connected with their mission (see 6:52; 7:14-21). Jesus stays with them, ready to teach them.

The crowd has played an important role from the very beginning of the Gospel. The prologue had spoken of the crowd that came to John in the desert from the whole Judean countryside and from Jerusalem (1:5). Coming from Galilee, Jesus was an exception, and not one of the crowd.

The first section (1:14–3:6) showed how a huge crowd of Galileans came to Jesus at home (1:32-33), in desert places (1:45), and by the sea (2:13). At this point, the emphasis was on the rapid growth of the crowd and how it affected Jesus' life and ministry (1:35-39, 45; 2:1-4, 13).

In the second section (3:7–6:6a), the crowd continued to grow, but the emphasis shifted to how the crowd became much more diversified. The crowd included Galileans, Judeans, and people from Jerusalem, like those who had come to John in the desert (1:2-13), but also people from Idumea, from beyond the Jordan, and from the surroundings of Tyre and Sidon (3:7-9). As in the first section, the new crowd came to Jesus at home (3:20, 32-34) and by the sea (4:1; 5:21). The size of the crowd remains important, but greater prominence is given to the crowd's ethnic diversity.

Now, in the third section, the disciples felt overwhelmed by the crowd. In response, Jesus taught them to gather the crowd in communities of one hundred and fifty (6:40). In the first part of the section, the crowd included only Jewish men (6:44). In the second part, it included both Jews and Gentiles, as well as men and women (8:9).

From this development, we see how the Gospel used the crowd to set out the scope of the Christian mission. Jesus, the disciples, and the new Israel were to reach out to all peoples and welcome them to the breaking of the bread (6:34-44; 8:1-9). The crowd was not to remain without a shepherd (see 6:34).

As before, we meet Pharisees and scribes, and especially those who came from Jerusalem. These had first figured in the first section in a series of five conflicts with Jesus and his disciples (2:1–3:6). At the close of the fifth conflict, we saw how the Pharisees went to take counsel with the Herodians on how they might put Jesus to death (3:6).

In the second section, some scribes from Jerusalem accused Jesus of being possessed by Beelzebul and of driving out demons by the power of demons (3:22). Now in the Gospel's mission section, they object to the behavior of Jesus' disciples, who did not observe the Jewish traditions concerning eating and meals (7:1-16). They also test Jesus with a demand for a heavenly sign (8:11-13). Theirs is a bad leaven, like that of Herod (8:15; see 3:6). Their role in this third section is to uphold and represent traditions and practices incompatible with the mission of the Twelve to all peoples.

King Herod has an important part in the discussion of Jesus' identity (6:14-16), and an even greater part in a flashback describing the events and circumstances that led to the death of John the Baptist (6:17-29). The flashback tells about Herod's birthday banquet, attended by Herod's courtiers, military officers, and the leading men of Galilee, with Herodias in the wings, and Herodias' daughter in the limelight. The story includes some of the finest and most highly developed characterization in the Gospel.

Mark's individual personages tend to be stock characters. Wearing a mask, they are personally nameless and faceless. They enter the Gospel as representatives of a people, a segment of society, a way of life, or a particular affliction or attitude.

So with a woman, who was Greek and Syrophoenician, and with her daughter, who was afflicted with an unclean spirit (7:24-30). With this woman, both the Gentile world and the world of women enter the Gospel. As a Greek woman, a Syrophoenician, she brings meaning and excitement to her dialogue with Jesus.

The same is true of a deaf man suffering from a speech impediment (7:31-37). Besides his infirmities, it is significant that he was from the Decapolis, the land of the Ten Cities, presumably a Gentile, and that Jesus cured him.

Jesus the Teacher (6:6b)

Like the two previous sections, the third opens with a brief summary of Jesus' life and ministry. First, Mark had introduced Jesus as a proclaimer of the gospel of God (1:14-15). Second, he introduced him as a healer, boldly confronting evil spirits (3:7-12). In the third section, he presents Jesus as an itinerant teacher (6:6b).

This third summary is by far the briefest: "He went around to the villages in the vicinity teaching" *(didaskon)* (6:6b). Nothing is said of the content of his teaching (compare with 1:14-15) and of the villages where he taught (compare with 3:7-13). It was enough to say that Jesus was a teacher, one who went about teaching in the villages of the vicinity.

This is not the first time the Gospel presents Jesus as a teacher. After placing the entire first section under the banner of Jesus as a proclaimer (1:14-15), Mark referred to various events and activities of Jesus as teaching (1:22-27), healing, and exorcising (1:32-34). Later, after summarizing Jesus' mission anew in terms of healing (3:7-12), he included the long discourse, where Jesus teaches in parables (4:1-34).

As an effective proclaimer and healer, Jesus was a good teacher. As an effective teacher, he was a powerful proclaimer and healer. The difference between these ministries is not so much in the nature of the activities as in their primary purpose and the needs they met.

There were those who needed to be awakened with good news, those needing to be healed, and those needing to be taught. Jesus' ministry responded to those distinct and overlapping needs. For some, his ministry was preaching. For others, the same ministry was healing. For still others, it was teaching. Accordingly, Mark's summary of Jesus as an itinerant teacher (6:6b) does not introduce a new set of activities. It simply views his preaching or proclamation and his healing or exorcising from a different angle, that of teaching or catechesis.

The most remarkable thing about this summary is its brevity, and this alone alerts us to a major shift in the Gospel's focus. Until now, Jesus dominated Mark's literary stage. Now the Twelve remain with him at the center. Taught by Jesus, they will pursue his mission beyond the confines of Galilee to all nations (see 13:10).

Right along, we have seen how Mark told the story of the early Church while telling that of Jesus and his first followers. The conflicts between the disciples and the Pharisees and the struggle of the new Israel to welcome all peoples were told as the story of Jesus. At the same time, they reflected the experience of the apostolic Church.

As we move into the third section, the emphasis on the early Church is even stronger, a fact reflected in the very short summary of Jesus' ministry (6:6b) and the very long account of the apostolic mission (6:7-30). Mark helps us to see the life of the Church in light of the story of Jesus and the life of Jesus in light of the story of the early Church.

Jesus Sends the Twelve on Mission (6:7-30)

The mission of the Twelve (6:7-30) unfolds in three units. First, Marks tells how Jesus sent the Twelve in pairs and how they fulfilled their mission (7:7-13). Second, interrupting the story line, Mark tells what Herod and others thought of Jesus (6:14-16, 17-29). This second unit includes a long flashback telling of John's imprisonment, Herod's birthday feast, and the event that led to John's execution (6:17-29). Third, as the account of John's death and burial comes to a close, Mark returns to the original story, and tells how the apostles returned from the mission and reported to Jesus (6:30).

We are familiar with this sandwiching format from the story of Jairus' daughter (5:21-24, 35-43), which was interrupted by that of the women with a hemorrhage (5:25-34). The same literary technique was observed in Jesus' teaching regarding his true relatives (3:21, 22-30, 31-35) and in the parable discourse (4:2-9, 10-25, 26-33).

In each case, the story that interrupts the main narrative line provides a significant commentary on it. The two stories, therefore, need to be read in light of one another. In the present case, our biggest challenge is to see how Jesus' identity and the story of John's death and burial are related to the mission of the Twelve.

The Commissioning of the Twelve (6:7-13)

The Gospel already had referred to the mission when Jesus called the first disciples and told them he would make them fishers of human beings (1:17). It did so again when Jesus made the Twelve that they might be with him *(met' autou)* and be sent to preach with authority to drive out demons (3:14-15). The call of the first disciples and the constitution of the Twelve (3:13-19) thus announced the theme of the Gospel's third major passage on the disciples (6:7-30). The disciples had been called (1:16-20) and constituted as the Twelve (3:13-19) in view of the apostolic mission (6:7-30).[1]

The story of the commissioning of the Twelve is found in Matthew 10:5-15 and in Luke 9:1-6, as well as in Mark 6:7-13. Of these, Mark's account is the oldest, that is, written prior to the other two. However, the accounts in Matthew and Luke, while written later, refer to a historical context that is older than the one in Mark. Mark adapted the traditional story to address a new situation at the time of his writing *(circa* A.D. 70). Matthew and Luke recalled situations that had long disappeared by the mid-80s when they were writing, as they distinguished the historical periods of Jesus and the early Church.[2]

---

[1] The mission of the apostolic community is consequently one of the main themes of Mark's Gospel. This needs to be emphasized. In recent decades, the study of Mark has focused on the gospel's Christology and the cost of discipleship. Both are important, but so is the Gospel's missiology. For a synthesis of Mark's missiology, see Donald Senior, C.P., and Carroll Stuhlmueller, C.P., *The Biblical Foundations for Mission* (Maryknoll, N.Y.: Orbis Books, 1983) 211–32.

[2] From this point of view, like John, we can describe Mark as more symbolic and Matthew and Luke as more historical.

The principal differences between Mark and the other Synoptics are these. Jesus' instruction in Matthew and Luke does not allow for a walking stick and sandals (see Matt 10:10; Luke 9:3 and 10:4). In Mark, Jesus not only allows these but explicitly orders the Twelve to take them along: "He instructed them to take nothing for the journey but a walking stick—no food, no sack, no money in their belts. They were, however, to wear sandals but not a second tunic" (6:8-9).

Further, in Matthew, Jesus instructs the Twelve not to go into Gentile territory or in a Samaritan city but only to the lost sheep of the house of Israel (see Matt 10:5-6). As he told a Canaanite woman, Jesus himself had been sent only for the lost sheep of the house of Israel (see Matt 15:24). Only after his passion and resurrection would Jesus send the Eleven to all nations (see Matt 28:19).

In Luke, nothing is said about this restriction but it seems to be assumed. The mission to the Samaritans begins only with the great journey to Jerusalem (see Luke 9:51-56), and the mission to the Gentiles, announced after Jesus' passion and resurrection (see Luke 24:47), is told in the Acts of the Apostles.

In Mark, the mission of the Twelve had no such limitations. It did develop in stages, as we can see from the two stories of the breaking of the bread (6:34-44; 8:1-9) and the events from the first to the second. But in Mark, the mission to the Gentiles did not wait for Jesus' passion and resurrection or the descent of the Holy Spirit.

The first story of the breaking of the bread took place in Jewish territory where Jesus nourished five thousand men (6:34-44). The second took place in Gentile territory where Jesus nourished four thousand people (8:1-9). Between the two events, the Gospel shows how the mission moved from the restricted Jewish context to the broader Jewish and Gentile context of the Decapolis (6:45–7:37; see especially vv. 24 and 31). Both events are presented as part of the disciples' mission during the earthly life of Jesus. From a historical point of view, Mark took an event that followed Jesus' passion and resurrection and inserted it within the story of Jesus' Galilean ministry.

The first thing to notice is that the mission is about the Twelve, not the disciples in general (6:7). First, Jesus called the Twelve to himself *(proskaleitai tous dodeka)*. The Twelve were to be with him, committed to him, and with him committed to the kingdom of God. This first aspect sums up the meaning of their call (1:16-20) and their constitution as the Twelve (3:13-19).

Second, Jesus sent them out in pairs *(erxato autous apostellein dyo dyo),* as witnesses to his life and teaching. For the early Christians, this surely included the passion and resurrection.

Third, Jesus gave them power *(edidou autois exousia)* over unclean spirits. Committed to Jesus and commissioned to be his witnesses, the Twelve had the authority and the power to silence and banish the power of evil. Jesus himself had this power (1:21-28, 32-34, 39; 3:11-12) as he went about proclaiming the kingdom of God (1:14-15), and he now bestowed it on the Twelve to continue and extend his mission in the world.

The story continues with Jesus' instructions for the mission. The first part is taken up with what the Twelve were to bring or not bring on their missionary journey (6:8-9). As was noted earlier, the Twelve were to carry a walking stick, a staff, and to wear sandals. They were also to have one tunic, not two. All of these details are significant.

The staff, the sandals, and the tunic evoke the instructions given to the Israelites on the eve of their flight from Egypt. "This is how you are to eat it: with your loins girt, sandals on your feet and your staff in hand, you shall eat like those who are in flight. It is the Passover of the LORD" (Exod 12:11).

These instructions for the Passover were given in the historical context of the exodus. They were meant for the annual commemorative renewal of the Passover, a family liturgical celebration in which the early disciples and many of the early Christians had participated. The Jewish customs surrounding the celebration may have changed, but the instructions for the celebration remained the same, evoking the ancient tradition of Israel's great journey from bondage to freedom.

In setting out on their Christian missionary journey, the Twelve were like the Israelites going forth in the Exodus. Their Christian journey would be a new exodus, a personal passage from slavery to freedom. However, their exodus journey would not be just personal, but missionary. Liberated, the new Israel would be a liberator.

The Twelve were also to wear a tunic, which, like all garments (see 1:6; 2:21; 5:15) was symbolic of a person's identity. In this context, the one tunic spoke of their life as witnesses committed to Jesus and the kingdom of God. That is why they were not to have second tunic, which might have indicated a divided allegiance. Nothing was to render their witness ambiguous.

Like the Israelites, with staff in hand, sandals on their feet, and their loins girt, the Twelve were to have a staff, wear sandals, and have one tunic. But they were told explicitly to take nothing else for the journey, no food, no traveling bag, and no money in their belts. These negative instructions are very different from those given to the Israelites for the Exodus.

If the Israelites did not have food, it is only because of their hasty departure: "They had been rushed out of Egypt and had no opportunity even to prepare food for the journey" (Exod 12:39). Besides, they were to provide themselves with all the riches they could amass at the expense of the Egyptians: "Instruct your people that every man is to ask his neighbor, and every woman her neighbor, for silver and gold articles and for clothing" (Exod 11:2).

In the Old Testament, attention focused on the land the Israelites were leaving. They were an exploited people, forced to leave a land they would not otherwise have left. Their journey was one of liberation. In the New Testament exodus, attention focused rather on the people to whom the apostles were being sent. The Christians were not forced to leave. They accepted to leave because they were being summoned by the demands of the Kingdom. Here, too, there is liberation, but not in relation to the place and the people left behind, but in relation to the people to whom they were sent.

The second part of the instructions for the mission (6:10-11) deals with hospitality. Those who went on mission did not rely on anything they brought with them, but on the hospitality of those to whom they were sent. They came not to give, but receive food, money, and shelter. There would be no confusing the gift they brought on their mission, Jesus' gospel of repentance *(metanoia),* faith, peace, and spiritual healing. They were simply to accept the hospitality offered them. When none was offered, they were to leave the place and go on. The implications of this demand will be spelled out in the stories of the breaking of the bread (6:34-44; 8:1-9).

The story now tells how the Twelve fulfilled the mission Jesus gave them (6:12-13). They went and preached repentance, cast out many demons, and anointed the sick with oil, curing many of them. Their proclamation of repentance recalls the mission of John the Baptist (1:4), but the repentance they proclaimed was for all human beings in the context of the new Israel.

The anointing with oil was a common healing practice in the Hellenistic world. The early Christians adopted it, and by the time of Mark's writing it was a Christian tradition. Elsewhere in the New Testament, its clearest expression is in the letter of James, which asks: "Is anyone among you sick?" That person "should summon the presbyters of the church, and they should pray over him and anoint [him] in the name of the Lord" (James 5:14).

Jesus' Identity and the Mission of the Twelve (6:14-29)

Many factors, both religious and secular, contribute to the shape of the mission. Some have to do with culture, social context, economic conditions, and religious background. Others come from tradition, history, Church teaching, and theology. Still others are connected with the person, life, mission, and teaching of Jesus.

Of all these factors, none is more fundamental than the person of Jesus. While respecting all the others and giving them their due weight, the nature and scope of the Church's mission ultimately depends on the question, "Who is Jesus?" How we answer the question is the single most important factor for defining the mission. Consequently, it was extremely important that, after describing the mission of the Twelve (6:7-13), the Gospel should focus on the identity of Jesus (6:14-16).

It is in this connection that King Herod enters the Gospel. He had heard about the Twelve and how they were preaching repentance, driving out demons, and curing the sick. Through the ministry of the Twelve, Jesus' fame was spreading further and further. On all sides, people were asking who he might be. Answers varied. For some, Jesus was Elijah, for others, a prophet, one among many. For Herod, Jesus was John, the one he beheaded, now risen from the dead.

Were any of these opinions right? Did some at least approximate the truth? At this point, the Gospel does not answer directly. It was enough to raise the question. The answer is left for later when Jesus himself raises the question of his identity (8:27-30). At the same time, however, the Gospel gives an indirect answer in the story of the death of John the Baptist (6:17-29).

The story of John's death is like a historical parable, prefiguring the death of Jesus and its implications for the disciples. It enters the Gospel as a flashback, telling how Herod had arrested, imprisoned, and beheaded John, and how John's disciples had come to take his body and laid it in a tomb.

The story of John's death is very rich in descriptive detail, movement, characterization, and dialogue. The most colorful part of the story is Herod's birthday banquet, which evokes a wide range of emotions and responses. Rarely is Markan story so visual.

Very often, Mark is content with summarizing activities, events, and reactions to them. He has so refined the art of summary in the Gospel that very often we hardly notice that all we have been given is a summary. The account of how the Twelve fulfilled their mission is a good example (6:12-13). Mark presented what was surely a sequence of events in general terms. The same is true of the series of opinions regarding the identity of Jesus (6:14-16).

By comparison with the summary (6:14-16), the story of the death of John (6:17-29) stands nearly alone. Outside the story of Jesus' passion and resurrection (14:1–16:8), the only story that approaches its narrative qualities is that of the Gerasene demoniac (5:1-20).

Who Is Jesus? (6:14-16). This is not the first time the question of Jesus' identity has come up in Mark's Gospel. We were first alerted to its importance in the prologue, where we learned that Jesus, who came from Nazareth in Galilee, was God's beloved son (1:9-11).

Then in the first section of the Gospel we heard a man with an unclean spirit cry out: "What have you to do with us, Jesus of Nazareth? Have you come to destroy us? I know who you are—the Holy One of God!" (1:24; see also 5:7). The reader answers the rhetorical question: "Jesus of Nazareth, the Holy One of God, has indeed come to destroy you." We then watch it happen as Jesus expels the unclean spirit and reduces its power to nothing.

In the prologue and in Jesus' first confrontation with demonic evil, the question itself is presupposed rather than raised. Instead of the question, we are given an answer. Jesus is a man from Nazareth of Galilee, but there is more to Jesus than that. Jesus of Nazareth is actually God's beloved Son, the Holy One of God. In this, both the Spirit of God and the unclean spirit concur.

For the reader, the proclamation raises further questions. How can Jesus of Nazareth be God's beloved Son, the Holy One of God? What does Jesus' divinity mean in relation to prior biblical tradition? How does it reveal itself in Jesus' life and ministry? What does it say about the identity of those who become followers of Jesus?

Although at first the question itself is presupposed, it does not take very long before it comes up explicitly. The context is always experiential. In the synagogue at Capernaum, when Jesus drives out the unclean spirit, those in the synagogue are filled with amazement: "What is this? A new teaching with authority. He commands even the unclean spirits and they obey him" (1:27).

In this context, the question of Jesus' identity arises from what he does. Confronted by this extraordinary manifestation of authority and power, the synagogue assembly questions its previous assumptions concerning Jesus' identity. The narrator leads us to believe that they had thought of Jesus as a scribe comparable to other scribes. They now see that this was not the case (see 1:22).

Later in the Gospel, when Jesus says to a paralytic that his sins are forgiven, the scribes are the ones who raise the question: "Why does this man speak that way? He is blaspheming. Who but God alone can forgive sins?" (2:7). Recalling the baptism of Jesus and the hopeless acknowledgment of the unclean spirits in defeat, the reader answers the scribes' question and protest.

For the scribes, Jesus was only "this man." For them, he was certainly not God, who alone forgives sins. For the Christian reader, Jesus is not an ordinary man. He is God's beloved Son, endowed with the authority to declare a person's sins forgiven. As God's beloved Son, he is also the ultimate human being, the Son of Man, the epitome of human creation, fulfilling all that human beings were called to be, and more. That is why he was able to answer the scribes objection: "The Son of Man has authority to forgive sins on earth" (2:10).

Still later, in the second section, the question of Jesus' identity arises when he commands the winds and calms a great storm at sea. The disciples were with him in the boat. The disciples thought of him as a teacher: "Teacher, do you not care that we are perishing?" (4:38). But once the wind had ceased in obedience to Jesus' command and there ensued a great calm, they were filled with awe and they asked one another: "Who then is this whom even wind and sea obey?" (4:41).

The disciples' experience of Jesus, whose authority extended over creation, led them to question their prior assumption that he was just a teacher, albeit one whose authority far exceeded that of the scribes. For Mark's story, it was enough at this point to raise the question. No answer was attempted. By itself, raising the question has brought the reader much deeper into the mystery of Jesus' identity.

Finally, the Gospel showed how the people of the synagogue in Jesus' native place reacted when Jesus taught there. They recognized that Jesus' powerful teaching could not have come from the person they knew as "the carpenter, the son of Mary, and the brother of James and Joses and Judas and Simon." As they put it, "Are not his sisters here with us?" (6:2-3). Earlier on, Jesus' own relatives had thought that he was out of his mind (3:21). The people of Jesus' native place thought they knew who Jesus was. They really did not know. Instead of questioning their prior knowledge, they took offense at him.

From all these examples, bound up with the basic fabric of the Gospel, we see how important the question of Jesus' identity was for Mark. It arose both in and out of the synagogue. It was voiced by religious Jews who frequented the synagogue, by the scribes, by the disciples, and by the people of Jesus' native place. In all of this, we considered the most obvious instances. With them in mind, however, we can easily sense that the question of Jesus' identity pervades the entire Gospel.

As the question came up over and over again, explicitly and implicitly, it became very plain that faith was critical for anyone to answer the question properly, that is, in the manner called for by Jesus' teaching and ministry. Demons could know who he was, but their knowledge, which was not knowledge of faith, arose from their distance from Jesus. It led to their banishment. For human beings, who knew Jesus in various ways and through a variety of relationships but without faith, he remained just Jesus of Nazareth, a teacher and a carpenter. All of this provides the background for the question of Jesus' identity.[3]

John the Baptist, Elijah, One of the Prophets. People thought that Jesus was John the Baptist raised from dead (6:14) and continuing his mission. Herod thought the same way (6:16). Many, including Herod, accounted for Jesus' identity in relation to that of John. There were some grounds for this, since Jesus had been a follower of John. When Mark and early Christian tradition said that Jesus came after John (see 1:7-8), they meant that he was John's follower.

The same people, however, did not think that Jesus was actually John *redivivus,* the one they had known, again going about his mission. The historical John was not adequate to say who Jesus was, so they thought of Jesus as John raised from the dead. That way, they accounted for the "mighty powers" at work in Jesus (6:14).

The importance of this lies not so much in the statement's adequacy or lack of it, but in the way it pointed to the future. Jesus was not John the Baptist. John was "not worthy to stoop and loosen the thongs of his sandals" (1:7). Referring to Jesus as John raised from the dead, however, said something important about Jesus. To know Jesus in faith and to understand the gospel story, one has to be attuned to Jesus as the risen Lord and not merely as a historical figure.

The account of the opinions concerning Jesus' identity is thus closely associated with the story of John's death and burial. The flashback concerning the death of John can be understood as the passion of John the Baptist, one that was unique and very different from that of Jesus.

There were also those who thought of Jesus as a new Elijah. That is also how John the Baptist was perceived, as we saw from the clothing he wore. The garment of camel's hair and the leather belt in Mark 1:6 were meant to evoke the figure of Elijah (see 2 Kgs 1:7-8).

---

[3] The question Mark raises is one of identity not of identification. Identification has to do with externals, such as someone's appearance, history, family, and achievements. Identity has to do with who a person really is. Knowing a person (identity) is not only knowing about a person (identification).

Elijah had been a prophet with extraordinary powers in his earthly life and he was expected to return before the Lord's definitive coming.

We can understand, therefore, why some thought of Jesus in terms of Elijah. But if the life of John the Baptist could not provide an adequate interpretation of Jesus' personal identity, how could Elijah have done so? In John, people knew Elijah. In the follower who far surpassed John's greatness, they knew more than Elijah.

Finally, there were those who thought of Jesus as merely one of the prophets. As with John the Baptist and Elijah, certainly this was not adequate to express the identity of Jesus. Jesus was much more than a prophet.

At this point in the Gospel, Mark passes no judgment on these opinions. They are simply presented as what some people thought. Later, the Gospel would return to Jesus' identity (8:27-29). At that point, it will state not only what people in general thought, but also what the disciples thought. As their spokesman, Peter confessed his belief in Jesus as the Messiah, the Christ (8:29).

The Death of John the Baptist (6:17-29).[4] Was Jesus John the Baptist risen from the dead? Is that why he had extraordinary powers? For Herod, it was clear. Jesus was John whom he had beheaded. John had been raised up (see 6:14-16).

The various positions concerning Jesus' identity focus the attention primarily on the resurrection, but also on death. Both are important for understanding the death of John the Baptist.

Looking back, the question of Jesus' identity recalls how Jesus raised Simon's mother-in-law from illness to a life of ministry (1:29-31), how he raised a man suffering from paralysis to the forgiveness (2:9), and how he also raised a young girl from death to new life (5:41-42). The question also points ahead to Jesus' resurrection from the dead and the various contexts in which he and others would proclaim it (8:31; 9:31; 10:33-34; 14:28; 16:6; see also 9:9).

But the question of resurrection presupposes that someone has died or at least was suffering from illness or had an infirmity. Raising someone from illness is not the same as raising someone from death. And from a literary and rhetorical point of view, raising someone from death is not the same as raising someone who was beheaded.

---

[4] See Roger Aus, *Water into Wine and the Beheading of John the Baptist, Early Jewish-Christian Interpretation of Esther 1 in John 2:1-11 and Mark 6:17-29* (Atlanta: Scholars Press, 1988) 39–74.

In 6:14, the powers operative in Jesus evoke the image of John the Baptist raised not just from illness or paralysis but from the dead. Then in 6:16, we are told how John died. When Herod heard about all the things Jesus was doing and what the people were saying about him, he exclaimed, "It is John whom I beheaded. He has been raised up" (6:16). With that, the focus shifted from John's resurrection (6:14) to his death by beheading.

The issue of John's resurrection (6:14) pointed to the resurrection of Jesus. In the same way, the violent death of John (6:16) announced the violent death of Jesus.

The story of John's death (6:17-29) enters the Gospel as a flashback providing the background for Herod's exclamation that Jesus must be John whom he had beheaded (6:14-16). Together with the questions of Jesus' identity, the story of John's death is inserted in Mark's story of the mission of the Twelve (6:7-13, 30). We have already seen several examples of this sandwiching pattern (see 6:21 [22-30] 31-35; 4:1-9 [10-25] 26-32; and 5:21-24 [25-34] 35-43).[5]

As a mere flashback giving the background for John's execution, the story is out of proportion. Its brilliant imagery, dramatic movement, and its very length captures the readers' imagination, and it is easy to forget why the story was told. Besides, this is the only story in the Gospel in which Jesus has no role and is not referred to. As such, one might expect a much shorter story, such as we find in Matthew 14:3-12, or a simple reference to it, as in Luke 3:19-20.

The story, however, is more than a flashback. In the larger context of the mission of the Twelve, it highlights the risk involved in the preaching of repentance (6:12). John had preached repentance (1:4), and for this he had been handed over (*paradothenai,* 1:14) and executed (6:17-29). Jesus also preached repentance, and for this he too would be handed over (*paradidotai*) and executed (14:1–15:47). The handing over and execution of John announced not only that of Jesus but also that of his followers, who like Jesus were sent to preach repentance (6:12).

The story of John's execution also prepared the Twelve for the death of Jesus. John's disciples took his body (*ptoma*) and laid it in a tomb (*kai ethekan auto en mnemeio,* 6:29). Joseph of Arimathea would receive Jesus' body (*ptoma*) and lay him in a tomb (*kai etheken auto en mnemeio,* 15:46).

---

[5] See James R. Edwards, "Markan Sandwiches, The Significance of Interpolations in Markan Narratives," *Novum Testamentum* XXXI, 3 (1989) 193–216.

From several points of view, then, the story of John's death does not appear as an unnecessary digression. On the contrary, it is an important narrative comment on the nature of the mission of Twelve and the new Israel.

A Historical Parable. A casual reading of the story of John's death might suggest that it consists of a historical reminiscence. Very little in the story, however, stands up to close historical scrutiny.

The story is historical in the sense that John the Baptist was a historical figure, an influential preacher and a baptizer with a large popular following. We know also that John spent his last days in prison and was put to death by order of Herod Antipas. All this we know from the New Testament and the corroborative witness of Flavius Josephus, the Jewish Roman court historian, in his *Antiquities of the Jews,* XVIII. 5. 2.

On many important points, however, Mark's story of John's death takes enormous liberties with history. To start with, King Herod was not a king but a mere tetrarch (see Matt 14:1; Luke 3:19; 9:7). His father, Herod the Great, had been a king, but when he died the Roman authorities did not transfer the title of king to his sons.

Even if Herod Antipas had been a king, his royal title, like his actual title of tetrarch, would have been entirely dependent on the emperor at Rome. As a Roman puppet, he would not have been in a position to offer anyone even the smallest part of his kingdom, let alone half, as he does to Herodias' daughter.

Further, Herodias was indeed the wife of Herod's brother—his half-brother, to be precise—but not the wife of Philip, the tetrarch of northern Transjordan after whom Caesarea Philippi (see 8:27) was named. Herodias was the wife of Herod Boethus, who had received no part in the inheritance of Herod the Great.

Then again, according to Josephus, Herodias did not figure in the execution of John the Baptist. Rather, John was put to death because Herod saw him as a potential threat to his political stability.

Like other prominent families, the Herodian family was known to celebrate birthdays with a great banquet to which they invited prominent guests, including military officers. However, as a tetrarch, Herod did not have an army, let alone tribunes (*chiliarchoi,* 6:21) in his service. Besides, that a Herodian princess would have entered the banquet room and performed a dance for Herod and his guests is unthinkable. The banquet described was a men's affair, and if women provided entertainment, as often happened after the meal, they were surely not respected members of the family.

Finally, Flavius Josephus situates the imprisonment and death of John at Machaerus, a Herodian fortress on the heights above the Dead Sea in Transjordan. Machaerus was in the district of Perea, which formed part of Herod's tetrarchy along with Galilee. For Mark, however, who mentions the presence of the leading men of Galilee, the event appears to have taken place in Galilee. Otherwise, we would expect the leading men of Perea to have been invited. Machaerus, it should be noted, was approximately a three days' journey from Tiberias, the Roman capital on the Sea of Galilee.

From all these points, it seems quite clear that Mark enjoyed great historical freedom in writing the story of John's death. This has led to considerable scholarly discussion concerning the story's literary form. Some see it as a legend, others as a piece of midrash, a type of traditional narrative commentary. I suggest it be read as a historical parable, a story with its roots in history but which allows full play to the author's creativity.

Drawing on various historical elements, Mark combined them in new ways in relation to the themes of the Gospel. As told by Mark, the story of John's death challenges Christians as they reflect on the mission of the Church. It confronts Mark's readers with the reality of persecution, and for this it addresses a wide range of emotions. That is why, like other parables, it must not be reduced to a lesson or a theological point. The whole story must be held up to the readers' imagination.

In creating this extraordinary historical parable, Mark, like the tradition from which he drew, found literary inspiration in the book of Esther and the traditional rabbinical commentaries on that book. To appreciate Mark's achievement, we must view his account through the lens of that exciting book and its Persian setting. There are many parallels, especially with the banquet scenes, the execution of Queen Vashti, and Esther's relationship to King Ahasuerus.

Taken in isolation, some of the parallels might be judged accidental, but not when they are taken together. Through a clever use of association and contrast, Mark dresses the history of John's death in the literary garb of the book of Esther and the Persian court.

The story unfolds in four sections. The first introduces the principal personages, Herod, John, and Herodias, along with the circumstances that led to John's arrest (6:17-20). The second describes the occasion for John's death at Herod's birthday banquet (6:21-23). The third tells how John came to be beheaded at Herodias' request (6:24-28), and the fourth concludes the story by introducing John's disciples and telling what they did immediately after his death (6:29).

John's Arrest (6:17-20). The story begins by introducing and identifying three personages, Herod, John, and Herodias, the only three in the story that are named (6:17). Although John is more significant theologically, Herod is the story's principal personage. It is he who had John arrested and bound in prison on account of Herodias, the wife of Herod's brother Philip, whom he had married.

Mark implies that, were it not for Herodias, Herod would not have arrested John and that somehow there was a connection between the preaching of John and her marriages. But for now we are not told what the connection might be.

The introduction also suggests that Herod was a weak man, a trait amply borne out later in the story. Herod's weakness contrasts with his powerful title as king (6:14). Herod is not just a weak man. He is a weak king, and kings ought not to be weak.

The background for Herod's royal title may lie in the book of Esther, where the title is used repeatedly in relation to King Ahasuerus. No other book in the Old Testament uses the title king so frequently, 136 times in Hebrew *(melek)* and 157 times in the Septuagint *(basileus),* including the additions. A reference to Ahasuerus is strongly supported by data that the story supplies later. For now, to appreciate Mark's story, it is best not to race ahead. It is enough to note that the association of a weak "king" Herod with a powerful Persian ruler was anything but complimentary for Herod.

After introducing the personages and the general situation that led to John's imprisonment (6:17), the story clarifies the position of the three personages (6:18-20). First, John had spoken to Herod. Just as Elijah had confronted King Ahaziah of Samaria (2 Kgs 1:1-8), John the Baptist, a prophetic reformer in the garb of Elijah (see 1:2, 6), had confronted Herod, concerning his unlawful marriage (6:18). By ancient Israelite law, Herod was not allowed to take his half-brother's wife as his own wife (see Lev 18:6; 20:21). John's prophetic word was the first step in the series that led to his death.

Second, after John's accusation, Herodias resented John to the point of wanting him killed, but for a reason undisclosed she was unable to bring this about (6:19). Herodias' deep-seated grudge continued unabated. We now know the connection between John's denunciation of the marriage and his imprisonment on account of Herodias. We also know that John's imprisonment was not enough for Herodias. What we do not know is what was blocking her desire to have John killed.

Third, we learn of Herod's complex and ambivalent attitude toward John (6:20). Herod feared John, knowing that he was a righteous and holy man. That is why he kept him imprisoned. Herod's fear, associated with John's righteousness and holiness, was not ordinary fear. It was religious fear. Consequently, it is not the reason why Herod refused Herodias' demand to have him put to death. In his religious fear or awe of John, Herod liked to listen to him, even though this left him perplexed and torn over John's denunciation of his marriage. So long as John remained alive, Herod's ambivalence threatened Herodias' marriage to him and fed her resentment.

In some respects, Herod's attitude evokes that of Pilate, a weak man who had Jesus killed, not because Jesus was guilty or because Pilate really wanted to kill him, but to satisfy the demands of the crowd (15:1-15). Against this background, Herodias evokes the attitude of the chief priests and the scribes, who sought a way to arrest Jesus and put him to death but were unable to do so, at least for a time. John, of course, evokes the figure of Jesus.

Herod's Banquet (6:21-23). Herodias' opportunity finally came (6:21-23). The occasion was a banquet *(deipnon)* Herod gave on his birthday for the princes of the court, the tribunes, and the leading men of Galilee (6:21). Herod's banquet recalls the one Ahasuerus gave "for all his officers and ministers: the Persian and Median aristocracies, the nobles, and the governors of the provinces" (Esth 1:3). Several ancient rabbinical commentaries *(midrashim)* present the banquet given by Ahasuerus as a birthday banquet.

Even the list of Herod's guests seems to have in mind that of the Persian banquet. The expression for Herod's princes *(hoi megistanes)* is a normal rendering in the Septuagint for the Hebrew word *sarim,* the term that appears at the head of the list in Esther 1:3. The tribunes *(chiliarchoi),* whose historical presence was most unlikely, may correspond to the military commanders that were substituted for the nobles in the first Targum, an interpretive retelling in Aramaic, of Esther 1:3. The leading men of Galilee *(hoi protoi)* recall the princes who held first rank *(hoi protoi)* in the realm of Ahasuerus (see Esth 1:14).

"King" Herod's birthday banquet is thus associated with that of Ahasuerus, the Persian king. During the banquet, Herodias' daughter entered and performed a dance that pleased Herod and those reclining at table with him. Respectable women did not join in such banquets or dance for its participants, at least not in the Hellenistic and Roman world to which Herod's court belonged.

It was different among the Persians.[6] Even so, when King Ahasuerus ordered Queen Vashti, who was giving a feast for women elsewhere in the palace (Esth 1:9), to enter the banquet room and

---

[6] See Herodotus, Book V, 18.

display her beauty before his guests, she refused (Esth 1:10-12). Herodias, on the other hand, sensing her opportunity to have John put to death, sent her own daughter to dance before Herod and the men reclining at his table (6:22a).

Mark never named the young girl (*korasion,* see 5:41-42). She enters the story and remains throughout as Herodias' daughter. From her position outside the banquet room, Herodias is very much at the center of the action.

The girl's dance so pleased Herod that he invited her to ask for anything she wished. Herod would grant it to her, even if she asked for half of his kingdom (6:22b-23). Again the story alludes to the book of Esther: "then the king said to her, 'What is it, Queen Esther? What is your request? Even if it is half of my kingdom, it shall be granted to you'" (Esth 5:3; see also 5:6; 7:2; 9:12).

Herodias now had her opportunity. Esther also had a tremendous opportunity, which she used to save her people. Herodias would use hers to destroy her people in the person of John the Baptist.

John's Execution (6:24-28). The young girl left the banquet room and asked her mother what she should ask of Herod. The story implies that Herodias had sent her into the banquet room, but without telling her the reason. Herodias replied, "The head of John the Baptist" (6:24). The girl quickly brought the request back to Herod. The young girl repeated the gruesome request as a personal demand, "I want you to give me at once on a platter the head of John the Baptist" (6:25). The dance was over. So was Herod's pleasure.

In spite of Herod's distress, his weakness determined the outcome. Cowed by Herodias, he had arrested John and bound him in prison (6:17). Now he had to save face in front of his guests. He sent his bodyguard with the order to bring back John's head. The bodyguard beheaded John in the prison and returned to the banquet room with the head on a platter and gave it to the girl, who gave it to her mother.

The background for much of the story of John's execution is again provided by the story of Esther, not directly but through the *Midrash Rabbah* on Esther 1:9 and 1:21. The book of Esther itself does not say how Queen Vashti was executed or even that she was executed, at least not directly, but its ancient commentary does.

In the *Midrash Rabbah* on Esther 1:19, Memucan addresses King Ahasuerus as follows: "If it please the king, let there go forth a royal order . . . My lord the king, say but a word and I will bring in her head on a platter." The commentary on Esther 1:21 continues: "This advice pleased the king and the princes, and the king did as Memucan proposed. He gave the order. And he brought in her head on a platter."

Mark or the tradition on which he relied, simply transferred the rabbinical account of the execution of Queen Vashti to the execution of John the Baptist.

John's Burial (6:29). And so it is that Mark has brought us to the end of the story of the death of John the Baptist. Now we know why Herod could say of Jesus: "It is John whom I beheaded. He has been raised up" (6:16). We also know how John, God's messenger (1:2-6), was handed over (1:14), preparing the way for the handing over of Jesus (1:3). It was a magnificent flashback.

It was also a great historical parable, filling and enlarging the imagination. With a brilliant interplay between history and literature, between the death of John the Baptist and the book of Esther together with its ancient rabbinical traditions and commentaries, the story pointed repeatedly to the passion of Jesus.

But there was one more thing to tell. John's disciples, the ones who used to fast while Jesus' disciples feasted (2:18-20), came, took John's body, and laid it in a tomb (6:29). With the arrival of John's disciples, the story takes an unexpected turn. John prepared the way for the passion of Jesus. John's disciples also prepared the way for the role of Jesus' disciples in Jesus' passion. They too would survive the death of Jesus and see to his burial.

For John, the burial was the end, not the beginning, at least not in the same sense that the end would be the beginning for Jesus and his gospel (1:1; 16:6). Unlike Jesus, John did not rise from the dead. The new life into which he entered was not the definitive event through which God saved his people. But then, we have been told that one mightier than John would come after him, one who would baptize with the Holy Spirit, not just water (1:7-8). Nevertheless, John and his story did become part of "the beginning of the gospel of Jesus Christ [the Son of God]" (1:1).

The Return of the Twelve (6:30)

After showing that Jesus was not John the Baptist and Elijah (6:14-29), the Gospel returns to the mission of the Twelve (6:7-13). The first part of the story showed how Jesus sent them on mission with a set of instructions (6:7-11) and how they accomplished their mission (6:12-13).

The question of Jesus' identity and the story of John's death (6:14-29) were intimately connected with their mission. Their mission was much greater than the mission of John's followers. John prepared the way. Their mission came from Jesus, the one for whom John prepared the way.

It took time to tell the story of the death of John the Baptist. We have been given the impression that mission of the Twelve took a long time. Now they returned (6:30). Returning, the apostles *(hoi apostoloi)* gathered together *(synagontai)*[7] with Jesus and "reported all they had done and taught" (6:30). The rest of the section (6:31–8:21) would show the implications of their mission.

Earlier, when Jesus called the disciples together and sent *(apostellein)* them on mission, Mark referred to them as the Twelve *(hoi dodeka)*. Now as they rejoined Jesus, Mark refers to them as the apostles *(hoi apostoloi)*, a term rarely used in Greek-speaking antiquity. However, when Mark used the term, it already had become traditional among the early Christians.

Many years earlier, when Paul referred to the apostles (see Gal 1:19; 1 Cor 15:7), the term did not need an explanation. Paul may have had to insist that he himself was an apostle, albeit the least of them (1 Cor 15:9), but he expected the Christians to know what he meant.

The Gospel summarized the apostles' report as "all they had done and taught." The description corresponds to the two basic facets of Jesus' ministry and that of the early Christians. Like Jesus, the apostolic Church spread the gospel not in words alone, but in deeds. Later, the expression would become a leitmotiv in Luke-Acts (see Luke 8:21; 24:19; Acts 1:1), for whom the gospel had to be seen as well as heard (Luke 1:20; 7:22; 29:39-44).

Like the first and second sections of the Gospel, the third is divided into two parts. The first presents the culmination of Jesus' ministry in Galilee (6:31–7:23). The second presents the beginning of the mission to the Gentiles (7:24–8:21).

The Culmination of Jesus' Ministry in Galilee (6:31–7:23)

Jesus, the itinerant teacher (6:6b), had sent the Twelve on mission (7:7-13) with a detailed set of instructions regarding what they should bring and not bring with them and how they should respond to those who welcomed or refused to welcome them (6:7-11). In Mark's story, these instructions were followed by a short summary of how the Twelve carried out their mission (6:12-13), and with that the story of their mission was interrupted.

---

[7] The verb *synago* (to assemble or gather together) is related to the noun *synagoge* (synagogue).

Reports concerning Jesus and the Twelve raised some important christological questions. Who was Jesus? What was his mission? What bearing did Jesus' identity have on the life and mission of his followers? The questions concerning Jesus' identity evoked the life, mission, and death of John the Baptist. Was Jesus John the Baptist raised from the dead, as Herod maintained (6:14-16)? For the mission of Jesus' followers, the answer was critical.

The answer lay in the story of John, whose imprisonment and execution was told in great detail. In a way, Jesus was like John, who also met a violent death by execution. But John did not rise from the dead. Jesus' disciples, like those of John, would have to deal with the death of the one they followed. But for Jesus' disciples, unlike John's disciples, the story would not end with his burial (6:17-29). After the story of John's death, the story returns to the mission of the Twelve (6:30).

The first part of the third section includes three sections, the breaking of the bread for the five thousand (6:31-44), the coming of Jesus to the disciples in the midst of the sea (6:45-56), and a discourse of Jesus concerning the tradition of the elders (7:1-23).

Signs and Wonders in the Desert (6:31-44)

Once the apostles completed their report (6:30), Jesus invited them to come away by themselves to a desert place in order to rest a while. As it was, a huge crowd surrounded them, and they had no opportunity even to eat (6:31). And so, the apostles left in a boat by themselves for a desert place (6:32). But some saw them leave, the news spread, and people hurried on foot and arrived there ahead of them (6:33). With these few simple indications, Mark has set the stage for our oldest written account of the breaking of the bread (6:34-44).

The two-part introduction (6:6b, 7-30) for this third section of the Gospel (6:6b–8:21) is over, and the main part of the story has now begun. With the opening verses (6:31-33), Mark has also reintroduced four major themes, well known from the earlier parts of the Gospel.

The first is the location, a desert place *(eremos topos)*. Mark emphasized the severity of this physical environment *(topos)* which was a desert *(eremos)*. The disciples accepted Jesus' invitation to go to the desert.

The desert had entered the Gospel in the prologue (1:2-13), where it played a prominent role as the place where large crowds went to hear John the Baptist, "a voice of one crying in the desert" (1:2) and where Jesus stayed for forty days after his baptism (1:12-13). Jesus had also returned to the desert *(eremos topos)* after his first day's ministry in Capernaum to find a place for prayer away from the crowd (1:35). For Jesus, the desert was a place of testing and formation, as it had been for the Israelites in the Exodus. It would be a place of testing for the disciples as well.

The second theme is the large crowd. The crowd has been an important component in the story of Jesus from the very beginning. Sometimes the crowd and its size seemed problematic, even overwhelming, but even then it provided an opportunity for Jesus to fulfill his mission. The story of the crowd's growth and its changing composition was also essential for understanding the nature and the scope of Jesus' mission. Now it becomes a significant factor for the mission of the disciples. From the point of the disciples, the crowd was an overwhelming problem, but from the point of view of Jesus, it was but a challenge and a wonderful opportunity.

The third major theme is that of bread and eating. There was a time when the disciples were unable to eat bread because of the crowd (3:20). Now when they were in the same situation, he asked them to go to the desert where they could have an opportunity to eat. The story shows that in the perception and the understanding of the disciples, the desert was not a normal place to find bread. But if this desert is meant to evoke that of the Exodus, when the people of Israel also were tested with hunger (Exod 16:3; Num 11:4-6; 21:4-5), we begin to understand. The crowd would be nourished in a new and wonderful way that would reveal God's loving presence to his people.

The fourth and final theme is the boat, which we have seen so often in this whole first part of the Gospel, beginning with the call of the first disciples (1:16-20). The boat helped Jesus to fulfill his mission (4:1) and enabled him and the disciples to unite the Jewish and Gentile shores of the Sea of Galilee in a single new Israel (4:35-41; 5:1, 21). Now, it would enable the apostles to cross the sea for the mission to the Gentiles.

The Breaking of the Bread for the 5,000 (6:34-44)[8]

Everything has been put in place for a story of signs and wonders, like those told in the story of the Exodus. Mark never mentioned the word manna, but the story of how the hungry people of God was

---

[8] See E. LaVerdiere, *The Eucharist in the New Testament and the Early Church* (Collegeville: The Liturgical Press, 1996) 46–64; and "Feed My Sheep: Eucharistic Tradition in Mark 6:34-44," in *Bread from Heaven, Essays on the Eucharist,* Edited by Paul J. Bernier, S.S.S. (New York: Paulist Press, 1977) 45–58.

tested and wondrously nourished in the desert fills the atmosphere. Elsewhere in early Christian tradition, the bread that Jesus gave is compared to the manna given to God's people in the desert during the Exodus (see John 6:32-35, 48-51).

Sheep without a Shepherd (6:34-36). The story opens by contrasting Jesus' reaction to the crowd (6:34) with that of the disciples (6:35-36). Jesus' reaction was simple and direct. When he saw the huge crowd, his heart reached out to them. He was deeply and audibly moved *(esplagchnisthe)* because they were like sheep without a shepherd, and he responded immediately to their need. He himself would be a shepherd to them. As shepherd, he began to teach them as he had taught his disciples and the crowds that came to him.

The story did not spell out or even mention what Jesus taught. Instead, it moved on to the disciples' reaction. Unlike Jesus, who reached out to the crowd and taught them, the disciples wanted to send them away. The disciples approached Jesus and asked him to dismiss the crowd since the place where they were was a desert and the time was already very late. People needed to eat but there was no food in the desert. The crowd should therefore be sent into the farms and villages to purchase for themselves something to eat (6:35-36).

With the contrasting reaction of Jesus and the disciples, the setting is complete and the story is engaged. Jesus accepted to be shepherd for the crowd, but the disciples, overwhelmed by the size of the crowd and the harsh conditions of the desert, refused. They even asked Jesus the shepherd to send the crowd away.

There is much irony in the contrast. Jesus had sent his disciples to a desert place where they might rest and find nourishment (6:31). The disciples wanted the crowd sent away from the desert back to the farms and villages to find themselves something to eat (6:35-36). It did not occur to them how they would find nourishment for themselves in the desert.

Earlier Jesus had sent the disciples on mission with instructions to take no food, no money, not even a sack for their Exodus journey. Jesus' intention was that they should not rely on such things to fulfill their mission. But now with the vast crowd in the desert, and without food and money, they felt totally unable to fulfill their mission and were prepared to abandon it.

During the Exodus, God had given instructions to Moses that "the Lord's community may not be like sheep without a shepherd" (Num 27:17). In the course of their subsequent history, Israel oftentimes would find itself shepherdless, and the Lord himself became a shepherd for them (see Exek 34:1-31; Psalm 23). Later, Jesus too became a shepherd for the shepherdless crowd (6:34). Would his followers, his disciples, the apostles, now refuse to do the same? Would they leave Christ's flock shepherdless in the new Israel?

No Bread, No Money (6:37-38). Beginning with 6:35-36, when the disciples asked Jesus to dismiss the crowd, the story focused primarily on the disciples and their relationship to the crowd. Earlier it had focused on Jesus and how he related to the crowd (6:34).

Jesus' response to the disciples was intentionally enigmatic: "Give them some food yourselves" (6:37a). Is this the same person who told them not to take any bread with them on their missionary journey? The same who told them to come apart to a desert place when they could not find time to eat? Without bread and unable to provide for themselves, how could they possibly give this vast crowd something to eat?

The disciples might have responded as Jesus' relatives had done earlier that he was out of his mind (3:21). Like the people of his native place, they might have found him altogether too much for them (6:2-7). Or they might have concluded they did not understand what he meant. Instead they balked at the impossibility of the request: "Are we to buy two hundred days' wages *[denarion diakosion]* worth of food *[artous]* and give it to them to eat?" (6:37b).

When you consider that a *denarion* (denarius) was a day's wage for an average laborer, two hundred denarii represented a considerable sum, well beyond the disciples' means. The disciples, now oblivious of Jesus' earlier command that they not bring money with them, assumed that Jesus did not understand the situation. Their assumption added further irony as the story begins to show the disciples' own lack of understanding (see 6:52; 7:18; 8:14-21).

Jesus ignored the disciples' protest: "How many loaves *[artous]* do you have? Go and see" (6:38a). After finding out, they said, "Five loaves and two fish" (6:38b). Undeterred, Jesus continued as one who knew precisely what he was doing. The disciples had responded with dismay, "Five loaves and two fish." Their response was not a simple report, as it might have been in another context, but a defiant protest. What could anyone do with five loaves and two fish for such a large crowd?

At this point we become aware of another story in the background (2 Kgs 4:42-44). A man had come from Baal-shalishah bringing Elisha the prophet twenty barley loaves and some fresh grain in the ear. "Give it to the people to eat," Elisha had said. But Elisha's servant had objected, "How can I set this before a hundred men?" Elisha had insisted, "Give it to the people to eat. For thus says the LORD, 'They shall eat and there shall be some left over.'" The servant did so, and that is what happened, giving a good intimation of what is about to happen in the Mark's story.

From the start, the Exodus story of the murmuring Israelites and the heavenly manna gave Mark's story of the breaking of the bread a lot of biblical depth and resonance. Now with the evocation of Elisha, the hungry soldiers, and the twenty barley (see John 6:9) loaves the story of the breaking of the bread acquired even more.

On the Green Grass (6:39-40). Still undeterred, Jesus ordered that the people recline by *symposia* on the green grass (6:39). This they did, in orderly arrangements by hundreds and fifties (6:40). The language for these two verses was very carefully chosen to evoke a number of cultural and literary settings.

In the ancient world, a *symposion* (symposium) was a formal banquet at which people reclined on dining couches. These banquets had two major components. The first included various courses served on platters on small tables or carried by servants from person to person. After the last course, the tables were removed and the second part of the *symposion* began. Wine was served, some form of entertainment was provided, or the gathering joined in a serious discussion on a chosen theme.

The Greek *symposion* influenced the early Christian practices for the breaking of the bread or the Eucharist. Because of its association with the Eucharist, Mark wished to evoke the ancient *symposion* and this determined his choice of the verb *anaklinai,* to recline. Following Mark, it would be quite appropriate to call the ancient celebration of the Eucharist a Christian *symposion*. Given the story's context, Mark contrasts the starkness of the desert with the abundant nourishment of the Christian banquet.

In the story, the evocation of the Christian *symposion,* with its participants gathered into orderly groupings of hundreds and fifties, also brings to mind the story of Moses, who appointed leaders over groups of thousands, hundreds, fifties, and ten during Israel's desert Exodus (see Exod 18:21-25). In Mark only the hundreds and fifties were retained, since they alone corresponded to small Christian communities and their assemblies for their eucharistic *symposia*.

Finally, the reference to the green grass can be surprising, given the story's desert setting, but only when it is read as a realistic description. Early in the account we saw how Jesus became a shepherd for a flock without a shepherd (6:34) and how he wanted the

Twelve, the apostles, to do the same. We need not wonder that Jesus has led the flock into green pastures and that he is about to set a splendid table before them (Ps 23:2, 5).

The story shows the influence of a meditative reflection on Psalm 23 and Ezekiel 34. The early Christians in Mark's time may have found themselves in a desert, like the ancient Israelites before them, but in their eucharistic *symposion* they reclined in the green pastures of messianic fulfillment (see also Isa 35:1-2).

The Breaking of the Bread (6:41-42). With everyone reclining by *symposia* in groups of hundreds and fifties, Jesus proceeded to take the five loaves and the two fish. Looking up to heaven, he offered a blessing, broke the loaves, and gave them to the disciples to place before the people. He also divided the two fish among them (6:41).

The story has reached a high point, and its language, simple but solemn, is drawn from the liturgical tradition. We recognize the introductory elements of a liturgical text from the account of the Last Supper (14:22-25). There was no need to cite the whole text. The few opening words saying how Jesus took the loaves, said the blessing, broke and gave the loaves to the disciples were enough to evoke the entire liturgical text and the Eucharist to which it referred.

In biblical times, the normal way for people to refer to a work was by quoting the first line or the opening words. For example, in order to associate Jesus' last words with the whole of Psalm 22, a psalm of hope, it was enough to cite the beginning of the first verse: "My God, my God, why have you forsaken me." To associate John's Gospel with the Book of Genesis, it sufficed to say, "In the beginning." In the same way, to associate the story of the breaking of the bread (6:34-44) with the Eucharist, all Mark needed was to cite the beginning of the community's liturgical text.

Mark used the Greek verb *eulogein* (to bless) and not *eucharistein* (to give thanks) that is used in his second story of the breaking of the bread (8:6). Beneath these two Greek verbs lies the single Hebrew verb *barak,* which includes both notions and shows how closely they were related. Even today, we may thank someone by responding, "Bless you."

In modern times, however, we also use the verb "bless" in relation to impersonal objects. We speak of blessing a statue or even a home. By this we recognize an object's divine provenance and we want the object to remind us of God who gave it to us. But in biblical times, blessing an object was completely foreign to Israelite and Jewish practice.

The Hebrew word *barak,* meaning to thank as well as to bless, excluded it. Gratitude was given to persons not to things, and blessing also was given exclusively to persons. In the literary context of 6:34-44, whose tradition remains close to its Jewish origins, Jesus could not have blessed the bread. Raising his eyes to heaven, he blessed God.

The source of the eucharistic nourishment was Jesus himself and the eucharistic action was attributed to him. But the disciples, like the priest and the Christian community today, were very much part of the action. The request to send the crowd away was their initiative. It sets the story's ecclesiological focus. Accordingly, it is the disciples, not Jesus, who had to give the people to eat, assemble them in *symposia,* and have them recline on the green grass. And it was also they who placed the bread before the people and divided the fish among them.

The disciples served at the Christian *symposia,* joining the various Eucharistic communities into a single great community, a *symposion* of *symposia.* But where did the disciples find the bread to nourish the crowd? "How many loaves do you have? Go and see" (6:38). They themselves had no bread to give. Jesus had asked them not to bring any. The bread that was shared came from the crowd.

As shepherds of the flock and servants at the breaking of the bread, the disciples were not meant to be great benefactors (see 10:42-44; Luke 22:25-26) but to facilitate sharing among those who had gathered. Such was their mission. When this happened, though the food itself may have been very simple and meager, five loaves and two fish, the desert became a green pasture and all were able to eat and be satisfied (6:42). Remembering this, they would never again be overwhelmed by the demands of their ministry. At the Last Supper, Jesus would declare that the bread was his body (14:22), no meager fare.

Twelve Baskets for the Twelve (6:43-44). We have come to the end of this extraordinary story. In the story of Elisha (2 Kgs 4:42-44), God had promised that all would be nourished and that there would be bread left over. Once everyone had eaten, the disciples now picked up twelve baskets of bread broken *(klasmata)* and some fish as well (6:43). The abundance of this desert meal sufficed for future generations in the development of the Christian mission. In this story of the mission of the Twelve (see 6:7), the twelve baskets of bread broken evokes the Twelve. Here is bread for the new Israel. It is the gift of Jesus, but its sharing is the work of the Church.

At first, the concluding words may appear enigmatic: "Those who ate [of the loaves] were five thousand men" (6:44). In our day, the tendency is to substitute the term "people" for "men." This is understandable. In this case, however, the Greek term is not the generic *anthropoi* but *andres,* which refers to men as opposed to women.

The reason Mark used "men" *(andres)* was to show how at the beginning the Church stayed close to the Jewish and male environment from which it sprang. But as the Gospel continues to unfold, we shall see how the Church moved beyond those limitations to include women as well as men and Gentiles as well as Jews. For these later developments, the second story of the breaking of the bread (8:1-9) will prove very significant. Respect for Mark's intention, therefore, requires that in 6:44 we retain the limited expression "five thousand men."

Signs and Wonders on the Sea (6:45-56)

Jesus, the itinerant teacher (6:6b), sent the Twelve out on mission (7:7-30). On their return, he invited them to a desert place where they might rest, but the crowd saw them leave and hurried there ahead of them (6:31-33). That desert place became the site for the miraculous breaking of the bread (6:34-44).

They had come to the desert place by boat. After the breaking of the bread and the gathering of enough bread broken to fill twelve baskets, it was time to get back into the boat. Jesus was asking them to precede him to the other side toward Bethsaida, a town on the northeastern shore of the Sea of Galilee at the border of Galilee and Gaulanitis (4:45).

With that, we are well into the body of the section (6:31–8:21), where the Twelve come to grips with the many important challenges confronting the new Israel. The first challenge had already surfaced in the desert when the disciples felt overwhelmed by the demands of the mission and asked Jesus the Shepherd to dismiss the sheep *(apolyson autous)* to find food for themselves (6:36). Jesus did not dismiss the sheep, that is, the crowd of five thousand. Only later, once the crowd had been superabundantly nourished did he dismiss them *(apolyei ton ochlon* 6:45).

To nourish the crowd in the new Israel, the disciples had to accept a new vision. Their mission would not be limited to the lost sheep of Israel (see Matt 10:6). Symbolically, they had to cross to the other shore (6:45-56). And for this, they had to abandon some of the traditions of the elders and come to a new understanding (7:1-23). In both matters, they experienced strong resistance.

The Disciples' Resistance and Jesus' Prayer (6:45-46). The disciples resisted from the very start of the journey, and Jesus had to compel them to get into the boat and precede him to other side *(eis to peran)*. The verb for compel, *anagkazo,* is very strong. Jesus does not ordinarily need to force or compel the disciples.

Is it that the disciples did not want to go ahead *(proagein)* of him? Jesus is usually the one who precedes *(proagein)* the disciples, not vice versa (see 10:32; 14:28; 16:7). Is it that they were awed by the wonders of the new exodus and fearful of what lay ahead? Or is it that they did not want to leave without Jesus? On another occasion, they had left the crowd and crossed the sea with Jesus with them in the boat. When they ran into a storm, he calmed it (4:35-41).

It is best to leave such questions open. Motives for resistance are usually complex. Besides, the narrative moves on more than one level, and the story's main emphasis may not be on Jesus' first disciples but on the new Israel and its need to cross over toward a new shore in the Christian mission.

Jesus did have to compel the disciples to get into the boat, but no pressure was required to dismiss the crowd. Once Jesus bade them leave, he went to the mountain to pray (6:46). Earlier, Jesus had gone up the mountain to appoint the Twelve for the new Israel and its mission (3:13-19). On that occasion, the mountain was not a particular geographical and localizable mountain but a symbolic place of divine revelation and great initiatives, evoking Sinai and Horeb. This time the mountain is a symbolic place of prayer as it was so often in the stories of ancient Israel. Jesus went to the mountain to pray as he had gone to the desert to pray in preparation for his mission beyond Capernaum (1:35-38). His prayer is now in preparation for the great new developments in the Christian mission.

Far out on the Sea (6:47-48a). Jesus had compelled the disciples to get into the boat and precede him to the other side. He had also taken leave of the crowd and gone to the mountain to pray. With that introduction, we can anticipate a great event in the mission of the new Israel.

The event (6:47-52) recalls an earlier crossing of the sea, when Jesus and the disciples went by boat from the Jewish to the Gentile shore and the territory of the Gerasenes (4:35-41). On that occasion, Jesus was in the boat with the disciples. When a bad storm arose, the terrified disciples were certain they were about to perish, while Jesus slept in the stern. Awakened by the disciples, Jesus commanded the sea to be still, and immediately all was calm.

This new crossing is very different. First, they did not actually cross from the Jewish to the Gentile shore. The disciples were to precede Jesus to Bethsaida, which is on the northeast shore of the Sea of Galilee (6:45), but they actually landed at Gennesaret, which is on the western shore (6:53). At Bethsaida, they could easily have been on their way to Gentile territory, but Gennesaret was way off course.

We saw how the disciples at first resisted going on this journey and how Jesus had to apply pressure for them to go (6:45). At the end of the story, even after they experienced wonders in the midst of the sea, their hearts were hardened, an attitude hearkening back to the Pharisees when they began conspiring with the Herodians to find a way to destroy Jesus. They too had resisted Jesus and hardened their hearts (3:1-6). Everything indicates that Jesus had intended a missionary journey toward Gentile territory but that the disciples resisted going. Eventually, they would go with Jesus via Tyre and Sidon (7:24, 31), and there would be a second breaking of the bread in the Decapolis, the land of the ten Greek cities, but first other issues had to be dealt with. For example, there was the question of "the tradition of the elders" (7:1-23; see vv. 3, 5).

Second, this new crossing differs from the first in that the disciples were to go in the boat without Jesus (6:45). Jesus did join them deep in the night at the fourth watch (6:48), sometime between three and six in the morning, but that was because they were not making any progress. The original plan was that they should precede Jesus to the other side and he would meet them there, but the disciples simply were not ready to move out into that mission on their own.

Earlier, overwhelmed by the demands of the ministry, they had asked Jesus to dismiss the crowd to find themselves something to eat. Ignoring their request, Jesus had indicated to them what to do. They had followed his instructions and seen everything work out. Everyone was wonderfully nourished. They were even able to gather an abundance of bread broken, twelve baskets full, for the new Israel (6:34-44). Still they failed to understand the breaking of the bread in which they had participated (6:52). They needed more formation in the company of Jesus as he continued to exercise his ministry.

This need was met at Gennesaret (6:53-56) when Jesus healed many and answered the objections of the Pharisees regarding "the tradition of the elders." Only afterwards, would the mission finally move into the Gentile territory of the Decapolis, where the Gerasene had prepared the mission of Jesus and the Twelve (5:1-20; see v. 20).

There is a third difference between the two stories. This time, there is no storm, only a contrary wind. To understand and appreciate

Mark's story at this point we need to pay close attention to its Old Testament background.

The disciples were out on the sea for quite some time, and by evening the boat was "far out on the sea," while Jesus was alone on the shore (6:47). The Greek expression for "the middle of the sea" *(en meso tes thalasses)* calls to mind the Septuagint's reference to the Israelite passage through the Reed Sea in their flight from Pharaoh's army as they made their way to the promised land. For the Israelites, the crossing "in the middle of the sea" was one of God's wonders. Protected by God, they made their way "in the middle of the sea" on dry land, with the water rising like a wall on their right and on their left. Once they had passed, their enemy was destroyed "in the middle of the sea" as the water flowed back and covered them (see Exod 14:16-31).

As told by Mark, the story thus continues to evoke the exodus that was introduced in the instructions regarding what the disciples were to take on the missionary journey (6:7-13). The evocation of the exodus was also pursued in the story of the breaking of the bread for the five thousand (6:34-44). Unlike the Israelites, who made their way in faith to the other shore, the disciples had to be forced into the boat, and they made little headway because the wind was against them. But Jesus did see them from the shore (6:48).

Jesus Walks to them on the Sea (6:48b-49). In the desert, the disciples were not able to cope with the demands of the mission (6:35-37), but Jesus showed them the way (6:38-44). Once again, when Jesus asked them to expand the scope of their mission, they were unable to cope, and again Jesus came to their assistance, now in the middle of the sea. He came at the fourth watch, deep into the night as dawn was approaching, walking on the sea (6:48).

The image of Jesus walking on the sea evokes a number of poetic passages from the Old Testament, at least two of which refer to the Exodus and God's passage through the Reed Sea:

> Through the sea was your path;
>> your way, through the mighty waters,
>> though your footsteps were unseen.
> You led your people like a flock
>> under the care of Moses and Aaron (Ps 77:20-21).

> Thus says the LORD,
>> who opens a way in the sea
>> and a path in the mighty waters,

Who leads out chariots and horsemen,
    a powerful army,
Till they lie prostrate together, never to rise,
    snuffed out and quelched like a wick (Isa 43:16-17).

Deutero-Isaiah uses the ancient exodus event as an image for Israel's liberation from Babylon.[9] Mark applies the exodus event and Isaiah's image to the new Israel's liberation for the mission to the nations.

Jesus' walking on the sea also recalls biblical images of God's eternal wisdom. Especially significant is this passage from the book of Sirach, which emphasizes the universality of God's dominion:

The vault of heaven I compassed alone,
    through the deep abyss I wandered.
Over the waves of the sea, over all the land,
    over every people and nation I held sway (Sir 24:5).

With this passage in the background, Jesus' walking on the sea points directly toward the mission to every people and nation.

Finally, there is an important passage from the book of Job, which also sheds light on an otherwise enigmatic element in Mark's story: "He meant to pass by *(parelthein)* them" (6:48b).

He alone stretches out the heavens
    and treads upon the crests of the sea . . .
Should he come near me, I see him not;
    should he pass by, I am not aware of him (Job 9:8-11).[10]

God walks on the crests of the sea, but he might pass Job by, leaving him unaware.

Jesus saw the disciples in the middle of the sea, like the ancient Israelites, except that they were making no headway. He came out to them walking on the sea, but mysteriously meant to pass them by. But he did not.

---

[9] For the setting and the message of Deutero-Isaiah, see Carroll Stuhlmueller, C.P., "Deutero-Isaiah and Trito-Isaiah," *The New Jerome Biblical Commentary* (Englewood Cliffs, N.J.: Prentice-Hall, 1990) 329–31.

[10] See also the Lord's address to Job in Job 38:16:
    "Have you entered into the sources of the sea,
        or walked about in the depths of the abyss?"

Jesus Reveals Himself as I AM (6:49-52). The association with the passage from Job tells us that Jesus, the one who was coming on the sea, was divine. In the terms already presented by Mark, he was the Son of God (1:1), God's beloved Son (1:11), and the Holy One of God (1:24). But the disciples did not recognize him as such. They thought he was an apparition *(phantasma),* and shouted out *(anekraxan,* 6:49), for all saw him and were terrified *(etarachthesan,* 6:50a). Jesus' identity as the Son of God escaped them. As the Son of God, Jesus was passing them by.

It is then that Jesus spoke with them and said, "It is I," or more literally, "I AM" *(ego eimi),* an expression the Septuagint attributed only to God. The most famous usage is in Exodus 3:14, when God discloses his name to Moses, "This is what you shall tell the Israelites: I AM sent me to you."[11] Speaking to the disciples, Jesus takes the divine name and makes it his own.

To Mark's first readers and to us, Jesus' divine self-disclosure is clear, and all those who know him in faith accept it and proclaim it. However, even when Jesus got into the boat and the wind died down, the disciples were astounded (6:51), because they had not understood about the loaves *(epi tois artois,* 6:52b; see also 8:16-20).[12] They resisted to the very end of the story. They did not want to understand. Their hearts were hardened *(he kardia peporomene,* 6:52c).[13]

For those steeped in the language of the Septuagint, the divine disclosure in the "I AM" statement is supported by the introductory statement, "he spoke with them" *(ho . . . elalesen met' auton),* an expression that the Septuagint applied to God and divine revelation.[14] In the Markan context, we would expect the story to say that Jesus called out to them. Instead, Mark employed the classic Septuagintal turn of phrase. Precisely because the expression is a bit jarring in this context, it calls attention to its special Old Testament context.

Jesus had wanted the disciples to precede him to the other shore and to the lands of the Gentiles. This intention corresponds to the

[11] Besides Exodus 3:14, see Deuteronomy 32:39; Isaiah 41:4; 43:10.

[12] What they did not understand about the loaves of bread, will be clarified in 8:14-21 and 14:22.

[13] For the hardness of the heart in Mark's Gospel, see also 3:6; 8:17; 16:14.

[14] See, for example, Genesis 35:13, 14, 15; Exodus 3:10; Numbers 11:17; Judges 6:17. As Edward J. Mally, S.J., commented, "This expression further enhances the epiphanic character of the miracle," "The Gospel According to Mark," *The Jerome Biblical Commentary* (Englewood Cliffs, N.J.: Prenctice-Hall, Inc., 1968) II:36.

history of the early Church and its actual mission, which was to prepare the way for the final coming of Christ. As we learn from Luke, and even more explicitly from Matthew (see Matt 10:6; 15:24), the mission developed exclusively in the Jewish sphere during the lifetime of Jesus. Only after Jesus' death and resurrection was the apostolic Church commissioned by the risen Lord to bring their mission to the Gentiles, that is to all nations (see Luke 24:46-49; Acts 1:8; Matt 28:16-20). The apostles were to precede Jesus, the Lord, to the nations and proclaim the Gospel until his return (see 13:10, 26).

Mark, however, as I have suggested on several occasions, is telling two stories at once, that of Jesus with his disciples and that of the Lord with apostolic Church. His Gospel makes little or no effort to distinguish these two periods in our Christian origins. Rather, they interpenetrate one another. Accordingly, Jesus, as I AM, but not recognized as such, joins the disciples in the boat. The statement must have been especially meaningful to Mark's early readers, many of whom may have felt that the Lord was passing them by, while in fact he was with them in the boat of the Church, but unrecognized.

At Gennesaret (6:53-56). And so, they came to land and tied up at Gennesaret on the western shore of the sea, instead at Bethsaida, which was on the northeastern shore. People recognized them, and once again the crowd started to gather, as it had so often. From everywhere, from villages, towns, and the countryside, they brought their sick people on mats (see 2:4, 11) and laid them in public places, begging to touch at least the tassel of his cloak (see 5:27). All those who did were healed (6:53-56).

As I have already noted on several occasions, clothing expressed a person's identity. So, for example, John the Baptist's garment of camel hair and his leather belt revealed him as Elijah (1:6). Clothing also community Jesus' identity. To touch even the tassel of his cloak, the tiniest element in his clothing, was to touch him. A close parallel can be found in the story of the woman with the hemorrhage who reached out to touch Jesus' clothes. When she did so, she was healed (5:25-34).

The cures at Gennesaret are presented in the form of a general summary, of which we have already seen several in the course of the Gospel (e.g. 1:12-13, 14-15, 32-34; 3:7-12; 6:6b). Such summaries cover many events. They brought the sick "to wherever they heard he was" (6:55). With the summary, Jesus resumes his ministry in Galilee after the failed attempt to cross over to Bethsaida. The disciples needed more formation before taken on the Gentile mission.

The disciples' stay at Gennesaret and in its environs also provides a context for reintroducing the Pharisees and some scribes from Jerusalem. The disciples were not prepared to move into the Gentile mission before coming to grips with "the tradition of the elders" (7:1-23). Beyond that, there would be other hurdles as well, but they would accompany Jesus to the Decapolis (8:31) and eventually to Bethsaida, where Jesus opened the eyes of a blind man (8:22-26).

Tradition, Traditions, and the Word of God (7:1-23)

What would we Christians do without traditions? What would anyone do without traditions? Traditions are part of life wherever people gather in community or join in common celebration, whether religious or secular. Traditions are also intimately connected with a family's identity. The same is true of a community.

Traditions are pervasive, tenacious, and very important, but they are not absolute, and their value can be questioned. Traditions spring from a particular history and shaped by common beliefs. They nourish a community's ideals, and they in turn are nourished by those ideals.

When a life context that inspired a set of traditions dies or is drastically altered, traditions it once sustained become lifeless and meaningless. That does not mean they are immediately abandoned. The roots of traditions may run very deep, and it is very difficult to set them aside. There is nostalgia, of course, and sometimes just plain fear of letting them go. But then, a tradition may also have tapped a hidden spring granting it life and a purpose still to be disclosed. Traditions are connected with a community's identity.

The early Christians were a people of tradition, of practices and beliefs that they received and handed on. At first, while still close to their Jewish origins, they remained faithful to the Jewish traditions of their forbears. However, as the various communities gradually welcomed Gentiles as well as Jews, new traditions common to both sprang from the new identity they found in Christ. The Jewish traditions so dear to them had to be set aside lest these stifle or even destroy their oneness in Christ, which did not admit a distinction between Jew and Gentile.

Some traditions had to be set aside and new traditions adopted, but there was never any question about the early Christians being a people of tradition.

The transition from Jewish traditions to specifically Christian traditions did not come without a struggle. Many would not let go of the old. Where change did occur, many wanted to return to the old. Had their attitude prevailed, Christianity could not have developed into the inclusive community called for by the death and resurrection of Jesus Christ. It could not have embarked on its historical mission to the ends of the earth.

Mark 7:1-13 is an extraordinary witness to the early Christian struggle over the traditions of their Jewish forbears. The passage shows how they resolved the struggle and gives the rationale enabling them to set aside traditions that had once been an important part of their lives.

Context in Mark 6:6b–7:21. After their first missionary journey (6:7-30), the apostles still had much to learn. When a large crowd gathered, Jesus saw that they were like sheep without a shepherd, and he became a shepherd to them. His disciples were meant to follow him in this, but instead they asked that he send the crowd away (6:34-36).

Then when Jesus led the apostles in the breaking of bread, they failed to understand what it said of their mission and what it demanded of them. They even resisted Jesus' instruction to precede him to the shore and the region of Bethsaida. And when they did set out, a strong contrary wind prevented them from making any headway. When Jesus came to them across the sea and joined them in the boat, they were terrified after the wind died down (6:37-52).

Had the disciples understood about the bread (6:52a), they would not have resisted crossing to the other shore. But as it was, their hearts were hardened (6:52b), not unlike the Pharisees (3:5).

Hardness of heart was not something that could be lightly dismissed. It led the Pharisees to take counsel with the Herodians to find a way to destroy Jesus. Hardness of heart could also turn the disciples against the new Israel and its mission, which transcended the distinction between Jew and Gentile.

Before the disciples embarked on their mission to the Gentiles, Jesus had to deal with the disciples' hardness of heart. Their mission and the new Israel were at stake. Jesus' encounter with the Pharisees and some scribes from Jerusalem (7:1-23) addresses the disciples' lack of understanding concerning the bread and their hardness of heart.

Form and Purpose. The passage is a discourse, composed for the Gospel from various elements of traditional teaching with roots in the ministry of Jesus. Like the other discourses in Mark, it clarifies an important issue confronting the Christian community.

In the great discourse on parables (4:1-34), the issue was the meaning and purpose of Jesus' teaching in parables, questions that did not arise during Jesus' ministry, at least not in the same way. From the beginning, Jesus' parables were very challenging. They opened people's minds in wonder and moved them to reflect on simple but profound things, which gradually yielded their meaning as people continued to ponder their implications. This first happened in the context of Jewish life and tradition.

However, as the early Christians moved out of the Jewish context into the Gentile world and came to see themselves as a new Israel, transcending the distinction between Jew and Gentile, the parables lost the meaning they once had and needed to be reinterpreted for the new context.

In the discourse on parables (4:1-34), Jesus provided that new interpretation for all who joined in the vision of the new Israel, for those who were with the Twelve. Using a quotation from Isaiah, he also showed why the parables became totally opaque for those who remained outside the new Israel.

In the mini-discourse on feasting and fasting (2:18-22), the issue consisted in the radical newness of the following of Christ. From the very beginning, the disciples' way of life had differed from that of the disciples of John and those of the Pharisees. Whereas the disciples of John and the Pharisees fasted, those of Jesus did not. That was during Jesus' life, when the bridegroom was still with them. After the passion and resurrection, when the bridegroom was taken away, they fasted, but this was not a mere adoption of the practice of the disciples of John and of the Pharisees. When they fasted, they were inspired by the passion and resurrection of Jesus. At no time was the life of Jesus' disciples comparable to the disciples of others, neither during Jesus' historical life nor in the years following his passion and resurrection.

In the short discourse on Satan (3:22-30), the issue consisted in the forgiveness of sins. In general, it could be said that all sins and blasphemies would be forgiven. But this presupposed recognizing the source of Jesus' power to forgive, namely the Holy Spirit. Those who attributed his power to Satan cut themselves off from the source of forgiveness. In Mark, the discourse addressed those claiming that the development of the community of disciples into the new Israel was the work of Satan.

In the discourse on tradition (7:1-23), the issue centered on the Jewish traditions handed on to the disciples by their forbears. Should the early Christians cling to such traditional practices? If they had already abandoned them, should they return to them?

The discourse shows the relationship between tradition and God's commandment, the word of God. It also shows how traditions can actually be destructive. Appealing to the teaching of Jesus, it applies it to the community's mission beyond Israel to all peoples.

The discourse on tradition consists in a rethinking of Jesus' teaching concerning tradition. Like all the other discourses, it provides a bridge from the community's earliest days to the days of Mark and the new challenges confronting the community. That is what discourses do.

Literary Structure. From the literary context, we saw how the discourse dealt with the resistance to move beyond the Jewish context into the Gentile mission. From the literary form and purpose, we then saw how the discourse enabled the early Christians to reinterpret Jesus' teaching for the new Israel.

To discern the flow of Jesus' message and its main concerns, we now look at the discourse's literary structure, which broad lines are quite simple. After a narrative introduction (7:1-5), Jesus' message unfolds in two parts (7:6-13, 14-23).

The discourse opens with a narrative introduction that provides a concrete setting for Jesus' message (7:1-5). The Pharisees and some of the scribes who came from Jerusalem gathered around Jesus and observed that some of his disciples *(tinas ton matheton)* ate their meals with unclean hands (7:1-2). At this point, Mark interrupts the narrative to provide background information on Jewish traditions regarding ritual purification (7:3-4). The narrative then resumes. The Pharisees and the scribes objected: "Why do your disciples not follow the tradition of the elders but instead eat a meal with unclean hands?" (7:5).

The form of the objection, a question in two parts, is noteworthy. They provide the basic outline for Jesus' two-part response in the discourse proper. First, Jesus deals with the broad issue of following the tradition of the elders (7:6-13). Second, he addresses the particular question of eating with unclean hands (7:14-23).

Jesus did not answer the first issue directly (7:6-13). Instead, he denounced the Pharisees and the scribes as hypocrites for the way they themselves followed the tradition of the elders. In doing so, he showed how they made a total sham of those traditions. In his response, Jesus began by quoting a prophetic denunciation from Isaiah (7:6-7). He then applied it to the practice and the teaching of the Pharisees and the scribes (7:8-13).

For the second issue, eating with unclean hands (7:14-23), Jesus first summoned the crowd and gave them a parable on what cannot defile and what actually defiles a person (7:14-15). Later at home away from the crowd, he explained the parable to his disciples and refocused their concern away from ritual defilement toward moral defilement, the only defilement that should concern them (7:17-23).

The Setting (7:1-5). The setting for Jesus' discourse focuses on the gathering of Pharisees and the scribes from Jerusalem, on their observation that the disciples ate without purifying their hands, and on their question to Jesus. The discourse itself makes no effort to localize the event or situate it in time. That was also true in the short discourse on fasting and eating (2:18-22).

The context, however, requires that we situate the event sometime after the unsuccessful crossing of the sea (6:45-54), somewhere in the Jewish villages, towns, or countryside (6:56), and before Jesus went to the district of Tyre (7:24).

In Mark, a discourse is situated in place and time only when these are theologically and literarily significant. In 4:1, the land, the sea and the boat are just as significant as the crowd on the shore. In 3:22-30, Jesus' home is in the background (see 3:20). In these and other cases, what is important is the symbolic and literary association, not the historical reminiscence.

The discourses are composed of diverse traditions that had distinct settings in Jesus' ministry and in the early Church. For that reason, only the most general historical and geographical context could be retained.

While the introduction does not give a specific location for the event, it does refer to Jerusalem, the place from which the scribes came. For Mark's Gospel, this was far more important than the place where they gathered around Jesus.

The Pharisees. The Pharisees have already figured prominently in the Gospel's first section in a series of conflicts and controversies (2:1–3:6). We first encountered them at Levi's table, where scribes who were Pharisees *(hoi grammateis ton Pharisaion)* objected to Jesus' eating with sinners and tax collectors (2:16). In 2:18-22, Jesus responded to the contrast between his own disciples who did not fast and the disciples of John and of the Pharisees who did. In the next story (2:23-28), the Pharisees objected that Jesus' disciples picked heads of grain on the Sabbath. Finally, angered over Jesus' healing on the Sabbath and their hearts hardened, the Pharisees went out to confer with the Herodians for a way to destroy Jesus (3:1-6).

In all these instances, as here in 7:1-5, the Pharisees objected that Jesus or his disciples did not observe traditional practices. In most cases, the tradition concerned eating and meals (see also 8:11). The same is true concerning the tradition of the elders (7:1-23).

As we saw in 2:16, some Pharisees were scribes. The Pharisees, like the Sadducees and the Essenes, constituted a kind of party or sect in early Judaism, whereas the scribes were a class of religious scholars, who could simultaneously belong to one of the parties. Apart from 2:16, the Pharisees are associated with scribes only twice in the whole Gospel, and in both cases the scribes came from Jerusalem (3:22; 7:1-5). Elsewhere, Mark associates the Pharisees with Herod and the Herodians (3:6; 8:15; 12:13).

The role of the Pharisees in 7:1-5 is very significant. In 3:5, their hardness of heart announced that of the disciples in 6:52. In 7:1-23, their shadow falls on some of the disciples and as such on a party in the early Church. Jesus' response to the Pharisees was intended to move the disciples out of their shadow.

The Scribes from Jerusalem. The scribes are far more prominent than the Pharisees in Mark's Gospel. The first time they are mentioned highlights the contrast between Jesus and the entire class of scribes. Jesus taught "as one having authority and not as the scribes" (1:22). After this, we are not surprised to see them in conflict with Jesus (2:1-12 and 2:13-17). We next meet them in 3:22-30 at Jesus' home and then here in 7:1-23. In both cases, the Gospel specifies that the scribes came from Jerusalem (*hoi grammateis hoi apo Hierosolymon katabantes,* 3:22; *tines ton grammateon elthontes apo Hierosolymon,* 7:1).

The scribes that came from Jerusalem represented greater authority than ordinary scribes. That is true, but it is not Mark's emphasis. The scribes from Jerusalem plan their most important role in the second part of the Gospel (8:22–16:8), beginning with Jesus' first prophetic announcement of his passion, death and resurrection (8:31). Since the passion took place in Jerusalem, there was no need to state explicitly that the scribes came from Jerusalem.

Beginning with 8:31, the scribes are regularly associated with the chief priests and the elders, with whom they formed the Sanhedrin (see 15:1), Judaism's religious governing body in Jerusalem. They figure prominently in Jesus' teaching on the passion and the following of Christ (8:31; 9:11, 14; 10:33), in his teaching in the temple in Jerusalem (11:18, 27; 12:28, 32, 35, 38), as well as in the story of the passion (14:1, 43, 53; 15:1, 31).

In 7:1-23, the Pharisees evoke those who hardened their hearts and joined the Herodians seeking a way to destroy Jesus. The scribes from Jerusalem, condemned by their blasphemy against the Holy

Spirit (3:29), evoke those who would join the chief priests and the elders in rejecting Jesus, condemning him to death and handing him to the Gentiles. Their presence at this point in the Gospel shows how strongly Mark felt about the new Israel and its mission to the Gentiles. Blocking that mission was like a new assault on Jesus' life.

Some of the Disciples. Mark does not use words and expressions lightly. His main concern in 7:1-5 is not with the scribes in general but only with those that came from Jerusalem. In 7:5, when he refers to the Pharisees and the scribes, the designation "the scribes" presupposes the more specific indication from 7:1.

There is a similar pattern in Mark's references to the disciples. In 7:2, the first time they are introduced, we find "some of his disciples" and not "the disciples" pure and simple. The Pharisees and the scribes "observed that some of his disciples *[tinas ton matheton autou]* ate their meals with unclean, that is, unwashed hands." The later reference to "your disciples" (7:5) presupposes the more limited one in 7:2.

A simple expression such as "some of his disciples" can be very significant. In the present case it points to a major difference among the members of the Christian community. At some point in the history of the community and very likely in Mark's own time, there were those who did not observe Jewish tradition regarding meals and there were those who did.

It is not possible to say whether those who did not follow the tradition were Jewish or Gentile. That the community included many Gentiles is clear from the fact that Mark needed to explain that "unclean" meant "unwashed" and provide some background for the Jewish traditions regarding ritual purification (7:3-4). Gentiles may even have constituted the majority. We may assume that these Gentiles did not follow the Jewish traditions. Had they done so, Mark would not have needed to explain them. It is also possible that some Jews had abandoned the tradition of the elders as the community reached out to the Gentiles.

The distinction between those who followed the tradition and those who did not gave rise to conflict in the community. A good assumption from 7:1-23 is that some were appealing to the tradition of the elders in an effort to restore practices associated with the early days of their community. The situation may consequently have been very much like the one described in Galatians 2:1-14, where Paul argues against Judaizing tendencies. For his part, Mark saw very well that for Christianity to develop and survive as a new

Israel, the community had to come to terms with the whole issue of Jewish tradition.[15]

Meals, Bread, and the Loaves. The particular issue in 7:1-23 is eating with unclean hands. The general issue is observing the tradition of the elders. In 7:1-23, both of these come to the fore in relation to the Christian meal in which Jewish and Gentile Christians participated.

Some Greek expressions are very difficult to translate. For example, the Greek in the New Testament can use the same word, *artos,* to mean "bread," "a loaf of bread," and even "a meal." In the plural, *artoi* can mean "loaves" and "meals." The same Greek word can consequently carry more than one meaning, while English need to use a different word for each of those meanings. By selecting one word, we necessarily exclude the others. That is what happens in 7:1-5. In the process, the passage can lose its intended relationship to the eucharistic meal.

We read in English that the Pharisees and the scribes from Jerusalem observed how some of Jesus' disciples ate their meals with unclean hands. The Greek expression for "their meals" is *tous artous,* meaning the loaves of bread. The disciples ate the loaves of bread with unclean hands. "Their meals" is a normal and good translation, but unfortunately it loses any association with the loaves Jesus broke for the five thousand, from which the disciples gathered twelve baskets of the bread broken (6:34-44). It also loses any association with the disciples' failure to understand about the loaves when Jesus came to them on the sea.

The same is true in the objection by the Pharisees and the scribes: "Why do your disciples . . . eat a meal *[ton arton]* with unclean hands?" (7:5). In the immediate context, the Pharisees and the scribes ask about "eating a meal." In the larger context and from the story teller's point of view, the expression acquires deeply Christian meaning and is associated with "the breaking of the bread."

In 7:1-5, the problem raised has to do with more than ordinary meals. It has to do with the Christian community's very special "breaking of bread." The discourse on the tradition of the elders is consequently at the heart of Mark's story. Before moving on to the other shore of the sea and gathering both Jews and Gentiles as well as men and women in the breaking of the bread, the disciples and

---

[15] Luke deals with this issue in the book of Acts, first in the story of Cornelius and his household (Acts 10:1–11:18), then in what is popularly called the council of Jerusalem (Acts 15:1-35).

the Christian community had to deal with the tradition of the elders. At stake was the very nature of Christianity as a Church, representing a new Israel.

By Markan standards, Mark 7:1-5 is a fairly ample introduction, particularly for a discourse. First, Mark notes the presence of the Pharisees and some scribes from Jerusalem who objected that some of Jesus' disciples ate with unclean hands (7:1-2, 5). He then provides background for the ritual washing of hands and similar practices which the Pharisees and other Jews observed as part of the tradition of the elders (7:3-4).

With that, all is now ready for Jesus' response, which comes in two parts. The Pharisees and scribes objected that Jesus' disciples did not follow the tradition of the elders (7:5a). Jesus deals with this general objection in the first part of the discourse (7:6-13). In their objection, the Pharisees and scribes specified that Jesus' disciples ate their meals (*ton arton,* bread) with unclean hands (7:5b). Jesus deals with this more specific matter in the second part of the discourse (7:14-23).

The Tradition of the Elders (7:6-13). Jesus' response opens with a very strong denunciation regarding the tradition of the elders. It is not that there was a problem with the tradition in itself. The problem lay rather with the Pharisees and the scribes who made the tradition absolute and imposed its observance even if it meant disregarding the word of God and breaking the commandments.

Tradition draws its value from the word of God and the life of faith it inspires. Its purpose is to interpret God's word and apply it to particular cultures, conditions, times, and places.

The Pharisees and the scribes would not accept that the tradition of the elders was secondary and relative to the word of God. Turning tradition into a set of absolutes, they moved away from the deeper reality that gave it life and meaning. In so doing, the also broke away from the elders and actually abandoned the tradition as it had been understood and handed on to them. All this was done in defense of the tradition of the elders.

That is why in his response Jesus never referred to "the tradition of the elders" *(he paradosis ton presbyteron),* the expression used by the Pharisees and the scribes (7:5). Instead he spoke of "human tradition" *(he paradosis ton anthropon,* 7:8) and even more pointedly of "your tradition" *(he paradosis hymon,* 7:9, 13). For Jesus, the Pharisees and the scribes were clinging to merely human tradition, their own personal tradition, and not to the tradition of the elders.

A Prophetic Message from Isaiah (7:6-7). Jesus began by introducing a prophetic passage from Isaiah and applying it to the

Pharisees and the scribes: "Well did Isaiah prophesy about you hypo-crites" (7:6a). The text of Isaiah is an adaptation of 29:13.[16]

Isaiah plays a very prominent role in Mark's Gospel, especially in the teaching of Jesus. This is the second time a formal quotation from Isaiah appears in the context of a discourse of Jesus. The first was in the discourse on parables, where Isaiah 6:9-10 was applied to the purpose of Jesus' parables for those who refused to gather around Jesus and remained apart from the Twelve (4:12).

The term "hypocrite," on the other hand, while quite frequent in Matthew, appears only this once in the whole of Mark. It refers to the perverse, willful masking of one's true attitude and intentions. The use of so harsh a term to denounce the Pharisees in conjunc-tion with the very strong condemnatory passage from Isaiah high-lights the importance of this conflict for the Christian community.

The quotation from Isaiah 29:13 in Mark 7:6b-7 follows neither the Septuagint nor the Hebrew Massoretic text, but is closer to the Septuagint. The distinctive elements in the New Testament ren-dering could stem from a loose quotation done from memory or rep-resent a traditional Christian form of the text. Those elements probably constitute a deliberate adaptation of Isaiah 29:13 for the present Markan context.

The most substantial departure from the Hebrew Massoretic text is in the last part of the verse. The Hebrew said, "And their rever-ence for me has become routine observance of human precepts." Mark 7:7 reads, "In vain do they worship me, teaching as doctrines human precepts" *(didaskontes didaskalias entalmata anthropon)*, which is not the same as the corresponding statement in the Sep-tuagint, "In vain do they worship me, teaching precepts and doc-trines" *(didaskontes entalmata anthropon kai didaskalias)*.

The text in Mark 7:7 allows us to think of the doctrines as divine, or at least intended to be, and of the precepts as human, a very im-portant distinction for the purposes of Mark 7:6-13. Whereas Isa-iah 29:13 referred to the people of Jerusalem, Jesus turned the prophecy into an indictment of the Pharisees and the scribes, who taught human precepts as divine doctrines. The conclusion (7:8) for 7:6-8 leaves no doubt regarding this interpretation. Addressing the Pharisees and the scribes directly, Jesus accuses them of clinging to human tradition while disregarding God's commandment.

---

[16] Paul cited the following verse, Isa 29:14, in 1 Corinthians 1:19 in con-nection with the paradox of the cross. Paul's message to the Corinthians is similar to Mark 4:10-12, where the Gospel quotes Isa 6:9.

The last words of the quotation from Isaiah, "teaching as doctrines human precepts," set the stage for the conclusion in 7:8 as well as for the next segment of the discourse (7:9-13), which includes an example regarding the use of the *qorban* formula (7:10-12).

A Triple Escalation (7:8-9, 13). The rhetorical force of Jesus' denunciation springs largely from a triple escalation of the indictment. The escalation is seen both in the choice of the words, especially the verbs, and in the sentence structure:

> 7:8 "You disregard God's commandment
>   but cling to human tradition;
> 7:9 "You have set aside the commandment of God
>   in order to uphold your tradition . . . ;
> 7:13 "You nullify the word of God
>   in favor of your tradition."

The first of the three accusations applies the Isaian passage concerning "teaching as [divine] doctrines human precepts" to the Pharisees and the scribes and their way of enforcing tradition. The Pharisees and the scribes teach human precepts as divine doctrines. When they abandon God's commandment, the human tradition to which they cling replaces it.

The second accusation goes further than the first. The Pharisees not only forsake God's commandment while clinging to human tradition. They set aside God's commandment in order to maintain their tradition. Tradition was meant to serve God's commandment. By giving priority to their tradition, the Pharisees and the scribes reversed the order.

The third accusation goes further yet. Not only do the Pharisees and the scribes set aside God's commandment, they actually nullify the word of God in favor of their tradition. In their life and teaching, they reduce the word of God to nothing, whereas they are careful to hand on a tradition that has become purely their own.

Jesus' denunciation takes one final step: "And you do many such things" (7:13b). With this *etcetera* or *kai ta loipa,* the rest is left open to the imagination. Not that a further escalation would have been possible—Jesus does seem to have exhausted the possibilities—but that many examples other than the traditional use of the *qorban* formula could be given.

The *Qorban* Formula (7:10-11). The first accusation (7:8) applied the passage from Isaiah (7:6b-7) to the Pharisees and the scribes. The second and third accusations (7:9, 13) frame Jesus' teaching concerning the *Qorban* formula. From a literary point of view, 7:9-13 can be considered a sub-unit of 7:6-13. The unit is introduced by, "He responded" (7:6a). The sub-unit is introduced by, "He went on to say" (7:9a).

After the second accusation, Jesus provided an example contrasting the teaching of the Pharisees and the scribes with that of Moses, that is, God's commandment. Brief introductions set up the contrast:

7:10 "For Moses said . . ."
7:11 "Yet you say . . ."

Two statements are quoted from "Moses," that is from the Torah (Law). First there is a commandment: "Honor your father and your mother" (7:10a; see Exod 20:12; Deut 5:16). Then comes a closely related threat: "Whoever curses father or mother shall die" (7:10b; see Exod 21:17). In the present context, the commandment may be a veiled accusation. Using the *Qorban* formula, the Pharisees and the scribes do not honor their father and their mother. If so, the accompanying threat might well apply to the Pharisees and the scribes.

Then comes the practice of the Pharisees and the scribes showing how they set aside the commandment of God to uphold their tradition (7:11-13). Honoring father and mother includes supporting them especially in their old age. But some appear to have found a way around the obligation. By declaring something *qorban,* that is dedicated to God, it became sacred and could no longer be used for any other purpose. By declaring *qorban* whatever might have been used to support mother and father, children freed themselves of their obligation to support them.

Jesus accuses the Pharisees and the scribes of accepting this practice as part of what they called "the tradition of the elders," but in reality it was no more than their own tradition, which they handed on as the tradition of the elders.[17]

And so we come to the end of the first part of Jesus' discourse (7:6-13). The Pharisees and the some scribes who came from Jerusalem had objected that some of Jesus' disciples did not follow the

---

[17] If the Pharisees and the scribes represent a segment of the Christian community, Jesus' teaching concerning his true relatives could have influenced them (see 3:31-35). If everyone who "does the will of God," including Jews and Gentiles, was Jesus' "brother and sister and mother" (3:35), this could have weakened the obligation to "Honor your father and your mother" (7:10). Hence the tendency to declare property and money *qorban*.

tradition of the elders (7:5a). Jesus responded quite directly. What some of the disciples failed to follow was no more than the personal tradition of the Pharisees and the scribes, something they handed on as the tradition of the elders, but which was quite different from the genuine tradition of the elders.

Personal Defilement (7:14-23). The discourse now moves away from "the tradition of the elders" and takes up the second part of the objection. The Pharisees and the scribes had asked Jesus why his disciples ate a meal *(ton arton,* bread) with unclean hands (7:5b). Instead of responding directly to the Pharisees and the scribes, Jesus "summoned the crowd again *(palin)*"[18] and addressed the answer to them in the form of a parable (7:14-15). Later, away from the crowd, he explained the answer to the disciples (7:17-23).

A similar pattern was observed in the discourse on parables, where Jesus' teaching for the crowd (4:1-9) had to be explained to his disciples (the Twelve) once they were by themselves away from the crowd (4:10-20). In the discourse on parables, Jesus also taught the crowd in parables (4:2), and the Twelve asked about their meaning (4:10).

The same is true in the discourse on tradition. Jesus taught the crowd with a parable (4:14-15), and his disciples asked about its meaning (4:17). Mark 7:14-23 is thus another example of Jesus' general practice in which he taught the crowds in parables but explained everything to his disciples in private.

Jesus spoke the word to the crowd in parables, that is, according to their ability to understand it (see 4:33). His disciples, however, had been granted the mystery of the kingdom of God (see 4:11a). They consequently were able to understand the explanations that would have been opaque for the crowd of outsiders (4:11b-12). The distinction between the crowd and the disciples also enabled Mark to interpret the early parable tradition for the new and challenging situation created by the Gentile mission.

The similarity between 4:1-34 and 7:1-23 is also indicated by the repeated calls for the listeners to hear and understand (4:3, 9, 13, 24; 7:14, 18). The parallelism in this matter is so clear that a num-

---

[18] Jesus had dismissed the crowd after nourishing the five thousand and making his disciples get into the boat to precede him to other side (6:45). Now he summons the crowd again. This is the seventh time Mark employed *palin* to connect an event to a previous event (see 2:1, 13; 3:1, 20; 4:1; 5:21; and 7:14). In 7:14, *palin* connects Jesus' teaching concerning "the tradition of the elders" with the breaking of the bread for the five thousand (6:34-44) and the sea journey (6:45-52).

ber of ancient manuscripts inserted an expression from the discourse on parables into the discourse on tradition: "Anyone who has ears to hear ought to hear" (7:16).[19]

A Parable for the Crowd (7:14-15). Jesus had dismissed the crowd after breaking the bread with the five thousand (6:34-44) and making the disciples get into the boat and precede him to the other side toward Bethsaida (6:45). He now summoned the crowd again and pleaded with them to hear him and understand.

The crowd Jesus summoned again is the one to whom he had already taught many things (6:34) and with whom he had broken the bread (6:41). There was now something they needed to hear and understand about personal defilement and how it was related to eating the bread Jesus broke.

Jesus spoke to the crowd with a parable (7:17). In this context, the term "parable" refers to a succinct teaching, a general principle, such as we expect to find in a collection of wisdom sayings. In the Gospels, the meaning of the word parable is much broader than we find it used in modern scholarly discussions. The Gospels simply followed contemporary usage. Recent scholarship is more concerned with their literary form.

The parable to the crowd contains two contrasting statements. The first speaks of what cannot defile, the second of what does. Nothing that enters a person from outside can defile the person (7:15a). Only those things that issue from inside a person do so (7:15b).

No reason is given for either statement. Nor is there any indication of how defilement is to be understood in this context. In relation to ancient Jewish laws and traditions concerning ritual defilement and purification, Jesus' parable was very enigmatic. Like Jesus' disciples, we are left with questions and wondering what Jesus meant, which is precisely what parables are meant to do.

An Explanation for the Disciples (7:17-23). In a brief introduction, the disciples ask Jesus about the parable (7:17), and Jesus, presupposing that the crowd had not understood, asks if the disciples too *(kai hymeis)* were without understanding (7:18a). We recall that the previous time Mark indicated that the disciples did not

---

[19] Verse 16 is omitted from critical Greek editions of the Gospel of Mark. See Kurt Aland, Matthew Black, Carlo Martini, Bruce M. Metzger, and Allen Wikgren, *The Greek New Testament,* 2nd ed. (New York: American Bible Society, 1968). That is why the Greek edition and modern translations in various vernaculars go from 7:15 to 7:17.

understand, it was concerning the bread and because their hearts were hardened (6:52).

Like the parable itself, the explanation is given in two parts. The first is on what cannot defile (7:18b-19). It corresponds to the first part of the parable (7:15a). The second part of the explanation is on what does defile (7:20-23). It corresponds to the parable's second part (7:15b).

As soon as Jesus begins his explanation, it becomes very clear that the parable was not about ritual defilement but moral and spiritual defilement. The objection of the Pharisees and the scribes had been based on accepted notions and traditions of ritual defilement that certainly could come from outside a person. The Law itself contained many prescriptions regarding foods and eating practices that made one ritually unclean. For clean and unclean foods, see for example Leviticus 11.

The reason things entering someone from outside could not defile that person is that those things merely entered the stomach and not a person's heart *(kardia)*. Jesus' reference to the heart recalls the hardness of heart *(he porosis tes kardias)* of the Pharisees (3:5) and the disciples' lack of understanding about the bread because the hearts also were hardened *(auton he kardia peporomene, 6:52)*. Jesus' explanation consequently called the disciples to confront their hardness of heart in the matter of the breaking of the bread and called them to a new moral stance.

Mark notes that with this explanation, Jesus declared all foods clean (7:19b).[20] The Jewish laws and traditions of ritual defilement constituted a major obstacle for the mission among the Gentiles. Jesus' parable, together with his explanation, was meant to remove that obstacle.

It was not enough to abolish the laws and traditions concerning ritual purity and defilement. It was necessary to fulfill them in a law of moral purity and defilement. So it is that the discourse ends with a statement of what constitutes moral defilement.

For this, we are given a list of evil actions (sins) and a list of vices. At the head of the double list, Jesus speaks of evil thoughts (7:21a). Both sins and vices flow from evil thoughts that issue from the heart. The first list includes six evil actions or sins: lustful acts, acts of theft, acts of murder, acts of adultery, acts of greed, and acts of

---

[20] For a parallel, see Acts 10:11-15, where a mysterious voice tells Peter: "What God has made clean, you are not to call profane" (Acts 10:15; see also 10:28; 11:7-10).

malice (7:21b-22a). Each sin is given in the plural. The second list includes six vices, all given in the singular: deceit, licentiousness, envy, blasphemy, arrogance, folly, or perverseness.[21]

And so we come to the end of the entire discourse. The Pharisees and some scribes from Jerusalem had objected that Jesus' disciples did not follow the tradition of the elders but instead ate a meal (bread) with their hands unclean. In his response, Jesus took the two parts of the objection one at a time.

For the first part, he showed how in fact the question did not have to do with the tradition of the elders but with the personal tradition of the Pharisees and the scribes. In doing this, he revealed the hypocrisy of their objection.

For the second part, he did not deal with the washing of hands as such but with the more general question of ritual defilement, which also included laws and traditions regarding particular foods that could not be eaten. In so doing, he responded to the whole matter regarding unclean foods, a critical issue that had to be resolved in relation to the Gentile mission.

In the discourse, Jesus did more than answer the objection of the Pharisees and the scribes. By placing their question within the larger contexts of tradition and defilement, he met the broader issues of this section of the Gospel. As it was, the disciples had been unprepared to cross from the Jewish shore to the Gentile shore. They were now one step closer to being able to do this.

As Mark's Gospel advances, it becomes clearer and clearer that to understand a particular event, we need to place it in the context of the whole Gospel. Each story moves the Gospel forward and contributes to the whole.

The Mission to the Gentiles (7:24–8:21)

To take on the Gentile mission, the disciples and the early Church had to deal with the tradition of the elders, especially regarding ritual purification and defilement. The tradition of the elders weighed heavily on the disciples, enough to block the mission to the Gentiles. Among the Gentiles, the tradition of the elders would have no meaning (7:1-23).

The disciples and the early Church also had to deal with other issues. There was the question of breaking the bread at a common table with Gentiles, a practice that challenged the Jewish identity

---

[21] For similar lists, see Romans 1:29-31; Galatians 5:19-21; and 1 Peter 4:3.

of the early disciples. Mark's Gospel takes up this issue in the story of the woman who was a Greek, a story that unfolds in the district of Tyre (7:24-30).

With that it was finally possible to go into the Decapolis, the district of the Ten Greek Cities, and take on the mission to the Gentiles. First, the ears of the Gentiles had to be opened to hear the word of Jesus and their lips unsealed to proclaim it (7:31-37). Then, Jesus had to show the way by breaking the bread with Gentile men and women (8:1-9), as he had done earlier with Jewish men (6:34-44).

After the breaking of the bread for the four thousand (8:1-10), there would be another crossing (8:10), after which Jesus would deal again with the Pharisees (8:11-13). Leaving them, Jesus and the Twelve "got into boat again, and went off to the other shore" (8:13). This crossing would again deal with the disciples' understanding about the bread. The event ends with a rhetorical question: "Do you still not understand?" (8:21). With this question, the first part of the beginning of the Gospel of Jesus Christ (1:14-8:21) ends.

The Woman Who Was a Greek (7:24-30)

The story of the woman who was a Greek is most extraordinary for the brief exchange of sayings between Jesus and the woman. The exchange clears the last obstacle for the Gospel to move into the Gentile mission.

The Setting (7:24). A brief introduction provides the setting. "From that place," that is, from the villages, towns, and countryside around Genesareth (6:53-56), Jesus "went off to the district of Tyre" (7:24a). This is not the first time the district of Tyre is mentioned in the Gospel. We remember that part of the crowd that gathered around Jesus along the sea came from the district of Tyre (3:8). They were among those who made it necessary for Jesus to establish the Twelve (3:13-19). They also formed part of the crowd that gathered at Jesus' home in Capernaum (3:20). Now, instead of their coming to Jesus, it is he who went to Tyre and entered one of their homes (7:24b).

Nor is this the first time Jesus went into Gentile territory. He had already been to the territory of the Gerasenes, where he had banished a Legion of unclean spirits from a Gentile swineherd (5:1-20). The man had subsequently returned to his home and family, announcing what the Lord had done for him. As a forerunner for the future mission to the Gentiles, he proclaimed what Jesus did for him throughout the Decapolis. This time, Jesus came to the Gentile world to establish the mission that had already been prepared by the anonymous forerunner, the man exorcised of the unclean Legion.

It is interesting to note that though Jesus did not want anyone to hear of his presence the word did spread (7:24c). Something similar had happened earlier in the Gospel, at the very beginning of Jesus' mission in Galilee (1:45). At this point, Jesus' intention underscores that there was no repressing the good news. Even Jesus could not prevent its diffusion. Some things were reserved to the Father (13:32).

The Woman and Her Daughter (7:25-26). The story itself is about a woman and her daughter who had an unclean spirit (7:25-30). The woman was among those who heard of Jesus' presence. She came and threw herself at Jesus' feet, pleading that he drive the demon from her daughter (7:25-26).

If these were the only elements in Mark's introduction of the woman and her daughter, we would move on immediately to the heart of the episode. This is not the first time a woman enters Mark's Gospel. Recall Simon's mother-in-law (1:29-31), Jairus' daughter (5:21-24, 35-43) and the woman with the hemorrhage (5:25-34). Indeed, up to this point women have already played quite a prominent role in Mark's Gospel.

But Mark also places great emphasis on the identity of the woman. She was a Greek. Besides, she was a Syrophoenician by birth (7:26a). The story thus focuses on the fact that she was both a woman and a Gentile. Recall that Jesus broke the bread for five thousand men *(andres)* early in this section (6:34-44). At this point, the introduction of a Gentile woman must be very significant.

An Exchange of Sayings (7:27-28). The dialogue that follows confirms the Gentile woman's significance. We normally would expect the dialogue to deal directly with the woman's request that Jesus expel the demon from her daughter. Instead, we have an exchange of sayings between Jesus and the woman. Only afterwards does Jesus announce that the woman's request has been granted and that the unclean spirit has gone out of her daughter.

There are two sayings, the first from Jesus, and the second from the woman. After telling the woman that the children must be fed first, Jesus adds, "It is not right to take the food *[ton arton]* of the children *[ton teknon]* and throw it to the dogs" (7:27). To this the woman answers with a counter saying, "Lord *[Kyrie],* even the dogs under the table eat the children's *[ton paidion]* scraps" (7:28).

We notice immediately that the sayings revolve around the image of bread, the dominant theme in Mark's account of the Christian mission. This is especially striking in the immediate context where we might expect sayings involving healing. Such sayings are not foreign to the Gospel literature.

In Luke's presentation of the mission of Jesus, those in the synagogue at Nazareth appeal for Jesus' attention with the simple saying, "Physician, cure yourself" (Luke 4:23). More striking still is Mark's own use of a healing saying in Jesus' response to the scribes when they objected that he was eating with tax collectors and sinners: "Those who are well do not need a physician, but the sick do" (2:17).

Sayings communicate in a very special way. It is important not to apply the terms included in the sayings to those who figure in the narrative itself. The tendency here is to jump to the conclusion that Jesus refers to the Gentiles and to Gentile woman and her daughter as dogs. With this interpretation, the further conclusion is that the woman, accepting the metaphor, grovels at Jesus' feet.

Were this not an exchange of sayings, the metaphor would indeed apply directly. But the metaphors used in sayings follow the laws of communication that apply to sayings. Above all, sayings must be understood as a whole and not through their particular elements. As such, sayings correspond to entire situations, independently of their metaphorical content.

A few examples will make this clear. A number of years ago, Western journalists chided Deng Xiaoping about allowing elements of free trade in China. He responded: "It does not matter whether the cat is black or white so long as it catches the mouse." No one inquired whether the black or the white cat represented the capitalist or the communist system.

We also have similar sayings in our own culture, for example, "You can lead a horse to water but cannot make it drink"; and "A bird in the hand is worth two in the bush." Both sayings comment on an entire situation. No one is offended or repulsed by the metaphors of the horse or the bird, which are understood only within the saying. The saying itself, not the metaphors, comments on the situation.

The same applies to the exchange between Jesus and the woman. It would be wrong to apply the dog metaphor to her and her daughter. It would destroy the effectiveness of the sayings.

Equally important is the source of the saying. We should ask whether this is a saying that Jesus speaks in his own name or whether he is the literary spokesman for those in the Christian community who object to the presence of Gentiles and women at the breaking of the bread.

If Jesus was speaking in his own name, we would expect a more judicious choice of saying, one that would effectively silence the woman at his feet. Instead, he provides her with an opportunity to respond with a related saying. The woman takes the opportunity and counters Jesus' saying and neutralizes its effectiveness.

The Cure of Her Daughter (7:29-30). Because of her word, she may go: "For saying this *[Dia touton ton logon]*, you may go. The demon has gone out of your daughter" (7:29).

We are reminded of Jesus' response to the woman who was cured of hemorrhages: "Daughter, your faith has saved you. God in peace and be cured of your affliction" (5:34). It is through her faith that the hemorrhaging woman was cured. It is through the Greek woman's word that her daughter was freed of the demon.

The story concludes with the woman going home and finding her child in bed and the demon gone (7:30). Through this story, Mark has eliminated the last reason why the apostolic community might have refused to proceed to the Gentile mission, where the Christian table and the breaking of the bread would be open to both Jews and Gentiles as well as to men and women. The response came from the Gentile woman's faith.

A Man from the Decapolis (7:31-37)

The story of the man from the Decapolis also is quite extraordinary. At the heart of it, Jesus opened the man's ears. The story is rich with images. It is a story of spitting, touching, and groaning. It even includes the Aramaic command *"Ephphatha,"* which Mark translated into Greek: *"Dianoichtheti* (Be opened)" (7:34). The story may well have its origins in the ministry of Jesus, but in its present form it may also reflect baptismal practices in the early Church.

The Setting (7:31). The story begins with the brief transitional statement that Jesus again *(palin)*[22] left the district of Tyre and went by way of Sidon to the Sea of Galilee[23] into the district of the Decapolis (7:31). The previous time, Jesus and the disciples left for Bethsaida and Gentile territories, they did not succeed (6:45-52). Instead they came to Gennesaret (6:53).

The geography of the journey is unusual. Sidon was not situated between Tyre and the Decapolis. From Tyre one went north to get to Sidon, but to get to the Decapolis, one went south.

Mark probably wanted to evoke the expression "Tyre and Sidon" when he described a crowd coming "from the neighborhood of *(peri, from around)* Tyre and Sidon" (3:8). The crowd came from around

---

[22] This is the eighth time Mark's employs the adverb *palin* (again) to connect an event with a previous event.

[23] Mark uses the full name, the Sea of Galilee, only for the first and the last time, he mentions the sea (1:16; 8:31). Otherwise he refers simply to the sea.

Tyre and even farther, from around Sidon. Now Jesus went to those who had earlier come to him from the regions *(ton horion),* that is, the surroundings *(peri,* 3:8), of Tyre and Sidon, not from the cities themselves.

The Opening of the Man's Ears (7:32-35). After telling a story about a woman (7:24-30), Mark tells a story about a man. The man was both deaf and unable to speak. As in the story of the healing of the Gerasene demoniac, which also unfolded in the Decapolis (5:1-20), Mark introduced a Gentile into the Gospel.

We should note that Jesus took the man off by himself *(kat' idian)* away from the crowd, as he had done for his disciples (4:10; 7:17). Recall that Jesus taught his disciples in private *(kat' idian)* away from the crowd (see 4:34). The story thus deals with the making of a disciple and not merely with a physical cure. What is significant in this case is that the disciple was from the Gentile world.

The manner of the cure is very physical. As in the case of the woman with the hemorrhages (5:30), Simon's mother-in-law (1:31), and Jairus' daughter (5:41), the cure involves touching. But in the present case, the touching is much more graphic. Jesus places his finger in the man's ear. He also spits and touches the man's tongue, looks up to heaven and groans (7:33-34). Later, when Jesus heals a man of blindness, he also puts spittle on his eyes and lays his hands on him (8:23). Even so, the cure of the man that was both deaf and mute remains the most graphic cure in the entire Gospel of Mark.

The story's association with the formation of Jesus' disciples invites us to see all of these indications as part of early Christian "sacramental" practice. The antiquity of such practice may be indicated by the use of the command in Aramaic, *"Ephphatha,"* which recalls Jesus' command to the little girl in the story of Jairus, *"Talitha koum"* (5:41). The earlier story was not only about Jesus' raising the dead girl to life. It was about raising her to Christian life. Correspondingly, when Jesus opened the deaf man's ears, he enabled him to truly hear (see 4:3, 9, 23, 24; 7:14). When Jesus removed his speech impediment, he enabled him to proclaim what he heard.

Reaction of the People (7:36-37). But as for those who observed the event, Jesus ordered them to be silent. They were not to tell anyone. As on previous occasions (see 1:34; 3:12; 5:43), the reason for this was quite simple. Those who were not followers of Jesus Christ could not properly reveal his identity or the true meaning of what he said and did. The mystery of the kingdom of God had not been given to them (see 4:10-12).

Proclamation presupposes faith, and faith consists in knowing Jesus, and not only knowing about Jesus. Knowing Jesus begins when people accept to be his followers, and it develops in the course of their life as followers. The second part of the Gospel (8:21–16:8) shows how the following of Christ was critical for knowing Jesus and his gospel.

But the people in the Decapolis, like the people of Galilee, ignored Jesus' command. The more he ordered them not to speak of what he did, the more they proclaimed *(ekerysson)* it (7:36).

Like the people in the synagogue at Capernaum, the people were extremely astonished *(exeplessonto,* 7:37a; see 1:22). When Jesus drove out a unclean spirit from someone in the synagogue, the people said, "What is this? A new teaching with authority. He commands even the unclean spirits and they obey him" (1:27). Later when Jesus healed a paralytic at the home in Capernaum, the people said, "We have never seen anything like this" (2:12).

Now the people in the Decapolis said, "He has done all things well. He makes the deaf hear and [the] mute speak" (7:37b). With that, the disciples are now prepared to break the bread with Gentiles that come to Jesus.

The Breaking of the Bread for the Four Thousand (8:1-9)

"In those days," that is, while Jesus was in the district of the Decapolis (see 7:31-37), "there again *[palin]* was a great crowd without anything to eat" (8:1a).[24] The Gospel had already told about a similar situation on the Galilean side of the sea (6:34-44). On that other occasion, the disciples asked Jesus to dismiss the crowd, but he ignored their request. Instead, he instructed them to organize the crowd and led them in an extraordinary breaking of the bread.

That earlier event took place with a crowd of Jewish men *(andres)* on the northwestern shore of the sea (6:34-44). After nourishing the crowd, Jesus made the disciples get into the boat and cross to the other side, where the population was mainly Gentile. The crossing proved too difficult (6:45-52). And so the mission continued among the villages and towns and in the countryside of Galilee (6:53-56), at least for a time.

Before they could take on the Gentile mission, the disciples had to be instructed concerning "the tradition of the elders," in particular

---

[24] This is the ninth time that Mark used the adverb *palin* (again) to connect a new event with a previous event. This time, he connected the breaking of the bread for the four thousand (8:1-9) with the breaking of the bread for the five thousand (6:34-44).

concerning ritual defilement (7:1-23). They also had to be exposed to the faith of the Gentiles, represented by a Syrophoenician woman (7:24-30). By opening the ears of a Gentile and by releasing his tongue (7:31-37), Jesus prepared the way for the breaking of the bread among the Gentiles (8:1-9).

Mark surely intended the breaking of the bread for the four thousand (8:1-9) to be seen as a new event, if not in relation to Jesus' historical life, surely in relation to the development of the Church. This is not to say that Jesus broke the bread only once or that his breaking of the bread was uneventful on other occasions. A meal with Jesus was always a prophetic event.

Meals with Jesus played a significant role in his ministry, and the memory of them profoundly marked early Christian tradition and the gospel accounts. But Matthew and Luke were quite right in situating those meals exclusively among Jews.

In Matthew, the second breaking of the bread does not take place in the Decapolis but on a Galilean mountainside near the shore of the Sea of Galilee (Matt 15:29-39). For Matthew, Jesus' ministry was "only to the lost sheep of the house of Israel" (Matt 15:24).

Luke omitted the second breaking of the bread altogether from his Gospel. For Luke, the mission to the Gentiles and the gathering of Jews and Gentiles at one Christian table developed Jesus' death and resurrection. Its story is not told in the Gospel but in the Acts of the Apostles.

Superficially, the new breaking of the bread (8:1-9) seems quite similar to the earlier one (6:34-44) but the stories are really quite different, as can be seen from their introductions (6:34-36; 8:1-3). In the first breaking of the bread, the narrator says that Jesus was deeply moved on account of the crowd *(esplagchnisthe ep' autous)* because they were like sheep without a shepherd, and so Jesus proceeded to teach them. It is only after this that the disciples enter the story, asking Jesus to dismiss the crowd.

In the second story, Jesus summons the disciples at the very start and tells them that he is deeply moved on account of the crowd *(splagchnizomai epi ton ochlon)* because they have been with him three days and have nothing to eat. Jesus then tells them why he cannot send them away to their homes. They were hungry and would collapse on the way. Besides, some had come a great distance. It is as though Jesus meant to anticipate a suggestion that he should dismiss the crowd.

In 6:34-36, the story contrasted the attitude of the disciples, who wanted to send the crowd away, with that of Jesus, who taught them and showed the disciples how to nourish them. The initiative to dismiss the crowd came from the disciples. In 8:1-3, the initiative came from Jesus, who called and told the disciples about the crowd's plight.

In the second story of the breaking of the bread, the disciples are no longer at the center of the story. Their role has become secondary. Instead, Jesus is now at the center and his role has become primary.

The disciples' initiative and their role in 6:34-44 point to the story's ecclesiological concerns. Jesus initiative and his role in 8:1-9 points to the story's Christological concerns. For the mission to the Gentiles, the Gospel needs to reach beyond ecclesiological considerations to their basis in christology.

Christological Emphasis. The christological emphasis in the breaking of the bread for the four thousand is evident not only in the opening verses (8:1-3) but throughout the story. In the breaking of the bread for the five thousand (6:34-44), the disciples, representing the Church, maintained their important role throughout the story.

The disciples' role in the breaking of the bread for the five thousand began when they asked Jesus to send the crowd away to buy themselves something to eat (6:35-36). When Jesus told them to give some food themselves, they asked, "Are we to buy two hundred days' wages worth of food and give it to them to eat?" (6:37). Then, when Jesus asked them to go see how much bread they had, they returned with the answer that there were but five loaves and two fish (6:38).

Jesus then ordered the disciples to have the crowd recline on the green grass by banquet parties *(symposia)* of fifties and one hundreds (6:39-40). After this was done, Jesus himself took the bread and the fish, spoke a blessing and broke the loaves, but he gave them to the disciples to distribute (6:41). Later, it is also they who gathered up the remaining fragments *(klasmata,* 6:43). Jesus' role is not unimportant, but in this first story, he does not act directly but through the disciples. The passage also emphasizes the role of the assembly.

By contrast, the role of the disciples in the breaking of the bread for the four thousand (8:1-9) is quite muted. As we have already seen, it is Jesus who summons the disciples, not they who approach him (8:1). He also brings up the matter of providing food for the crowd (8:2-3). Then, when Jesus inquires how much bread they have, they answered, "Seven." There was no need for them to go and see (8:5). Afterward, Jesus himself orders the crowd to sit on the ground. The disciples have nothing to do with organizing the crowd for the breaking of the bread (8:6). In this second story, Jesus generally acts directly rather than through the disciples. Nor is there any emphasis on the assembly.

The disciples' role is very limited. They ask Jesus where anyone might get enough bread to satisfy such a crowd in the desert (8:4). Their question was responding to Jesus' reflection on the hungry crowd and why it was impossible to send them away (8:2-3). The disciples retain their role in distributing the bread and the fish (8:6-7) and in gathering the remaining fragments (*klasmata,* 8:8), but this is not enough to draw them into the center of the story. From the beginning to the end, Mark 8:1-9 is very much a story of Jesus.

Now Three Days (8:2). The christological emphasis stands out most sharply in the story's reference to "three days." In 6:34-44, the disciples approached Jesus at the end of the first day. Here Jesus is deeply moved for the crowd after three days: "My heart is moved with pity for the crowd, because they have been with me now for three days *[ede hemerai treis]* and have nothing to eat" (8:2).

In Mark's Gospel, as in the rest of the New Testament, a reference to three days or the third day evokes Jesus' resurrection, his life in glory as risen Lord, and all that flows from that life for the life of the Church. In Mark's prophetic statements of the passion, for instance, Jesus states that the Son of Man will rise "after three days" *(meta treis hemeras)* (8:31; 9:31; 10:34). Elsewhere in the New Testament, the expression used is "on the third day" *(te hemera te trite)* with the ordinal numeral (see 1 Cor 15:3; Matt 16:21; 17:23; 20:19; Luke 9:22; 19:33). The expression in Mark, "after three days" has the cardinal numeral. The reference to the crowd that has been with Jesus "for three days" is in keeping with Mark's style.

Earlier, the Gospel dealt with objections against admitting Gentiles to the Christian table and the breaking of the bread (7:1-23). It also showed why Gentiles could be invited, how they asked for and received healing (7:24-30), and how they now had ears to hear and tongues to speak the gospel (7:31-37). With this reference to "three days," a symbolic evocation of the resurrection and the risen Lord, the Gospel now gave the reason why it was necessary that they join in breaking of the bread.

Like the people of Galilee, Judea, and Jerusalem, were they not with Jesus (3:7-8)? Were they not a brother, sister, and mother to him (3:31-35)? They came from far away, like those who had come from Idumea, Transjordan, and the regions of Tyre and Sidon (3:7-8), but this was no reason to exclude them. On the contrary, it was a reason not to send them away, as Jesus himself told the disciples at the beginning of the story (8:2-3).

The association of "the three days" with the resurrection comes from Jesus' new state as the risen Lord. As a historical figure, Jesus was a Jew, and to join him at table was to join in solidarity with his life and mission as a Jew. But as risen Lord, Jesus transcends all the limitations of being either a Jew or a Gentile. As risen Lord, Jesus is Lord of all, and that means that all human beings can identity with him directly. The table of the one who is Lord of all cannot be exclusive. It must be open to all, both Jew and Gentile. The table of the Lord of all must also be open to both men and women.

When Jesus broke the bread on the Jewish shore of the sea, the meal was restricted to men, five thousand men *(pentakischilioi andres)*. Now when he broke the bread in the Decapolis, the meal was for people, four thousand people *(tetrakischilioi)*. Matthew makes this more explicit when he describes the crowd as "four thousand men, not counting women and children" (Matt 15:38).

A Gentile Christian Tradition. The differences in terminology in the two accounts can be credited to distinct traditions. Underlying the breaking of the bread for the five thousand, there is a Jewish Christian tradition. Underlying the breaking of the bread for the four thousand, there is a Gentile Christian tradition.

In 6:34-44 and elsewhere in Mark, reference is made to a desert place *(eremos topos)*. The word *eremos* (desert) can be an adjective as well as a noun. In 8:1-9, we find *eremia* (desert), which can only be a noun.

Then there are the numbers. In 6:34-44, there were twelve baskets of fragments gathered, twelve baskets for the Twelve. In 8:1-9, there were seven. It is possible that the number seven is associated with the Seven referred to in the book of Acts in connection with Hellenistic mission (6:3, 5; 21:8).[25]

There is also the word used for the baskets. In 6:34-44, the word is *kophinos,* a term generally associated with a Jewish setting. In 8:1-9, the word is *spyris,* a common Hellenistic term without any Jewish connotations.

All of these differences might be circumstantial. But one additional difference is a clear indication of a Gentile Christian background. It has to do with the fish. In 6:34-44, where Jesus takes five loaves and two fish, the fish are very much part of the story. In 8:1-9,

---

[25] See E. LaVerdiere, *The Breaking of the Bread* (Chicago: Liturgy Training Publications, 1998) 111–26.

Jesus takes only the seven loaves, and later on we learn that they also had a few fish.

The fish have been relegated to the perimeter of the story. In this, we note the influence of liturgical practice. The tradition in 8:1-9 has been shaped in part by a liturgical setting in which fish were no longer part of the breaking of the bread. This influence, absent from tradition represented by 6:34-44, very likely occurred prior to Mark's Gospel.

Besides this, there is the fact that Jesus actually blessed the fish, a sure indication of a setting far removed from the story's Jewish origins. Jews did not bless objects, only persons. The Hebrew word for blessing is the same as the word for thanksgiving *(berakah)*. Just as one does not thank an object, one does not bless an object. In Greek, however, the verbs for blessing and thanking are different. The verb for thanking is *eucharistein,* for blessing *eulogein.* Two specific terms, loosely related, can be used in quite different ways. Greeks would not think of thanking a fish, but they might consider blessing a fish. In this context, to bless is to set something aside so that it will bring God to mind.

In 8:1-9, Mark has thus given us a story of the breaking of the bread among the Gentiles. He situated the event in the Decapolis, a predominantly Gentile territory on the eastern side of the sea. And to make his point even stronger, he drew on a Gentile Christian tradition in retelling the story. There was no question that the breaking of the bread had to be open both to Jews and Gentiles, men as well as women. In this, the very nature and scope of the Christian mission was at stake.

Crossing the Sea (8:10)

After breaking the bread, Jesus dismissed the crowd of four thousand (8:10) as he had dismissed the crowd of five thousand (6:45). He then got into the boat with the disciples and came to the region of Dalmanutha, a place whose identity is unknown to us. The name Dalmanutha, however, could be a popular corruption of Tiberiadaamathous, a combination of Tiberias, the Roman city built as the capital of Galilee, and Am(m)a thous, the ancient town that was replaced by Tiberias.[26] In any case, Jesus and the disciples did return to the Jewish shore of the sea to a place where they would meet up with the Pharisees.

---

[26] See Vincent Taylor, *The Gospel According to St. Mark* (London: MacMillan & Co. LTD, 1963) 360–61.

The sea crossing that followed the first breaking of the bread had been very eventful. Jesus had sent the disciples ahead of him toward Bethsaida. When contrary winds prevented them from making any headway, he had gone out to them in the midst of the sea and joined them in the boat (6:45-52). The disciples were clearly at the center of the story, as they had been in the story of the breaking of the bread for the five thousand (6:34-44).

After the second breaking of the bread, the story includes little more than the fact of the crossing. This time, however, Jesus is at the center of the statement, as he was in the breaking of the bread for the four thousand.

The Pharisees Seek a Sign (8:11-13)

After the first story of the breaking of the bread (6:34-44), the disciples never did reach their appointed destination. Instead they came to Gennesareth (6:53) and Jesus continued to minister in the Jewish villages, towns, and countryside (6:54-56). Without delaying on any one episode, Mark simply summarized Jesus' activities as a transition to a major encounter between Jesus and the Pharisees and some scribes from Jerusalem (7:1-13). The Pharisees objected that Jesus' disciples failed to observe "the tradition of the elders." Jesus' response was intended not so much for the Pharisees, but for the crowds (7:14-15), the disciples (7:17-23), and for Mark's readers.

The breaking of the bread in the Decapolis also was followed by an encounter with the Pharisees, presumably in the region of Dalmanutha to which Jesus had crossed with the disciples (8:11-12). But this time, the Pharisees did not come with a specific objection. Instead they argued with Jesus and tried to test him by seeking from him a sign from heaven (see Deut 13:2-6). Objecting to everything Jesus said and did, they demanded a sign from him that would establish his divine credentials (see John 6:30).

For the Pharisees, none of what Jesus had already done, including the two events of the breaking of the bread for the five thousand and for the four thousand constituted a sufficient sign. Listening to their request, we wonder what Jesus could possibly have done to satisfy them. We are not surprised that Jesus refused them a sign.

As in 7:1-23, Jesus' response to the Pharisees is intended for the crowd, the disciples and Mark's readers, that is, "this generation" (*he genea aute,* 8:12). This is the first time the Gospel refers to "this generation." The term returns several times in the second part of the Gospel.

Whenever the term appears, it tends to have negative connotations. In 8:38, for example, where Jesus spells out the conditions of discipleship, we read, "Whoever is ashamed of me and of my words in this faithless and sinful generation. . . ." In 9:19, it is used in an apostrophe, "O faithless generation, how long will I be with you?" Then, in 13:30, it appears in Jesus' discourse regarding apocalyptic judgment, "Amen, I say to you, this generation will not pass away until all these things have taken place."

Mark's reference to "this generation" in a context where exodus themes have a prominent role (6:6b–8:21) evokes a number of passages in the Old Testament. Notable among these is the poetic passage describing the generation that came out of Egypt, followed Moses into the desert, and strongly resisted him (Deut 32:5-20). The Pharisees and the generation of the new exodus resisted Jesus in the same way. The most important text is that of Psalm 95:7b-11:

> Oh, that today you would hear his voice:
>> Do not harden your hearts as at Meribah,
>> as on the day of Massah in the desert,
> There your ancestors tested me;
>> they tried me though they had seen my works.
> Forty years I loathed that generation;
>> I said: "This people's heart goes astray,
>> they do not know my ways."
> Therefore I swore in my anger:
>> "They shall never enter my rest."

In 8:12, Jesus addresses the generation of the new exodus, especially Mark's readers. Like the psalmist, he recalls those who came before them, in this case the Pharisees and the first disciples. The Pharisees also had tested Jesus. Their hearts were hardened (3:5) like the hearts of their ancestors at Meribah and Massah. Even the hearts of the disciples were hardened (6:52). Would the hearts of Mark's readers also be hardened (8:17)?

After announcing that no sign would be given to this generation, Jesus left the Pharisees, got into the boat, and went off to the other shore (8:13)

Disciples' Lack of Understanding (8:14-21)[27]

They were coming by boat from the region of Dalmanutha (8:10) on the way to the other shore (8:13). Jesus was in the boat with the

---

[27] See Norman A. Beck, "Reclaiming a Biblical Text: the Mark 8:14-21 Discussion about the Bread in the Boat," *The Catholic Biblical Quarterly* 43/1 (January 1981) 49–56.

disciples. Finally, they were going to Bethsaida (see 6:45; 8:22) at the border of Jewish Galilee and Gentile Gaulanitis.

There had been a lot of resistance to this crossing (6:45-56). Some of the resistance came from those who clung to "the tradition of the elders" (7:1-23). Some came from entrenched attitudes regarding the Gentiles as outsiders (7:24-30), and some from people who were not able to hear, let alone speak, Jesus' gospel of the reign of the God (7:31-37).

All that resistance had been dealt with, and Jesus had finally broken bread with a large crowd that had been with him for three days in the desert of the Decapolis (8:1-9). Jews and Gentiles, both men and women, were invited to share in the same breaking of the bread.

But that does not mean it would be clear sailing from then on. There were those who kept demanding an authenticating sign from heaven (8:11-13). Even the disciples that accompanied Jesus into the Decapolis and joined in the breaking of the bread failed to understand about the loaves. They still did not grasp who Jesus really is and what the breaking of the bread meant. Without such understanding, they stood in great danger of turning back to "the tradition of the elders," to the exclusive attitudes and the need for a heavenly sign, to all those things they had left behind (8:14-21).

So it is that Jesus warned them: "Watch out, guard against the leaven of the Pharisees and the leaven of Herod" (8:15). Mark inserted Jesus' warning between two observations regarding the disciples and their lack of bread (8:14, 16), thereby associating his warning with the breaking of the bread, a basic theme in this third section.

The disciples had forgotten to bring bread and had but one loaf in the boat (8:14). During the crossing, Jesus was warning them about the leaven of the Pharisees and the leaven of Herod (8:15), but all the while they were discussing and arguing about not having any bread (8:16). The disciples' situation, Jesus' warning, and the disciples' discussion provide the setting for an escalating series of seven questions in which Jesus focuses on the disciples' lack of understanding (8:17-21).

The episode (8:14-21) marks the conclusion of the Gospel's third section, which tells about the mission of the Twelve (6:6b–8:21). In the context of the first part of the Gospel (1:14–8:30), it parallels 3:1-6, the conclusion of the first section (1:14–3:6), which told of the Pharisees' hardness of heart. Their hardness of heart led them to consult the Herodians to find a way to put Jesus to death. It also parallels 6:1-6a, the conclusion of the second section (3:7–6:6a), which told of the lack of faith among the people of Jesus' native place. Because of their lack of faith, Jesus was not able to reveal the power of the gospel among them.

Context in the 6:6b–8:21. As we have seen, one of the basic themes in the story of Jesus and the mission of the Twelve (6:6b–8:21) is the breaking of the bread. For Mark and the early Christians, it was over the breaking of the bread that every issue eventually surfaced. It was in the breaking of the bread that they had to deal with the most difficult challenges confronting the Church.

At the beginning of the missionary journey, Jesus told the disciples to bring no bread with them (6:8). They were to accept the hospitality of those to whom they were sent (6:7-13). Then, when they returned to Jesus, they had no opportunity to eat because of the crowds (6:30-33). Then again, when they asked Jesus to send the crowd away to find something to eat, Jesus asked them how much bread did they have. When they returned and reported they had five loaves of bread, Jesus broke the bread. In the breaking of the bread, even five loaves could nourish a large crowd of five thousand men, with twelve baskets left over for others (6:34-44).

Later, when Jesus made them get into the boat and precede him to the other shore, the crossing proved too difficult for them (6:45-52). They did not understand about the loaves (6:52a). There was a problem with disciples—Pharisees and scribes from Jerusalem—who clung to the tradition of the elders regarding food, meals, and ritual purification. Were they to go to the Gentiles, they would have to accept their hospitality (6:10) and would not be able to maintain their traditions. Faced with this dilemma, they rejected the Gentile mission and remained apart from the Twelve (7:1-23).

The disciples' resistance had become embedded in a popular saying, "It is not right to take the food of the children and throw it to the dogs" (7:27). But a Gentile woman countered the saying with one of her own, "Even the dogs under the table eat the children's scraps" (7:28). With this (7:24-30), and after opening the ears and loosening the tongue of the Gentiles (7:31-37), Jesus and his disciples were able to break the bread with them. And when Jesus broke the bread with four thousand Jewish and Gentile men and women, there was again an abundance of bread broken to be shared with others (8:1-9). Even after all this, like their ancestors in the desert before them, the Pharisees demanded a sign (8:11-13).

No Bread, One Loaf (8:14). The disciples had forgotten to bring bread *(artous)* and had but one loaf *(arton)* with them in the boat (8:14). For some, Mark's opening observation causes difficulty. If the disciples had forgotten to bring bread, how is it they had the one loaf? And yet, this is not an unusual way to describe a situation like this, particularly in conversation. Having forgotten to bring bread, all the disciples had the one loaf! A similar situation existed when Jesus broke the bread for the five thousand men and then again for the four thousand. The crowd had nothing to eat, and yet they had five or seven loaves and some fish (6:34-44; 8:1-9).

In 8:14, Mark emphasizes the one loaf with a Greek turn of phrase, literally, "except for one loaf *(ei me hena)* they had none *(ouk eichon)* with them." That one loaf, however, went unrecognized. In 8:16, Mark summarizes the discussion with a simple statement: "They concluded among themselves . . . they had no bread" (8:16).

At this point, we need to recall that Jesus had told them not to bring any bread on the mission (6:8). Had they brought some, it might have been used as leaven in making new bread. The old bread would then transform the new. It could not be so in the Christian mission.

The one loaf the disciples had with them in the boat was the very person of Jesus, who offered himself as nourishment for all. But they could not yet understand. Jesus would present himself as the bread in the second part of the Gospel (8:22–16:8) at the Last Supper on the Feast of Unleavened Bread (14:12) when Jesus would break the bread (14:22) with the Twelve (see 14:17).

"Watch Out, Guard Against" (8:15a). Mark presented Jesus' warning as a repeated, quasi-continuous action, "He enjoined them," literally, "He kept ordering them." The warning thus summarizes Jesus' message to the disciples during the entire crossing from Dalmanutha to Bethsaida. Since the passage (8:14-21) is the conclusion for 6:6b-8:21, the warning also indicates one of the Gospel's key intentions for this whole section on the mission of the Twelve.

Jesus' warning began with an emphatic, "Watch out" *(horate,* see or look), a rhetorical device comparable to "Listen" *(akouete,* 4:3), calling attention to what follows. It continued immediately with the warning itself: "Guard against [*blepete apo,* watch out for] the leaven of the Pharisees and the leaven of Herod." Later, the same expression, "Beware *(blepete apo,* watch out for)" warns the disciples against the scribes (12:38) and still later against anyone who lead them astray (13:5). In each case, the intent is not to forewarn the disciples of possible harm at the hands of others, but of the danger that they themselves adopt the same behavior.

Leaven, Reality, and Metaphor. Jesus warned his disciples against particular forms of leaven *(zyme),* that of the Pharisees and that of Herod. He used the term metaphorically, but to understand the metaphor, which is open to several layers of meaning, we need to recall a number of things about leaven itself.

In the New Testament and elsewhere, the most basic metaphorical meaning of leaven from its gradual, pervasive, and transforming influence on the entire mass of dough. Such is its meaning in one of Jesus' parables of the kingdom: "The kingdom of heaven is like yeast (*zyme,* leaven) that a woman took and mixed with three measures of wheat flour until the whole batch was leavened" (Matt 13:33); see also Luke 13:20-21). Something is consequently to be learned about the kingdom of heaven from observing the pervasive action of leaven. The same meaning is found in the popular saying Paul quoted in 1 Cor 5:6 and Gal 5:9: "A little yeast *[zyme]* leavens *[zymoi]* all the dough." In itself, leaven is a neutral metaphor, open to a positive (Matt 13:33) or a negative (1 Cor 5:6) connotation.

Leaven, however, can also have a second layer of meaning, one stemming from its corrupting influence as an agent of fermentation. In such cases, the metaphor becomes negative. So it is in the case of Jesus' warning against the leaven of the Pharisees and the leaven of Herod (8:15; see Matt 16:6, 11-12; Luke 12:1).

The same is true in 1 Cor 5:6-8, where the leaven is that of malice and wickedness. Paul further emphasized this negative connotation by associating sincerity and truth with unleavened loaves *(azymoi)*. This added negative layer even appears in Gal 5:9, where the neutral saying acquires a negative meaning from the context. Paul used the saying to illustrate the corrupting influence of one who entices the Galatians from the following the truth (Gal 5:7-8).

In New Testament usage, leaven can also have a third layer of meaning, one based on the very nature of leaven. Besides pervasiveness and corruption, leaven can also connote something old, with the added implication that it cannot or ought not to be integrated in the new. For this third layer, we have to be familiar with what leaven actually consisted of.

We have an excellent source for this in the *Natural History* of Pliny the Elder (A.D. 23–79), of which Book XVIII is entirely devoted to cereal agriculture. Section 26 of Book XVIII describes six different kinds of leaven *(fermentum)* used in making bread.

During the vintage season, leaven could be made from millet soaked in unfermented wine. For gourmet bread, leaven could be made from the best fine bran of wheat steeped in unfermented wine for three days.

Then there was leaven made from cakes of barley and water, baked and allowed to sour. In times past, when bread was still made of barley, leaven consisted in the flour of bitter vetch or chickling. By the first century, however, barley was mainly fed to cattle and no longer used in making bread. Leaven could also be made of flour boiled into a kind of porridge and left to go sour. But ordinarily, one simply used some dough that was left uncooked from the day before.

This sixth and simplest form of leaven is referred to in Jesus' parable of the leaven (Matt 13:33; Luke 13:20-21). Very likely, it is also the kind presupposed in all the other New Testament references. At least, there is nothing in the texts that would indicate any other kind.

Leaven, a piece of dough put aside from an old batch for use in the new, could consequently be used as a metaphor for something old. Leavened bread was made from a mixture of the old and the new dough. Unleavened bread did not include anything from the old. This layer of meaning is clearly intended in 1 Cor 5:6-8, where Paul asks the Corinthians to "clear out the old yeast" (*ten palaian zymen,* leaven) that it might be a "a fresh batch of dough" (*neon phyrama,* new dough), since in fact they were "unleavened" (*azymoi,* unleavened loaves). The passage distinguishes between the old and the new person and warns against being corrupted by the old.

The same contrast between the old and the new is implied in Gal 5:1-10, where a neutral saying about the pervasive influence of leaven (Gal 5:9) is used in a negative context to illustrate the corrupting effect of the old. Christ set us free. The Galatians are to stand firm and never again submit to the yoke of slavery.

The Leaven of the Pharisees, the Leaven of Herod (8:15). Jesus' warning against the leaven of the Pharisees and the leaven of Herod (8:15) is very similar to Paul's warning in 1 Cor 5 and Gal 5. The leaven of the Pharisees and the leaven of Herod would be corrupting agents in the Christian community, but this is not the main point of the statement. Admitting such leaven into the community, the Christians would return to the old situation they had left behind when they opened their door to the Gentiles and embarked on the Gentile mission.

The old and the new were not compatible. This was clearly shown earlier with reference to Jesus' new teaching and way of life (1:27; 2:18-22). On that occasion Jesus offered two parables on the incompatibility of the old and the new. He spoke of unshrunken cloth and what happens when a piece of it is sewn on an old cloak (2:21). He spoke also of new wine and what it could do to an old wineskin (2:22).

In the first case, the tear in the cloak would become worse. In the second, the old wineskin would burst and the new wine would be spilled. In the case of the leaven of the Pharisees and the leaven of

Herod, the leaven would permeate and transform the new dough and gradually reduce it to the condition of the old.

Jesus' warning is twofold, as seen from the repetition of the word leaven. There is the leaven of the Pharisees, and then there is a different leaven, that of Herod. But what is that leaven of the Pharisees, and in what does the leaven of Herod consist?

Both Matthew and Luke identify the leaven explicitly. In the parallel text in Matthew, the warning refers to one leaven only, that of the Pharisees and Sadducees (Matt 16:6), who had come together to test Jesus by demanding a sign from heaven (Matt 16:1). At the end of the episode, Matthew states that Jesus was not warning the disciples against the leaven of bread but against the teaching of the Pharisees and Sadducees (16:12).

Luke contains a similar warning against the Pharisees, but unlike Matthew, the warning is related to the Sadducees (Luke 12:1). Like Matthew, Luke leaves no doubt about the meaning of the leaven. For Luke, it refers not so much to the teaching as to the hypocrisy of the Pharisees.

Unlike Matthew and Luke, Mark did not identify the leaven of the Pharisees and the leaven of Herod. It refers to everything the Pharisees and Herod stood for in the first part of the Gospel (1:14–8:21) and most especially in the section on the mission of the Twelve (6:6b–8:21).

The Pharisees first entered the Gospel in the story of Jesus and the call of the first disciples (1:14–3:6). Their role in four out of five conflict stories tells us much about the leaven of the Pharisees.

At the banquet following the Levi, the Pharisees objected that Jesus was eating with sinners and tax collectors (2:13-17). Afterwards, people objected that Jesus' disciples were not fasting like those of the Pharisees and of John the Baptist (2:18-22). Later, the Pharisees protested that Jesus' disciples picked heads of grain while walking through a field on the Sabbath (2:23-28). Finally, they found grounds to accuse Jesus when he healed a man with a withered hand on the Sabbath (3:1-6).

In every instance, the Pharisees clung to their legal observances and resisted the new teaching of Jesus. Entrenched in the old, their hearts were hardened.

The Pharisees next entered the Gospel in the story of Jesus and the mission of the Twelve (6:6b–8:21). In 7:1-23, they objected that disciples of Jesus did not follow the tradition of the elders, but ate with unclean hands. Then in 8:11-12, still resisting the mission of Jesus and the Twelve, they kept insisting they would need a sign from heaven.

Such is the leaven of the Pharisees. Jesus warned the disciples about this leaven. They must open their hearts to new understanding. They must disassociate themselves from the hardness of heart of the Pharisees. There can be no returning to the old traditions which would not allow them to go to the Gentiles (8:17-18).

The leaven of Herod is very similar. After having John the Baptist executed, Herod was not able to put John out of his mind. When Herod heard of the things Jesus did, he concluded Jesus was John the Baptist raised from the dead (6:14-16). He could not look beyond John and his reform movement within Judaism. For Herod, Jesus was in direct continuity with the old, not the beginning of the new.

Lack of Understanding (8:16-21). The disciples did not understand Jesus' warning about the leaven of Pharisees and the leaven of Herod (8:15). Nor did they understand the meaning of the one loaf that had in the boat (8:14). They concluded that Jesus was warning them about having no bread.

The passage continues with a series of rhetorical questions (8:17-18a), flowing directly from Jesus' warning about the leaven of the Pharisees and the leaven of Herod and the disciples lack of understanding. Jesus begins by questioning their conclusion: "Why do you conclude that it is because you have no bread? Do you not understand or comprehend? Are you hearts hardened? Do you have eyes and not see, ears and not hear?" (8:17-18a).

The question, "Do you have eyes and not see, ears and not hear?" evokes Jeremiah 5:21:

> Pay attention to this,
>> foolish and senseless people
> Who have eyes and see not,
>> who have ears and hear not.

It also recalls Mark's quotation of Isaiah in 4:12 concerning those who do not understand Jesus' parables:

> They may look and see but not perceive
>> and hear and listen but not understand,
>> in order that they may not be converted and be forgiven.

Jesus' warning summarizes the challenges facing the disciples in this part of the Gospel. The leaven of the Pharisees and the leaven of Herod would have separated them from the mission of Jesus. It would have transformed them into outsiders (see 4:11-12). Like Jesus' relatives, they would not have been able to enter Jesus' home and join both Jews and Gentiles at his table (see 3:21-22, 31-35).

Jesus' next two questions referred to the breaking of the bread for the five thousand (6:34-44) and the breaking of the bread for the four thousand (8:1-9). Jesus first asked them to remember the fragments left over when he broke the five loaves for the five thousand: "And do you not remember, when I broke the five loaves for the five thousand, how many wicker baskets full of fragments you picked up?" (8:18b-19a). Jesus did not ask about the breaking of the bread itself. He asked about the leftovers. They answered, "Twelve" (8:19b). With that, they should have understood. Twelve baskets for the Twelve! Twelve baskets for the universal Church!

Jesus then asked the disciples to remember the fragments left over when he broke the five loaves for the four thousand: "When I broke the seven loaves for the four thousand, how many full baskets of fragments did you pick up?" (8:20a). Again Jesus did not ask about the breaking of the bread itself. He asked about the leftovers. The answered, "Seven" (8:20b). With that, they should have understood. Seven baskets for the Seven! Seven baskets for the Church among the Gentiles (see Acts 6:1-7).[28]

Jesus concludes with a final rhetorical question: "Do you still not understand?" (8:21). With that, Mark introduces the second part of the Gospel, where Jesus would open the eyes of the blind and speak plainly about his passion and resurrection. To understand, the disciples have to follow him on the way to Jerusalem, to his passion and resurrection. At the Last Supper, Jesus would declare that the bread he broke was very his body (14:22). With that, the disciples would understand. But did the Church in Mark's time understand? They too have to remember about the leftovers, the one loaf in the boat, and the body of Christ.

---

[28] See Eugene LaVerdiere, *The Breaking of the Bread* (Chicago: Liturgy Training Publications, 1998) 111–26.

Index of Proper Names and Subjects

Index of Greek, Hebrew, Aramaic, and Latin Terms and Expressions